STATE POLICY CHOICES

LA FOLLETTE PUBLIC POLICY SERIES

The Robert M. La Follette
Institute of Public Affairs

Robert H. Haveman, *Director*

STATE POLICY CHOICES

THE WISCONSIN EXPERIENCE

EDITED BY

SHELDON DANZIGER

JOHN F. WITTE

THE UNIVERSITY OF WISCONSIN PRESS

The University of Wisconsin Press
114 North Murray Street
Madison, Wisconsin 53715

The University of Wisconsin Press, Ltd.
1 Gower Street
London WC1E 6HA, England

Printed in the United States of America

Library of Congress Cataloging-in-Publication Data
State policy choices.
   (La Follette public policy series)
   Bibliography: pp. 279–287.
   Includes index.
   1. Wisconsin—Economic policy. 2. Finance, Public,
Wisconsin. I. Danziger, Sheldon. II. Witte, John F.
III. Robert M. La Follette Institute of Public Affairs.
IV. Series.
HC107.W6S68   1988   338.9775   88-40232
ISBN 0-299-11710-3
ISBN 0-299-11714-6 (pbk.)

Contributors

Daniel W. Bromley
*Department of Agricultural Economics, University of
Wisconsin–Madison*
Sandra K. Danziger
School of Social Work, University of Michigan
Sheldon Danziger
*School of Social Work and Institute for Research on Poverty, University of
Wisconsin–Madison*
Nancy Cross Dunham
Associate Director, Health Research Program, New York University
Peter K. Eisinger
Department of Political Science, University of Wisconsin–Madison
Irwin Garfinkel
*School of Social Work and Institute for Research on Poverty, University of
Wisconsin–Madison*
John Goddeeris
Department of Economics, Michigan State University
Edward V. Jesse
*Department of Agricultural Economics, University of
Wisconsin–Madison*
Robert J. Lampman
*Department of Economics and Institute for Research on Poverty,
University of Wisconsin–Madison*
John F. Longres
*School of Social Work and Institute for Research on Poverty, University of
Wisconsin–Madison*
Timothy D. McBride
Urban Institute, Washington, D.C.
Ann Nichols-Casebolt
School of Social Work, Arizona State University, Tempe
David R. Riemer
Counsel, Cost Containment, Time Insurance Co., Milwaukee
Mark C. Rom
The Brookings Institution, Washington, D.C.
Arthur Sakamoto
Department of Sociology, University of Wisconsin–Madison

Gary D. Sandefur
  School of Social Work and Institute for Research on Poverty, University of Wisconsin–Madison
Kathleen Segerson
  Department of Economics, University of Connecticut, Storrs
Michael R. Sosin
  School of Social Work and Institute for Research on Poverty, University of Wisconsin–Madison
Paul R. Voss
  Department of Rural Sociology, University of Wisconsin–Madison
John F. Witte
  Department of Political Science and Robert M. La Follette Institute of Public Affairs, University of Wisconsin–Madison
Barbara Wolfe
  Departments of Economics and Preventive Medicine and Institute for Research on Poverty, University of Wisconsin–Madison
Patrick Wong
  School of Social Work, University of Wisconsin–Madison

Contents

**PART THREE: AGRICULTURAL AND NATURAL
RESOURCE POLICY**

Figures

Tables

Foreword

Since the late-1970s, policy initiatives in a variety of areas have devolved from the federal government to state-local governments. Major tax reforms, welfare initiatives, environmental legislation, economic development programs, policies to provide and finance health care, and agricultural and natural resources programs that have ultimately been reflected in federal policy had their incubation and testing at lower levels of government.

While Wisconsin has participated fully in this recent spate of policy reform, the idea of using the state as a laboratory for policy development is not a new one to its citizens. Indeed, the Progressive tradition for which this state has long been known holds this "state as policy laboratory for the nation" concept as one of its basic tenets. The papers in this volume reflect the recent rejuvenation of this policy initiation at the state level; in but few cases does one fail to find policy development within Wisconsin containing important lessons for other states and the nation.

A second proposition embodied in the Progressive tradition is also reflected in this volume. The "Wisconsin Idea" stresses the synergy that results when scholars and policy makers are jointly involved in policy debate and innovation. Academic notions become leavened by political realities and the obstacles to implementation. In turn, the bonds of these realities and obstacles are often loosened by the ideas and proposals—naive though they may at times appear—of scholars.

This volume has academics writing about policy, but the scholars represented all have histories of direct and "hands-on" involvement in the policy process. It, in a very real sense, is evidence that the "Idea" is still in action. The Robert M. La Follette Institute of Public Affairs is proud to have sponsored the volume.

Policy issues wax and wane; what is reform today is reformed tomorrow. This fact is a danger that confronts all volumes that seek to speak to policy needs and processes. Although no such volume can avoid this danger entirely, this one comes close. It has done so by sticking to basic principles and long-run perspectives rather than addressing debate current in any season. Its contribution, therefore, should be a lasting one.

Robert Haveman
Director
Robert M. La Follette Institute
of Public Affairs
January 1988

Acknowledgments

This volume was made possible through the support of the Robert M. La-Follette Institute of Public Affairs and its first two directors, Dennis Dresang and Robert Haveman. Much of the research reported here was supported by grants and contracts between the Wisconsin Department of Health and Social Services and the University of Wisconsin–Madison. Particularly important has been the willingness of various state agencies to aid in the collection and analysis of data. We also wish to thank the chapter authors for their commitment to the Wisconsin Idea.

Michael Wiseman provided excellent comments on an earlier draft of all of these chapters. The coherence and content of the volume owe much to the editorial work of Elizabeth Uhr.

STATE POLICY CHOICES

1

Introduction

SHELDON DANZIGER AND JOHN F. WITTE

Reductions or slowed growth in federal expenditures have forced important decisions on state and local governments. This budget trimming has also increased pressure on state and local revenue systems. Few new programs have been generated at the federal level since 1981, leaving state and local governments greater opportunity to experiment. The Progressive axiom that the states serve as experimental laboratories for policy innovations seems to be returning after a long period of federal dominance.

The purpose of this book is to provide information on and evaluate critical Wisconsin policies from the perspective of university policy analysts. Although the issues examined here are all set in the Wisconsin context, the problems, and the innovative policy programs described in many of the chapters, will be of interest to those involved in or studying state and local policies in other states.

This volume does not attempt to canvass all major policy fields. It concentrates instead on those areas in which change has raised questions about the policies of the past. These areas include state budgets, finances, conditions for economic development, and demographic trends; human needs and services; and agricultural and natural resources policies.

Budgets, Finances, and Conditions for Economic Development

The first section links the processes by which money is raised and spent in Wisconsin with the population to be served and economic prospects.

Mark C. Rom and John F. Witte describe the historical evolution of the budget process, which has become so crucial for policy making in Wisconsin. Increasingly, new policies are introduced and existing policies are altered, expanded, or eliminated in the budget cycle. The Wisconsin budget system emphasizes power over participation: the power of the governor, the legisla-

3

ture's Joint Finance Committee, and the leaders of the majority party. The governor, with the help of the state budget director, submits a budget to the legislature. The JFC, which is dominated by the majority party, holds hearings and evaluates, alters, and approves the entire budget, which, with the amendments made by a majority caucus, is bound eventually to pass the legislature.

This system results in budgets that are passed on time and remain within the limits of the balanced budget provision so that, when shortfalls or surpluses occur, the system can respond. Compared to the federal budget process, the Wisconsin system is a model of efficient action. Yet it raises questions about bipartisan compromise, participation, and openness. It exemplifies the central struggle over how democratic decisions should be made: to what degree should closed, centralized decision making be built into the political process. The recommendations of the authors, who appreciate the effectiveness of the system, amount to a "slight nudge" to ensure greater proportional representation between parties.

Whereas Rom and Witte describe and evaluate the state budget-making process, Robert J. Lampman and Timothy D. McBride describe the shifts in state and local expenditures and revenues from 1960 to 1983. They analyze the changing roles of the federal, state, and local levels of government in funding and delivering state and local services. A series of graphs that standardize expenditure and revenue patterns as a percentage of personal income depict historical trends in the size of government programs and taxes and make possible comparisons with other states.

The authors report that Wisconsin taxes increased more rapidly than taxes in the rest of the United States during the period from 1960 to 1971, and that since that time the tax burden has been higher than the national average. The need for the high taxes is explained on the expenditure side of the ledger: Wisconsin's expenditures are higher as a percentage of personal income than those in most other states in the areas of education, social services, and transportation.

The authors report in a concluding section that these national comparisons have driven recent calls for reform in Wisconsin and may be crucial to future debates about taxing and spending by Wisconsin state and local governments.

Paul R. Voss describes and dissects population changes in the state from 1910 to the 1980s and projected through 1990. Voss reports an overall decline in population growth in the 1980s. Growth rates for both nonmetropolitan and metropolitan sectors are less than half those that prevailed just a few years earlier. He attributes a net migration loss of 100,000 people during the period from 1980 to 1985 to the decline in jobs in the state's manufacturing industries during the 1982 recession.

Continued slow growth will have both good and bad consequences. For the business community it means less growth in sales and less gross income, unless new products stimulate demand. A reduced tax base may result in higher costs for such social services as education and fire protection in some areas. Yet slow growth also generates less demand for higher-cost public sector services that tend to accompany rapid population growth and reduces the pressure for suburban sprawl, which almost always causes irreversible loss of farmland.

Voss addresses numerous population policy issues, including inheritance taxation, a hypothesized "brain drain," and whether or not Wisconsin is a "welfare magnet," and he stresses the need for policymakers to benefit from demographic "early warnings" to adjust the course of economic development.

The chapter on state economic development, written by Peter Eisinger, reviews the evolution of state policy toward economic development and describes the current policy tools available to aid private-sector expansion. Eisinger concludes with a discussion of a coherent plan for economic development that would target mature manufacturing industries, small business formation and expansion, new industry, and the least prosperous regions of the state.

Witte's chapter on income tax reform concentrates on the state's most important source of revenue and the most important legislative changes in the state's pioneering history of the income tax.

Since World War II, there has been agreement among both academic tax experts and practitioners on the basic contours of a "reformed" tax system. It would have a very broad base and few, if any, exclusions, exemptions, deductions, tax credits, or special rates or timing of tax payments. Its value would be judged in terms of horizontal equity, vertical equity, administrative efficiency, economic efficiency, and simplicity. Yet tax reform has generally proved elusive, for the theoretical criteria are difficult to apply in practice, and it has been difficult to generate the political momentum necessary to effect radical reform in a fragmented, pluralistic power system. In order to succeed, a reform must be radical enough that elected politicians can support the bill on general reform grounds and thus overcome the particularistic arguments of individual special interests. This is what took place in Wisconsin in 1985. Witte analyzes the new system, judging the individual provisions by the criteria of simplification, base-broadening, horizontal and vertical equity, and economic efficiency.

According to him, there is no question that the power-oriented budget process (described in an earlier chapter) facilitated the passage of tax reform. "Open tax legislation, where amendments are offered without restriction by all legislators and decided in open forums, produces abhorrent tax policy." Witte concludes his chapter with recommendations for further reform in light of the 1986 federal income tax reform.

Human Need and Human Services

The second, and longest, section of the book deals with the provision of human services. Health and Social Services, by far the largest department in state government, is an area in which many new issues have emerged in recent years.

A common theme that runs through this section is the problem of poverty among single women and their children. Their situation is first addressed in the chapter by Sheldon Danziger and Ann Nichols-Casebolt, who attribute the growth in female-headed families and their persistently high poverty rates to increased numbers of divorces and out-of-wedlock births, employment barriers, and poor performance of the child support system. Although employment is judged to be the best way for women heading families to escape poverty, it does not always guarantee a way out. Among the three-fourths of single mothers who work at least part time, one-quarter remain poor. Poverty remains high because on average women work fewer hours and earn lower wages than men.

Income transfer programs significantly reduce poverty, and Danziger and Nichols-Casebolt find that these programs are more effective in Wisconsin than in many other states. But although the transfer system, particularly its social security component, has succeeded in moving the elderly out of poverty, it has been less successful in helping single mothers with children. The authors therefore focus their policy recommendations on this group. They propose incentives for poor women to combine work with welfare; increased support services for women who participate in job training programs—including the opportunity to take jobs not stereotyped as "women's work"; a "workfare" that is a true work opportunity program; and a child support assurance system, described in a later chapter.

Sandra K. Danziger, John F. Longres, and Michael R. Sosin explore the question of whether changes in the economy and in the demographic characteristics of households—trends taking place in Wisconsin as well as in the rest of the nation—have altered and/or increased the needs of children.

The proportion of Wisconsin households containing children is decreasing (down from 56% of all families in 1970 to 53% in 1980). And within the category of families with children, the mean number of children under 18 has declined from three to two children per family. So there are now more adults per child in the state. But this does not translate into more adult resources available to children. Fewer adults are living in families with children; instead, they live alone or in adult-only households. The overall number of Wisconsin children (under 18) living with two parents has declined from 89% to 83%. Both the actual number of births to unmarried women and their percentage of all births almost doubled between 1970 and 1984. Add to this the fact that mothers (both married and unmarried) are much more likely to be employed, and the result may be less time available for children. Furthermore, fewer economic resources are available: median family incomes have not increased significantly since 1970, and the proportion of children in poverty has increased. What effects have such changes had on Wisconsin's children?

Danziger, Longres, and Sosin examine trends in the well-being of children over the decade 1970–80 and from one Wisconsin county to another, focusing on education (school performance and completion), youth employment, and such indicators of problems as juvenile arrests and births to teenagers. Although they find that the typical child is holding his own despite being forced to make adult choices at earlier ages, some subgroups seem to be facing severe problems. In pinpointing counties with the highest percentages of children in single-parent families, the authors reinforce the conclusion that reducing poverty among single-parent households is an important goal for state policy.

A major social policy innovation, the child support assurance system, is described in the chapter by Ann Nichols-Casebolt, Irwin Garfinkel, and Patrick Wong. Now instituted on a demonstration basis in the state, the program is designed to alleviate the poverty of single women and their children. Under the current child support system, less than 60% of mothers with children who have a living absent parent receive a child support award. When awards are established, the payments tend to be inequitable, inadequate, and in arrears. The result is that many women with children are forced to rely on welfare, which fosters dependence.

Under the child support assurance system, all parents living apart from their children are obligated to share their incomes with their children. The plan consists of four major features: (1) a standardized rate of income sharing; (2) automatic income withholding; (3) an assured minimum benefit for all children with absent parents; and (4) a custodial parent surtax in the event that the noncustodial parent pays less than the assured benefit.

The authors estimate that the system will reduce poverty and welfare dependency of single parents, and, depending on the size of the assured benefit, may save the state money.

Gary D. Sandefur and Arthur Sakamoto outline the history of Wisconsin's Indians as they were buffeted by various government policies, most of which, while putatively serving the interests of the Indian population, resulted in extracting land from them for white settlement: the reservation system, allotment, termination, and, since 1975, self-determination. Two important consequences of the shifting policies of government toward this group have been the placement of Indians in parts of the state that are far from major centers of population and commerce (although until the 1800s all of Wisconsin belonged to them) and a highly complex system of intergovernmental relations determined by federal policy reversals, Supreme Court decisions, federal legislation, and varying amounts of tribal governmental activism.

According to the authors of this chapter, it is not surprising that, given the inconsistencies and reversals in Indian policy, poverty continues to be a significant feature of life for Wisconsin's six Indian groups—the Chippewa, Menominee, Oneida, Potawatomi, Stockbridge Munsee, and Winnebago. Whereas 5% of the white residents of the state live in poverty, 22% of the Indians do. The Indians who live in cities (about one-third) are worst off; those on reservations have not fared much better. The unemployment rate for Wisconsin Indians was 16.1% in 1980, compared to 6.3% for whites.

Because a substantial proportion of poor Indian households in the state consists of single mothers and their children, policies to improve the circumstances of this group will ameliorate the circumstances of Indians. Policies should also be directed toward retaining Indian youth in the education system, training them for jobs, and providing them with health care and job opportunities. To accomplish these ends, Sandefur and Sakamoto see a need for more cooperation between the state government, tribal governments, and the private sector, and for both Indians and non-Indians to affirm the importance of Indian self-determination.

John Goddeeris and his colleagues focus on rate setting as a means of containing hospital costs, an increasingly important problem for all states as health costs have risen much faster than general inflation. They summarize the evidence on the effectiveness of setting hospital rates prospectively and describe the choices available to designers of rate-setting schemes—choices that often entail perverse incentives for hospitals to maximize their profits. One plan, for example, may encourage hospitals to keep patients longer than their health requires; another plan may encourage hospitals to discharge prematurely and then readmit patients.

The authors then explore the issues addressed by the short-lived Wisconsin Rate-Setting Commission, among them how to differentiate rates at different types of hospitals, whether to allow discounting to major payers (such as health maintenance organizations), and how to update rates to reflect changes in the quality of care.

Also discussed are the future of rate setting on the state level, now that Medicare has introduced its version of rate setting on a national scale, and the role of competition in keeping costs down.

Agricultural and Natural Resource Policy

The last two chapters examine two related areas of traditional importance to the state of Wisconsin—and the authors argue that both areas need increased policy attention. Indeed, Edward V. Jesse's chapter opens with a warning:

The state of agriculture in the state of Wisconsin is probably more uncertain now than at any time in recent history. The farm financial crisis of the mid-1980s affected Wisconsin less seriously than other midwestern states because of Wisconsin's heavy emphasis on dairying, which was more protected by federal programs from price drops than other farm commodities. But Wisconsin's dairy farmers now face the prospect of large cuts in dairy price supports and the reality of strong competition from rapidly expanding milk production in the southwestern United States. There is ominous evidence that financial stress in Wisconsin agriculture may intensify.

Jesse provides a profile of Wisconsin agriculture and reviews government policies that have shaped it. He then points to emerging problems. In dairy farming, for example, the Great Lakes states are losing their comparative advantage as population has shifted to the Sunbelt, and dairy farmers in those areas have benefited from federal water projects which subsidized the cost of irrigation. Sunbelt dairy farmers have benefited from cheap grain prices more than Wisconsin dairy farmers, who produce their own feeds. Finally, technological changes now provide substantial economies of scale for dairy farming.

Economies of scale are lessening the ability of all family farms to survive, and the continuing trend toward fewer and larger farms will create severe adjustment problems and high dislocation costs in some rural communities. In municipalities heavily dependent on farming, a snowball effect is likely, as loss of revenue combined with attrition of some businesses would be expected to increase the tax burden and/or reduce the quality of local services for remaining residents, thus accelerating the rate of exodus. The social implications of increasing farm concentration are also seen as a serious concern.

Jesse offers a number of policy suggestions to strengthen the comparative advantage of the state's agriculture and to promote family-sized farming.

Policy related to natural resources involves allocating a finite resource to meet several objectives that are often viewed as being incompatible. Kathleen Segerson and Daniel W. Bromley suggest that viewing the problem as one of costs imposed on one interest group by another is helpful in understanding the actions of the state, federal agencies, and the courts. So-called government intervention which circumscribes the rights of an individual, say a manufacturer who pollutes a river, is justified on the grounds that the polluter is interfering with the rights (to clean water) of those who live downstream. The policy challenge in this field is to take competing and often conflicting interests into account, not in an atmosphere of confrontation but rather in an atmosphere that tries to find as many common interests as possible and then develops a compromise with a broad base for acceptability.

How successful state policy has been is evaluated by the authors for four specific pollution problems: nonpoint source pollution (pollution of the waterways from dispersed sources), hazardous waste management, acid rain, and groundwater pollution.

Policies concerning natural resources need not be merely restrictive. The authors detail three areas—forestry, mining, and tourism-recreation—in which the natural resource base can generate increased income and employment as well as health, well-being, and aesthetic pleasure. The policy challenge here is one of proper management.

Taken as a whole, the chapters in this volume suggest that the problems of Wisconsin differ in degree but not in kind from those faced by some other states. They consist in maintaining a sound economic base, providing stability in a changing world, and protecting the vulnerable—whether children, family farms, or the environment. Owing to its Progressive tradition, Wisconsin has been in the forefront in taking stock of its needs and finding efficient and equitable means to provide them. We hope that this book is a contribution to that process.

PART ONE

BUDGETS, FINANCES, AND CONDITIONS FOR ECONOMIC DEVELOPMENT

2

Power versus Participation:
The Wisconsin State Budget Process

MARK C. ROM AND JOHN F. WITTE

Introduction

Legislators fight over budgets. Because of this, they also contest rules for making budgets: control over these procedures, while not meaning automatic victory in budgeting, provides a sturdy lever for moving state funds. This chapter describes and analyzes the Wisconsin state budgeting process, evaluates that process in relation to two competing sets of values, and suggests procedures to improve the system.

A Précis of the Wisconsin Budget Process

No universally accepted budgeting procedures exist; Wisconsin's system differs substantially from the ones used by Congress and the other states.[1] Several features are most noteworthy. The Wisconsin budget system begins and ends with a powerful governor. Every two years the State Budget Office, working closely with the governor, directs each state agency to submit a budget request. This directive contains the governor's broad policy initiatives. After the agencies submit their requests, the state budget director and the governor form one omnibus budget bill to submit to the legislature. This bill—the governor's budget—goes directly to the legislature's Joint Finance Committee (JFC) after the governor sends it to the legislature in his budget address at the end of every other January.

The JFC dominates the budget process in the legislature. It is here that Wisconsin's system differs most dramatically from those of Congress and many other states. Congress breaks the budget into thirteen functional areas, each considered by separate appropriations committees in each house. The

Budget and Impoundment Act of 1974 established budget committees in the House and Senate, and these committees oversee the general scope of government spending and set overall spending targets, but the appropriations committees remain Congress's budget makers. In Wisconsin, the budget is kept unified and legislative action centers almost completely on the JFC. Within that body, agency budgets are distributed to discussion groups, which hold public hearings and make recommendations to the whole committee. The JFC, comprising equal membership from the senate and the assembly, holds hearings, evaluates, alters, and approves the entire budget; though standing committees and the JFC's informal discussion groups may review portions of the bill, in the end it is the whole JFC's approval that is needed. The JFC sends the governor's budget, along with the changes it has made, to either the senate or the assembly. This stage takes about two months.

Next, the majority party caucuses become the main players. Though individual amendments may be added to the JFC budget on the floor, in practice one "super amendment" is created within the majority caucus. This amendment contains all the individual amendments approved within the caucus. This is done in order to build a coalition strong enough to approve the entire budget. Once enough votes are assembled in the caucus to ensure passage, the budget, along with the super amendment, is approved on the floor. All other amendments are routinely rejected. The same procedure is repeated in the other house. As the bills passed by the two houses will differ, a conference committee may be used to develop a compromise; more often, the bills are shifted between the houses with "narrowing" amendments considered until an identical bill is passed in each house. This process can also take several months.

When the final bill reaches the governor's desk, he has the power to delete portions of the budget through a line-item veto while signing the rest of the bill. He does this frequently; the legislature can override his vetoes but does so less often. If the timetable is successfully followed, the budget is completed by 30 June of each odd-numbered year.

Evaluation of the Budget Process

Wisconsin's budget process is marked by considerable centralized power. The governor clearly sets the path with his budget proposals and has an item veto to protect his decisions; increasingly the budget includes his substantive policy initiatives. Legislative activity is dominated by the majority party through a single committee (the JFC) and the party caucuses. Is this process a good one? We wish we could answer this question in terms of results, that is, the process creates "good budgets." But what is a good budget? Radically different answers are given by those with opposing political beliefs. Some would answer that the best budget spends least, while others would maintain that the best budget most fully provides for the needs of the citizens. On the other hand, most would agree that a responsible budget process completes a budget on time and within constitutional and fiscal limits. In that regard, the Wisconsin process, unlike the current national budget system, can generally be applauded.[2] Budgets are usually passed on time; they remain within the limits of the balanced budget provision which is mandated; and when short-falls or surpluses occur, the system responds. The response may not be pretty, but unlike the federal system, the Wisconsin system does respond.

The Wisconsin system thus appears to be a model of efficient action compared to the federal one. However, Wisconsin's budget system also exemplifies a central struggle over how democratic decisions should be made. The issue, which is a general and very old question of democratic theory, centers on the degree to which closed, centralized decision making should be built into the political process. The centralized system of power in Wisconsin has theoretical advantages and disadvantages as opposed to a decentralized system, which allows wider participation. Good arguments can be made that the budget process should be a powerful one controlled by the governor and majority party's members in the legislature. The theoretical benefits derived from such a powerful system are as follows:

1. *Accountability.* The majority party can take credit for its budget, while the opposition party can place the blame for that budget squarely on the majority party.
2. *Efficiency.* The budget can be approved by the legislature fairly quickly, without becoming bogged down in a procedural swamp.
3. *Effectiveness.* The budget can be part of a coherent program without becoming too open to the influence of special interests.
4. *Majority Rule.* The majority party represents the wishes of the majority of the electorate.

But these benefits carry procedural costs. A powerful majority party dominating the budget may reduce democratic participation. These costs, which provide arguments against tight legislative control, are the following:

1. *Partisanship.* The current system discourages (or prevents) cooperation of the two parties in forming the budget. The minority party, which represents almost half the state's citizens, may be effectively excluded from contributing to important decisions about the budget.
2. *Budget Packing.* Substantive policy issues (issues that are not strictly budgetary) can be pushed through the legislature as part of the budget.
3. *Inadequate Scrutiny.* Programs included in the budget may receive deficient evaluation relative to programs enacted through the separate standing committees. In addition, party caucuses, meeting in closed session, may alter the budget without public evaluation.

4. *Minority Control.* Crucial decisions regarding the budget are decided within the majority caucuses in the legislature. As only a majority of the majority caucus is needed to include an item in the budget, in effect a minority of the entire legislature can determine the shape of the budget.

It can be argued theoretically that in this context power and participation are conflicting values. By emphasizing accountability, bipartisanship is sacrificed. By promoting efficiency, the likelihood of budget packing is increased. As the system is more effective, it is less open. In allowing the majority party to dominate the budget, the chances that a legislative minority will control it are increased. We partially disagree with this assessment. There are times when power and participation are in direct conflict, but it is not necessarily the case that a direct trade-off between these two values must exist. By reducing one we do not automatically gain more of the other. With luck and skill, the process can be powerful and still provide a broad measure of participation. The trick—and it is a difficult one—is to weigh power and participation to obtain a suitable balance. Wanting both a powerful system and one providing for wide participation, we seek to balance them by asking: Can the budget process be made more participatory while retaining the benefits of a powerful system?

Carefully examining the current process and its historical development should reveal both features of the system worth preserving and those that need to be changed. Because power versus participation issues are interrelated, it is fruitless to consider each issue in isolation from the others or to separate them from the actual budget struggles. These issues will be examined as they arise in conjunction with recurring controversies over the budget. The controversies center on the powers of the governor and his ability to place policy in the budget, the Joint Finance Committee and how it should operate, and the party caucuses and their penchant for secrecy. Each institution and issue will be discussed in turn.

The Governor's Role in the Budget Process

The Expanding Role of the Governor

Since the late 1950s the governor's budgetary power has steadily increased. The creation of the Department of Administration (DOA) under Governor Gaylord Nelson, along with the growth in budget personnel throughout the bureaucracy, has clearly enhanced the governor's role. Although the budget office is housed in the DOA and not in the governor's office (as it is in many states), the DOA works very closely with the governor's staff in preparing the initial budget. Unifying the budget, rather than considering budget bills for each state fund separately, has strengthened the governor because it forces the legislature to consider his budget as an entire legislative package. Additionally, centralized budget power in the legislature has made it easier for governors to work for passage of their budgets and more difficult for groups within the legislature to derail executive initiatives.

There are clear advantages in this trend. The governor is the only figure elected statewide who has budget responsibility, and he is therefore the easiest target of a disapproving electorate. As Ira Sharkansky's (1968) analysis of state budgeting demonstrates, the governor must bear the brunt of tax increases and therefore should have commensurate responsibility for spending decisions. Without budget preparation centralized in the governor's hands, the system would be hopelessly inefficient. The line-item veto works well to control abuses in the system which can easily creep in during last-minute legislative bargaining.

The one countervailing problem we see is the potential, and indeed very strong temptation, for the governor to use the budget as the vehicle for new policy initiatives. This problem is most serious when the governor and the majority in the legislature are all from the same party. However, that is also when the majority mandate is most straightforward and the argument against the passage of such legislation is weakest.

A final change to consolidate the governor's budgetary power would be to move the budget office into the governor's office. This was briefly proposed at the beginning of Anthony Earl's administration (1982–86), but the arguments against that move appear sound. If it were to take place, more management levels in the agency would become appointive and not subject to normal civil service procedures. This not only makes transitions between administrations more difficult but also runs the risk of creating a highly politicized agency at the expense of professional competence. At present, the governor has considerable influence over the budget office within a permanent, professional department.

The Governor and Budget Packing: Policy in the Budget

The governor's ability to place substantive policy (or simply "policy") in the budget, which we call "budget packing," has been continually controversial. Advocates argue that policy is inseparable from the budget, and placing it there increases legislative efficiency and innovation while allowing the governor to develop a coherent program. Critics claim that putting policy in the budget permits the majority, by restricting sound legislative judgment and hindering public scrutiny, to jam numerous bills through the legislature that would not otherwise pass. Some also fear that "modest" programs slipped into the budget will be continually more costly as they expand in the future.

Both advocates and critics are partly correct. Clearly, each party can agree that budget packing is legitimate when *its* governor is in office, while opposing it when the governor is from the other party. The main questions to ask, then, attempt to show neither unequivocal support nor opposition to budget packing, but seek more tempered evidence. Are there adequate protections to budget packing, or is it increasing explosively? Are some types of policies more sensibly excluded from the budget? Do the policies included receive reasonable scrutiny? Do the policies that remain in the budget gain majority support?

History of Budget Packing

Through Governor Warren Knowles's administration in the 1960s, there were separate budget bills for each state fund: general purpose, conservation, and transportation. Budgets simply listed the amount of money needed to continue present programs. If a program was to be changed, such as by an alteration of the school aid formula, or a new program was proposed, a separate bill was required. In 1971, beginning with Democratic Governor Patrick Lucey, the budget was unified as an omnibus bill which included all appropriations and revenue measures. There was good reason to move to an omnibus bill: total revenue and spending requirements could be considered as a unified package rather than bit by bit.[3] However, once omnibus bills were used, inserting unrelated policy items became almost irresistible because the necessity of passing a budget made it highly likely that policy included in the budget would also become law.

The Republican-controlled senate initially voted to exclude all of Lucey's policy issues from the budget, even though Lucey had stated that his proposal to merge the University of Wisconsin–Madison with the other state universities was "nonnegotiable." After a lengthy stalemate, the merger was removed from the bill and passed separately before the budget was finished, and Lucey was able to marshal many of his other policies through a conference committee compromise. In the end, the stumbling block was not "policy" per se, but a major revision in the state tax-sharing formula, which was bitterly opposed by Republican conservatives but ultimately supported by six Republican moderates in the senate. The budget was signed on 3 November 1971—the latest a budget had been approved since the 1920s.

By 1973, budget packing was routine, if not routinely accepted. Senate Republicans proposed to hold public hearings on the policy issues within the established committees, and at least three senate committees did just that (*Capital Times,* 9 April 1973, *Milwaukee Journal,* 23 March 1973). A joint senate and assembly committee to evaluate the budget process, after assessing the policy-related delays in the 1971 budget, also affirmed a role for these committees: "The standing committees may hold public hearings in connection with their review of policy items in the budget bill and may invite agency personnel to appear upon these items" (*Milwaukee Sentinel*, 20 July 1973). These committee recommendations, along with minority reports, were to be submitted as nonbinding to the JFC (Wisconsin Legislature 1974). At least one legislator admitted that rules prohibiting budget packing were not essential. Representative Paul Offner (D-La Crosse), though a strong critic of Lucey's budget packing in 1975, thought that the blame for tolerating it was shared by the legislature. "After all, the legislature could always strip the budget of the nonbudgetary items, and require that these be considered as separate bills" (*Milwaukee Journal*, 23 June 1977).[4]

Governor Lee Dreyfus—who in his campaign pledged to limit policy in the budget—recommended few new policies in his first budget, and the bill emphasized current programs. He sent the legislature five "functional" policy bills (S.B. 110–14) for changing state government. All five died in committee at the end of the session (Wisconsin Legislature, 1979, pp. 120–23).

Dreyfus's 1981 budget bill was a hasty retreat from his earlier opposition to budget packing and included major policy proposals.[5] Having failed to pass his functional policy bills in the previous session, this time around he added his policies to the budget. The JFC, no stranger itself to budget packing, removed 111 provisions from Dreyfus's budget, declaring that since the items left spending unchanged, they had no place in the bill (*Milwaukee Journal*, 19 March 1981). Many were later restored. Despite a few legislative skirmishes since then, policy remains dug in. For example, Governor Earl's 1985 budget included major tax proposals (see Chapter 9) and a comparable worth program. Still, the future of budget packing is not certain. In June 1985, the Wisconsin State Appeals Court ruled that it was unconstitutional to place projects that are strictly "local" in nature (in this case, it was referring to the decision in the 1983–85 budget designating a site for a prison near Milwaukee County Stadium) in an omnibus budget bill. Though this ruling did not eliminate policy from the 1985–87 budget, it did open the possibility that those opposing certain policies could sue to have them removed.

Have policies been ramrodded into law via the budget? A great many no doubt have been. Still, little evidence exists that policies can be forced through in this way without limit. Policy can be—and has been—removed from the budget by the JFC (Dreyfus's policies), the party caucuses, the whole legislature (Lucey's merger), and the governor (such as when Earl used a line-item veto to eliminate a legislative reapportionment plan added by the Democratic caucus). However, a more complete evaluation of the budget-packing issue requires discussion of the types of policies included in the budget, the question of bipartisan participation, and the degree of legislative scrutiny policies receive.

Appropriate Budget Policies

Almost all policy—other than symbolic proclamations—costs money. One type of policy which has become pivotal in recent budget deliberations alters existing fiscal formulas such as state educational and municipal aids. Under anyone's definition, these alterations are substantive policy decisions, but because they critically affect state revenues and budget totals, it seems inconceivable that these decisions should be made apart from the budget process.

But there are numerous other policy decisions which cost something but whose expenses are incidental to their main purpose. The 1983–85 budget contains examples such as legislative reapportionment, creating a Transportation Projects Commission to recommend major highway projects, starting a hospital rate-setting commission to establish rates for all Wisconsin hospitals (see Chapter 11 in this volume), and allowing a town to issue a liquor license to an outdoor theater in excess of the town's quota. This category is a better candidate for removal. The National Council of State Legislatures (NCSL) found, in fact, that numerous states ban such policy from the budget.[6]

Between these two types of legislation there is a wide range of policy options that do not have the overwhelming budgetary impact of aid formulas, but are not as purely procedural (and political) as reapportionment or establishing commissions. Examples in recent budgets might include creating a farmland preservation program or initiating comparable worth. How these programs should be treated is not clear-cut, and the critical judgments involve issues in the power-participation trade-off. Key among these are the degree of bipartisanship and scrutiny these measures receive.

Bipartisanship

Few legislators—at least few in the majority party—cry for more legislative unity in writing the budget. The blunt fact is that in the Wisconsin legislature, unlike the U.S. Congress, the party lines are sharply drawn and pointedly kept. One legislator said he entirely rejected the other party's platform—so why should he ask their help in the budget? As far as he was concerned, the less influence they had, the better. If this did not please the voters, let them boot his party out. Others, no doubt, agree. Fortunately for this point of view, if not for some individual legislators, the boot does exist in Wisconsin, as neither party has a firm lock on control of the legislature.

Furthermore, when each party controls one house, bipartisan compromise is reached, if fitfully. Budget packing is also "bipartisan," as both parties do it when given the chance. As long as control swings from one party to the other, as it sometimes does, each party has the opportunity to put its policies into place through the budget. Consequently, efforts to remove policy from the budget may be seen as no more bipartisan than the desire to keep it in.

Scrutiny

Defining "adequate scrutiny" is not easy. Very few budget items receive anything like "full" public inspection, and in a document hundreds of pages long, only a smattering are studied even briefly in public hearings. And do public hearings ensure real scrutiny? Not necessarily. James Gosling, both a participant in and scholarly authority on Wisconsin's budget process, doubts the value of public hearings.

> Much of the proceedings [of public hearings] is of largely symbolic value, providing a widely publicized forum for a good deal of public staging, with attendance of committee members dropping off after the agency and major interest organizations have made their case (frequently corresponding to the termination of media coverage). (Gosling 1985, 4)

Controversial measures in the governor's budget bill do, however, undergo several months' publicity before they are signed into law. For measures introduced early, either in the governor's program or as part of the JFC's package, this may be good enough. Unfortunately, the later that policy is introduced, the less scrutiny it gets from the press, the public, and politicians.

Two checks prevent late introduction from becoming a severe problem. The governor can eliminate policy changes by means of the line-item veto. This power is used extensively[7] and is aimed mainly at last-minute additions (Gosling 1980, 109). This veto gives the governor a strong control over legislative ability to add policy. The second barrier is the party caucus leadership, which usually tries to limit caucus alterations of the JFC bill. Every additional amendment adopted makes passage more difficult because some legislators might find it unacceptable.[8] Still, policy changes do occur at the last minute. Should all policy be banned from the budget in order to keep these closing-time amendments out? We are not convinced. As some amendments are introduced in caucus to build consensus on the bill, perhaps it is better to allow "cheap" policy amendments than to rely on "expensive" fiscal amendments to create that consensus.

One good measure of "adequate scrutiny" might be the number of times a measure is voted on, or the number of places within the budget process that a measure is discussed. A measure that is explicitly approved at several different stages is more fully evaluated, because at each vote the merits of the policy can be debated. Do major policy proposals receive adequate scrutiny by this criterion? Consider Governor Lucey's proposal to merge the state university system. Before the budget was submitted, several senate Republicans offered a separate merger proposal, but no action was taken. During JFC deliberations, Governor Lucey publicly promoted the merger: "[It's] got to be in the budget. There's too much lethargy in higher education. It's a dramatic change. . . . It's the only way you're going to get it through" (*Milwaukee Journal,* 18 April 1971). In the assembly, Republicans brought to a vote an amendment to delete the merger from the budget; this proposal was defeated (*Milwaukee Journal,* 10 June 1971).

The senate did delete the proposed merger before passing its version of the budget. While the conference committee deliberated on the differences between the senate and assembly bills, the governor and prominent legislators again publicly discussed the merits of the merger.[9] Finally, the assembly and the senate passed the merger in separate legislation and Lucey signed it prior to final passage of the budget.

Comparable worth provided a similar lesson in the 1985–87 budget. This highly controversial policy was debated at every stage of the process. The JFC cut the governor's recommended funding almost in half, but retained it in the bill. Both houses heard arguments that it should be lifted from the budget before ultimately including a limited version in the approved measure.

The lesson is clear. Budget policy, if controversial enough, will usually receive separate discussion and votes at several stages. If opposition to including it in the budget is strong, the policy can be lifted from the budget and considered separately. Including the merger and comparable worth in the budget did not remove them from public scrutiny, but did force the scrutiny to move at a faster pace than it would have otherwise.

If the governor is going to shape state programs by altering taxing and spending formulas or creating new programs, there is a strong case for putting some policies in the budget. Two other possibilities exist. The governor can propose new policies after the budget has passed. In this case, the new policies make the just-passed budget obsolete—if he is able to get them through a worn-out legislature. Alternatively, the governor could wait until just before the next budget, but this would prevent policy innovation until late in the term. Because a new budget must be passed before the new biennium starts, the schedule for consideration of new legislation would be very tight and easily subject to procedural delay.

Although it is impossible to fully assess policy items before a newly elected governor submits a budget, it does make sense to have the JFC and the relevant standing committees consider major policy proposals—such as altering state revenue and local aid formulas—in the year before the budget is introduced. By doing this, the legislature could iron out many wrinkles from the governor's budget before it is officially submitted. This would match the Department of Administration's work in the off-budget years.

Majority Control

Are individual policies supported by a legislative majority when they are included in an omnibus bill? No legislator agrees with *all* portions of the budget, but must vote on it based on an overall assessment of its merits. Removing policy from the budget will not change this fact, as there will always be provisions in a large and complicated budget that are opposed by many, or even a majority. On the other hand, some contend that, if anything, legislators are more likely to vote against the entire budget if they strongly oppose only a few sections; a very unpopular policy measure will not gain majority support just because it is in a budget.[10] As the examples above hint, if a strong majority rejects specific policies, they can be removed and considered as individual measures.

What advantages are gained by excluding policy from the budget? It would force each measure to be considered on its own merit. This change would have conservative consequences, not by favoring one party over another, but by slowing government down. No majority party would be able to put its platform in place as swiftly, because many measures that would be approved under the current system would fail if considered apart from the budget. Yet policy in the budget can find bipartisan support, receive sufficient scrutiny, and obtain effective majority support. Budget packing is more than just an efficient way of putting programs into place.

Programs, once enacted, are likely to persist and grow. It is imperative that important policies receive the fullest possible evaluation. Every effort should be made to first consider and subsequently evaluate such legislation in the off-budget years using the normal standing committees. If these policies were approved separately from the budget, their legitimacy would be increased, and if defeated they would have fielded a true test of majority rule. However, if time or procedural delaying tactics forestall that consideration, the budget process offers an effective alternative.

The Joint Finance Committee

The Joint Finance Committee (JFC), which currently dominates the budget process in the legislature, exemplifies how power and participation can be balanced. Controversy has centered on committee membership: how many members should come from each house, and how should membership be divided between the Democratic and Republican parties. To understand these issues, it is necessary to review the JFC's evolution.

Recent History

In 1971, the JFC was composed of fourteen members, nine from the assembly and five from the senate. Seven of the nine assembly members were Democrats; the senate had four Republicans and one Democrat. The assembly controlled the JFC, and Democrats controlled the assembly. This would seem to give the assembly's majority party tremendous power over the budget process, and in fact the Democrats did have control over the JFC's actions. However, limiting the senate's participation also reduced the committee's power.

Because each house was unequally represented, the assembly had little reason to compromise with the senate in establishing the JFC's budget. In 1971, the assembly passed a budget almost identical to the JFC's proposal, but the senate adopted a budget very different from the JFC-approved one. A conference committee was required to develop a compromise between the two houses, and budgetary power shifted to this group. The assembly's power dissolved, as this conference committee had equal representation from each house. Its membership also reflected the divisions in party control: the assembly appointed three Democrats and the senate, three Republicans.

Similar problems cropped up in 1975. This time, the Democrats had a majority in both houses, and the JFC included seven Democrats and two Republicans from the assembly and four Democrats and one Republican from the senate. The senate, and even the senate Democrats, insisted that they were cut out by the "Secret Seven" assembly Democrats. The Secret Seven could block any proposal they opposed, but were one vote short of being able to pass measures they favored. Again, JFC power was reduced due to the unbalanced participation between the two houses. As in 1971, the assembly passed a bill very similar to the one approved by the JFC; the senate approved a bill that was substantially different; and a conference committee was appointed with equal representation from each house before a compromise emerged.

Legislators recognized that unequal representation for the two houses on the JFC delayed passing the budget. After a lengthy legislative battle—the assembly wanted to hang on to the illusory advantages of having a committee majority—each house finally received equal representation (seven members each) on the JFC for the 1977 budget.[11] This move has not resulted in a JFC that is ineffective or unable to act decisively, as some legislators warned (*Capital Times,* 2 May 1975). As opportunities for participation became more equally shared between the two houses, the JFC's power has increased. Still, despite equal representation between the assembly and senate, no consistent move has been made toward making representation on the committee equal to the partisan balance within each house. In 1979 and 1981 twelve Democrats and two Republicans were on the committee, and eleven Democrats and three Republicans served in 1983, even though this vastly overrepresented the majority party.

A study by the NCSL of twenty-four states found that Wisconsin had the most extreme case of nonproportional representation on its finance committee. The NCSL reported that twenty-two legislative bodies in fifteen states required that membership on standing committees reflect the party ratio in the whole chamber (National Council of State Legislatures 1983, 10). For the 1985 session, the JFC was expanded from fourteen to sixteen members, with each house having eight representatives on the committee. The assembly moved closer to proportional representation, with its ratio of five Democrats to three Republicans coming as close to equal representation as possible while still mirroring the Democratic majority found in the assembly. The senate tally was six Democrats, two Republicans.

Representation

The move toward proportional representation on the JFC should be applauded; it should also be required. Several representatives believe that since precedent has been established for roughly proportional representation on the committee, future appointments will reflect partisan divisions. However, this is not guaranteed. Unless proportional representation becomes a firm rule, it will not be followed if different parties control each house. For example, if the Republican party regained a senate majority, it would almost certainly appoint its members to the JFC—at best—to reverse the ratio it had previously suffered. If the senate Republicans placed six Republicans on the committee and only two Democrats, the assembly would quickly give up its proportional representation and also place six Democrats on the committee.

Why should there be proportional representation on the JFC? The procedural reason is evident: committee structure should reflect the electorally mandated partisan balance. Further, as with balancing the membership between the two houses, proportional representation from each house would increase both the participation of each party and committee effectiveness. Consider a few possibilities. If both houses had the current partisan balance, the committee would have ten majority party and six minority party representatives (a five-to-three margin in each house). The majority party would then be forced to maintain almost complete party discipline, as it could afford to lose only one vote and still muster a majority. This would pressure the committee to develop a budget bill basically acceptable to the entire party membership on the committee. (Unless, of course, the committee makes a sincere effort to create a bipartisan measure). This may be tedious, but it would go a long way to ensure that the committee's bill would be strongly supported by its members in each house, reducing the tinkering the bill receives in the party caucuses. This would minimize the little-evaluated amendments added to the budget.

If a different party controls each house by roughly the same proportion, the committee would have an exact eight-to-eight balance; thus, a bipartisan measure would have to be forged to eliminate ties. Exact balance on the committee would ensure that each proposal received fullest debate. It may be argued that this would sharply reduce the committee's efficiency—we could expect that the JFC's deliberations would be lengthier than they usually are— but it would probably not slow the entire process down. Remember that the slowest budget in recent years happened in 1971, when the JFC was not able to build a consensus acceptable to both houses. At that time, an equally balanced conference committee had to be created to do just that.

A third possibility is that each party controls one house, but one party has a narrow majority while the other has a large one. In this case, the party with slim control in the one house will have only a minority of the committee members. Again, the party that dominates the committee can cut the other party out of the process at the risk of seeing its plan sunk in the house that the minority committee members control. Bipartisanship within the JFC is promoted if the committee wants to pass a bill acceptable to both houses without extensive caucus rewriting.

While we believe that establishing more proportional representation on the JFC will create greater participation and improve the process, other, more dramatic changes are also worth contemplation. Because currently the JFC is really the only show in town, the remaining standing committees have atrophied considerably as the JFC's role has expanded. Informal links exist between discussion groups and standing committees, but because they remain informal the strength of the link depends on legislators' personalities. We believe that the role of the standing committees should be enhanced during the budget process. One way to accomplish this, as well as to consider new policy initiatives in the off-budget years, would be to have the standing committees formally review the functional budget sections, giving special emphasis to new spending provisions. This review could be made in February and March, running parallel with public hearings in the JFC.

We do not think Wisconsin should emulate Congress's dependence on individual appropriations committees. That system, which is certainly less centralized, has consistently failed to pass budgets in a timely manner and has been unable to contain spending. Timely passage has not improved following the Budget Reforming Act of 1974 (Wander et al. 1984). The established relationships between "clients" (constituent and bureaucratic) and appropriations committees are also critical in perpetuating spending even when the collective will seems to favor reduction (see Wildavsky 1979; Ippolito 1981). Therefore, Wisconsin's standing committee reviews would be nonbinding on the JFC. However, formal review would enrich the public record and possibly influence caucus proceedings. Budget timing would not be affected if a strict date were imposed. If the committees could not reach agreement on a report by the specified date, the JFC would simply proceed with its discussion group decisions.

The Party Caucuses

The majority party caucuses are probably the most criticized aspect of the Wisconsin budget process. Secrecy is little tolerated by the public, and the party caucuses maintain closed doors. Back-room deal-cutting is condemned, but the caucuses cut them to get the votes needed to pass the budget; in doing this, they appear to shut out the minority party. This negative image has roots in the Progressive tradition that all political decisions should be made in the full public gaze (Butler and Ranney 1978). Progressives believed that the only reason for making decisions secretly was to conceal some part of the process that politicians knew would be regarded as shameful. Venal bargaining at clandestine meetings discredited public policy.

As a result, Wisconsin has built a reputation for open government and opportunities for public participation. Laws were enacted requiring public bodies to meet openly, to hold public hearings with published records before adopting local budgets, and to grant public access to public records. The legislative process itself is unusually open, with printed copies of bills and amendments, public hearings, and open debate standard. Wisconsin has also significantly opened up its budget process in recent years. The major reforms followed the political uproar caused by Peter Bear and Senator Gary Goyke (D-Oshkosh) in the mid-1970s. Bear campaigned against—and beat—Speaker Norman Anderson, who defended closed JFC meetings; Goyke appealed against—and beat—the Secret Seven (the seven assembly members of the JFC who met privately to discuss budgetary items) in Wisconsin's Supreme Court. The formal procedures were opened up to public scrutiny.

But not all parts were to be entirely open. The party caucuses in each house are often open to the public, but they are not required by law to be open, and during important discussions they are routinely closed. Amendments are frequently introduced only by voice motion or a general written description. No document spelling out changes is generally available for immediate inspection. Often the subject of the amendment has not received a public hearing. Quickly adopting controversial measures through the caucus limits the opportunity for public reaction and also lets legislators off the hook without facing a roll call.[12]

Yet legislators defend the right to have closed caucus meetings, and indeed both parties use them. Political leaders often claim the need for some secrecy in order to maintain party discipline and to push their programs through, and

Wisconsin is not unlike other states on this point: fully twenty-nine others permit closed caucus meetings (National Council of State Legislatures 1983). Evaluating the caucus process involves several issues. First, can secrecy be readily eliminated and, if so, how would this likely affect the budget? Second, how much is the budget actually changed in the secret caucuses? Third, does a small minority of legislators use secrecy to control the caucus?

Eliminating Secrecy

The arguments made to eliminate secrecy in government rest on deceptively simple philosophical propositions, which nevertheless generate a powerful political conclusion. The propositions are: (1) because government is created by "the people," there is no reason to hide any act of government from its citizens; (2) better-informed citizens demand and receive better government; and (3) increasing government openness allows citizens to judge more clearly the performance of their elected officials. The political conclusion is that any politician who publicly defends secrecy in government risks defeat. And in Wisconsin, those politicians campaigning on platforms of reducing secrecy in government have scored stunning victories.

Few advocate secrecy on grounds that would be philosophically acceptable today. Practical reason suggests that undue emphasis on government openness is counterproductive, though. First, secrecy is virtually impossible to eliminate. The laws passed in the mid-1970s to ensure that all actions of the JFC are conducted in public encouraged the informal—and not always publicly open—budget discussion groups to form and caucuses to be used in each house. For example, in 1983 Senator Gerald Kleczka (D-Milwaukee) and Representative Mary Lou Munts (D-Madison) were ruled to have violated the openness-in-government laws by using informal discussion groups to study the budget. This ruling will not eliminate these groups, though it will make certain that future meetings do not involve a JFC quorum. Rather than eliminating secrecy, negotiations were just driven further from the public eye. The limited secrecy that does exist seems analogous to the federal government's "covert" operations that are secret in name only, with participants willing and able to discuss publicly the operations' more pernicious aspects. In Wisconsin, the "secret" meetings of caucuses are held in public places at times that are no secret; the actions at these meetings are usually well-publicized.

Furthermore, completely open proceedings may make compromise, which is an essential ingredient in a budget, difficult to achieve (Wildavsky 1979, 137). If all deliberations take place in public, legislators might find themselves accused of "selling out" if they make concessions. A related problem is that openness may promote "buying in," with individual legislators insisting on adding amendments giving some special advantage to their districts. This is the much-criticized "Christmas tree" effect. Though opening the budget process and eliminating the Christmas tree are often advocated in the same breath, several legislators believe that increasing the openness would make the "ornament" problem worse. As legislators' actions are increasingly open to public scrutiny, they feel pressure to have their constituents witness them adding specific items to the budget to help the district. If each legislator is seen by constituents as representing only the district, a completely open process may encourage the legislator to propose amendments that help the district though hurting other parts of the state. But if caucuses meet behind closed doors, no one can see—thus no one can blame—any particular legislator failing to bring home the budgetary bacon. Increasing openness encourages legislators to become increasingly skillful at doing this, so the ornaments may become larger and more ornate.

The Christmas tree effect has not gotten worse, close observers say, since closed caucuses have become more prominent. The number of amendments accepted by the caucus varies greatly from year to year and appears to depend largely on the legislature's partisan balance. The main example of the amendment process "blowing up" was in the senate in 1975, when amendment after amendment was debated and approved on the senate floor. The important point here is that the amendments were all added on the floor rather than in party caucus. Each amendment was considered separately, neither as part of a budget package nor in relation to the assembly-approved bill. Finally, so many amendments were approved on the senate floor that the entire budget was unable to gain majority support. The majority party returned to its caucus to build a bill with enough support to pass. Closed caucuses appear to have some advantages in limiting superfluous amendments.

Caucus Budget Changes

Still, it would be hard to defend closed caucuses *if* they significantly altered the JFC bill. Consequently, it is important to find out just how much budget alteration occurs within the caucuses. James Gosling studied this issue most closely in "The Wisconsin Budgetary Process: A Study of Participant Influence and Choice" (1980).[13] Gosling found that only a relatively small number of total budget items were altered or amended by caucus actions. However, 18% of approved budget items that had major policy and fiscal implications were initiated by floor amendments, most of which had originated within the majority's caucus. Major policy or fiscal items initiated through caucus amendments are much more likely to be approved than those items initially in the governor's budget. The governor's recommendations must pass JFC scrutiny, the caucuses, and floor voting, while caucus amendments must be approved only on the floor. Further, since caucus initiatives are often tied together into one "super amendment" when brought to the floor, party unity is strongly invoked there; thus caucus approval means floor approval.

Caucus amendments receive only minimal scrutiny within the caucuses. The purpose of the caucuses, in voting on budget amendments, is not to evaluate the merits of amendments but to develop a consensus that will hold on the assembly and senate floor. As it appears inevitable that some amendments will be necessary to build a consensus, the problem is how to limit the number and importance of these amendments so that consensus on the budget is gained in caucus with the fewest, most limited amendments. There are pressures to do just this. All proposed budget amendments are supposed to be brought to the JFC in time for their deliberations. This cannot always take place: some amendments proposed in caucus are designed to end stalemates, and their content cannot be foreseen before they are needed. Though it makes abstract sense to simply require that all amendments be sent to the JFC, doing this would take away some of the system's flexibility in forging consensus in the caucuses. However, adding significant amendments to the budget in one house's caucus makes it more difficult to compromise with the other house's bill. Recognizing this, the leadership in each house generally wants to add only enough amendments to gain a consensus within that house, without adding enough to complicate compromises between the houses.

Amendments approved by the legislature must also be able to withstand the governor's line-item veto. The more controversial and far-reaching the amendments are, the more likely it is that the executive will give them close scrutiny; the main task of the governor's staff after the budget has been approved by the legislature is to evaluate the portions of the bill that have been added to the governor's original proposal. This scrutiny is fairly heavy. In Gosling's study, a Democratic governor vetoed thirty-six separate provisions approved by a solidly Democratic legislature; his veto was upheld on twenty-eight measures (Gosling 1980, 173–74).

Minority Influence

Are closed caucuses bad because they allow the budget process to be dominated by a powerful minority? Within the caucuses, only a simple majority— in 1985, that simple majority in the assembly was twenty-seven—is needed to add an amendment to the budget. These twenty-seven votes represented only slightly more than a quarter of the assembly: a bare majority of a bare majority. In the extreme case, as the caucus attempts to fashion a majority, one or two representatives may be able to stall passage until their pet amendments are adopted. Critics claim that this subverts majoritarian principles and defense of this system seems to be based only on political expediency. Those who assert that a minority in the caucus can control the budget want all budget decisions to be made by a majority vote on the assembly floor.

But finding a majority can be tricky, as an example can show. Imagine thirty-three senate members evaluating a budget, to which three amendments have been proposed. A large majority favors each amendment and passes each one by votes of twenty-seven to six. The six opponents in each case, however, bitterly oppose one amendment, and vow to vote against any budget that contains that hated amendment. The six dissenters are also different for each amendment. When the amended budget is brought to a vote, it would fail by three votes, as the coalition of six dissenters on three amendments now forms a majority of the entire senate.

This paradox may appear artificial, but because in reality there are more amendments, and legislators learn the strategic value of their votes, this problem is very real. In 1975 the Democrats controlled the senate by a nineteen to fourteen margin. Had the Democrats voted as a bloc, the budget might have passed quickly. Instead, nine amendments were passed on the floor, several fiercely opposed by Democrats from Milwaukee and Dane counties. Even though each amendment was supported by a majority, only about twelve representatives were expected to support the entire bill, and stalemate was almost certain (*Capital Times,* 5 June 1975). The deadlock was broken only when the Democrats retreated to a party caucus and a budget acceptable to its majority was hammered out. There was apparently no way to gain a majority favoring the entire bill unless the legislators could bargain. Because Wisconsin's budget is highly partisan, bargaining will not likely carry across party lines. Amendments proposed in caucus may be added to the budget without a legislative majority supporting them, but in adding amendments high priority is given to developing a bill that will be supported by a majority of the entire body. By the time the amended budget is released from the caucus, that majority will have evolved.

No consistent argument can be made that floor action is "majority rule" and caucuses are "minority rule." The floor of the houses and the party caucuses are partly dominated by a majority and partly by a minority; however, one starts with majoritarian principles and ends in stalemate while the other starts with minority power and ends in majority acceptance.

Is the minority party completely excluded from budget deliberations? The amount of bipartisanship that has existed in creating budgets during this period is not easily measured. Very few legislators—especially in the minority party—have been willing to cross party lines on budget votes. Further, party lines are most clearly drawn for budget bills calling for tax increases, because the minority party has been unwilling to go on record as tax raisers. In these instances the minority party relishes its outsider role. For this reason, more than for any involving the budget procedure itself, there was bipartisanship in the final votes for the 1985–87 budget (at least in the senate), which called for pleasant spending increases without heavy new taxes.

Do opportunities for meaningful participation by the minority party exist? The minority can influence the budget at several levels, but, granted, this potential is limited. First, the minority party is represented on the JFC, and, depending on member personalities, a minority representative may be able to influence the bill. In the 1985 session, for the first time in recent years, a minority member (Representative Betty Jo Nelsen, R-Shorewood) chaired one discussion group. Second, several members suggested that it is possible for an adroit minority representative to have an amendment considered in the majority caucus, although technically the amendment is entered in the majority representative's name. Whether this happens depends largely on the relationship between particular members. Third, the minority party can make amendments from the floor, although in practice these amendments are usually rejected en masse. If the proposed amendment has substantial floor backing, it is sometimes tabled rather than rejected, and the majority party considers it later during caucus. The minority party most bitterly complains about being excluded at this point. Then assembly Minority Leader Tommy Thompson (R-Elroy) summarized this point in 1983—the majority party is "arrogant, drunk with power," trampling on the rights of the minority "because you don't have the guts to debate this [budget] on the floor" (*Wisconsin State Journal*, 26 June 1983).

Should minority amendments be considered more seriously? It depends, as two very different types of amendments are proposed. Amendments may be sincerely offered to address perceived flaws in the budget. Other amendments are offered not to "improve" the budget but to provide campaign material for the minority party simply because they will be voted down. Legislators recognize the difference between these types, and may grant serious amendments further treatment (by tabling them for caucus discussion) while summarily dismissing the amendments that are political ploys. For this reason, it is not necessary to create additional procedural safeguards to ensure that minority amendments receive consideration.

Using caucuses to develop majorities capable of supporting the budget may not appear to be an ideal system, but it is not viciously flawed. A trade-off between complete openness and political necessity has been reached. The budget is changed by the caucuses, but it is not rewritten by them, and most of the time the alterations are minor. Minorities are important, yet the caucuses hammer together a majority capable of passing the budget; there is no clean argument that using caucuses subverts majoritarian principles and leads to elite domination. The most serious problem in relying on caucuses is that their amendments receive little scrutiny. Still, there are some checks to prevent the caucuses from running wild in adding amendments, and the governor has the pen of last resort in scratching ill-considered items.

Conclusion

Since Wisconsin's budget system emphasizes power over participation, it is not surprising that our recommendations nudge the process in the opposite direction. Our nudge is slight, despite our initial enthusiasm for reform. The system that has evolved in recent years makes considerably more sense on careful examination than it first appeared. Thus, we do not recommend a drastic overhaul of the system, for example to emulate the federal system of budget, appropriations, and revenue committees. Such "reforms" are likely to get the state into the federal quagmire of delays, paralysis, and perpetual budgetary crisis.

American political scientists are wary of power, favoring procedural checks, openness, bipartisan compromise, and participation of many players. Those whom we consulted, many of whom have tasted power, fear it less, and are very conscious of problems arising from cumbersome procedures. We have reflected on the enormous web of problems that tangle the much more fragmented national budget process and have concluded that the power inherent in Wisconsin's budget system does not endanger the political process as political rhetoric often suggests. Rather, it often facilitates compromise, which in turn prevents stalemate.

Our recommendations are to protect against the most glaring problems of including major substantive issues in the budget, and preventing total atrophy of the standing committees. Specifically, we recommend requiring proportional party representation for each house for membership on the Joint Finance Committee, and for instituting formal, nonbinding review of budgetary proposals by standing committees in February and March of budget years. To do so preserves a system that gives government power to reach important decisions, while ensuring that participation is broad enough to represent the wishes of Wisconsin's citizens.

NOTES

1. For a more detailed account of Wisconsin's procedures, see Rhodes (1985).

2. For the most current and universally depressing anthology on the subject of federal budgeting see Wander, Herbert, and Copeland (1984).

3. The use of an omnibus appropriations and revenues bill was reaffirmed by the Special Joint Committee on the Budget Process as created by 1973 S.J.R. 77. Since that

time, there have been infrequent suggestions that the legislature should return to considering separate bills for the different programs.

4. Offner, it might be remembered, was the principal author of major policy proposals to check medical costs, which were included in the 1983 budget (*Wisconsin State Journal,* 3 June 1983).

5. His proposed budget was 714 pages long, topping Lucey's largest of 567 pages.

6. This study found that eight of the thirteen states examined constitutionally prohibit policy in the budget (National Council of State Legislatures 1983, table 1, p. 23).

7. Governor Lucey vetoed 20 items in 1971 and a similar number in 1973; in 1975 he penned 61 vetoes, and in 1977, 67 (though 21 of them were overridden by the legislature). Dreyfus item-vetoed 45 provisions in 1979. Governor Earl vetoed many items in 1983 and 1985, including the highly controversial legislative reapportionment plan that had been added to the budget in the Democratic Assembly caucus.

8. For example, in 1975 assembly Speaker Norman Anderson (D-Madison) pledged a "no amendment" policy for the Democratic caucus, and the caucus approved a budget very similar to the one passed by the JFC (*Milwaukee Sentinel,* 7 May 1975). In 1979, James Rooney (D-Racine) was a self-described "benevolent dictator" in his attempts to limit caucus amendments to the budget (*Wisconsin State Journal,* 24 June 1979).

9. For example, see the *Green Bay Press-Gazette* (6 August 1971).

10. See Robert Kasten's comments in the *Milwaukee Journal* (4 October 1973).

11. Senate Substitute Amendment 1 to S.B. 755. This amendment also balanced the power of the committee cochairmen. Previously, the committee was presided over by the cochairman of the house to which the budget had initially been referred. This provision was struck (Wisconsin Secretary of State 1975, 746–47).

12. Two highly controversial amendments added to the 1983–85 budget by the majority caucus were to reapportion legislative districts (in the assembly) and to increase unemployment compensation taxes by $61 million (in the senate).

13. Examining the 1977–79 budget, Gosling divided the document into several parts: (1) items of minor, medium, and major policy effect; (2) items of minor, medium, and major fiscal effect; (3) items proposed by the different actors in the process; (4) items approved by the different actors; and (5) items of local and nonlocal assistance. His counts give some indication of the relative importance of the legislative caucuses: of the 538 "decision items" initiated in the budget, 16 of them, or 3%, were legislative floor amendments; of the approved items, legislative floor amendments which modified earlier proposals accounted for 6%, or 26 out of the 446 approved decision items. Although Gosling counts "legislative floor amendments," these amendments are almost exclusively first considered and approved within the caucuses (data taken from tables 3 and 4, p. 78).

3

Changes in the Pattern of State and Local Government Revenues and Expenditures in Wisconsin, 1960–1983

ROBERT J. LAMPMAN AND TIMOTHY D. McBRIDE

Introduction

This chapter offers a factual account of broad trends in Wisconsin state and local government finances in the 1960s, 1970s, and 1980s. Here, a set of simplified graphs is used to describe what happened to revenues as a percentage of state personal income, what changes occurred in the relative importance of spending for education, social services, transportation, and other governmental functions, and what shifts were made in the roles of the state as opposed to local governments.[1]

This chapter presents a more complete, integrated picture of state and local government finances in one state than most studies attempt. Studies that concentrate on smaller parts of the complicated state and local government accounts may miss the subtle trade-offs and substitutions among revenue sources and expenditures and government levels that are captured by a larger study. It offers a framework to study often ignored revenue sources (e.g., charges and miscellaneous revenue) and expenditures (e.g., the trust-funds), and develops measures to capture the difference between funding and delivering a good or service or cash benefit.[2]

In most analyses of state and local government finances, the budgets of state and local governments are broken into two parts: (1) the general accounts and (2) the trust fund and utility accounts. This is the procedure used by the Census Bureau. The revenues and expenditures of the state and local governments of Wisconsin are depicted in this manner in table 3.1.

Revenues in the general government account are divided into those col-

Table 3.1. Revenues and Expenditures of State and Local Governments in Wisconsin, 1981 (millions of dollars)

	State	Local	Total
Revenues, Total	$7,200.8	$6,182.5	$10,562.7[a]
General revenues, Total	6,036.5	5,818.3	9,266.6[a]
Own-source general revenues, Total	4,380.1	2,900.8	7,280.9
Tax Collections	3,629.5	1,769.6	5,399.0
Property	92.2	1,743.1	
Income, total	1,910.5	—	
Individual income	1,654.9	—	
Corporate income	255.7	—	
Sales, general	901.5	—	
Sales, selective	477.8	—	
Licenses	186.3	—	
Death and gift	54.5	—	
Other	6.6	26.5	
Charges and miscellaneous	750.6	1,131.3	1,881.9
Charges	520.1	770.0	1,290.1
Education	312.8	104.4	
Hospitals	167.6	197.0	
Other	39.7	468.6	
Miscellaneous	230.5	361.3	591.8
Interest	174.0	176.7	
Other	56.5	184.5	
Intergovernmental revenues, Total	1,656.4	2,917.4	1,985.7[a]
From federal government	1,617.0	368.7	
From state government	—	2,548.7	
From local governments	39.4	[b]	
Trust fund and utility revenues, Total	1,164.3	364.2	1,296.1[a]
Utilities	—	288.9	288.9
Insurance trust funds	1,164.3	75.3	1,007.2[b]
Employe retirement	835.8	75.3	
Contributions	301.2	14.1	
Earnings on investments	534.7	61.3	
Unemployment compensation	322.6	—	
Contributions	299.8	—	
Earnings on investments	22.8	—	
Other	5.9	—	
Contributions	4.1	—	
Earnings on investments	1.8	—	

(*continued on following page*)

[a]Intergovernmental duplicative transactions, from state to local governments or from local governments to the state government, are excluded from totals.

[b]Intragovernmental duplicative transactions, from the state government to its trust funds or from local governments to one another, are excluded from totals.

Table 3.1. Revenues and Expenditures of State and Local Governments in Wisconsin, 1981 (millions of dollars) (*continued*)

	State	Local	Total
Expenditures, Total	6,838.4	6,241.6	10,277.8[a]
General expenditures, Total	6,092.8	5,815.2	9,105.9
Direct general expenditures, Total	3,267.2	5,809.7	9,076.9
Education	990.5	2,560.1	3,550.6
Social services	1,275.8	767.8	2,043.6
Public welfare	943.1	378.4	
Health and hospitals	263.7	389.4	
Employment security administration	64.1	—	
Veterans' benefits	4.9	—	
Transportation	319.2	674.7	993.9
Highways	308.4	629.6	
Other	10.8	45.1	
Public safety	163.5	471.4	634.9
Corrections	106.4	27.2	
Police protection	23.5	301.2	
Fire protection	—	128.8	
Regulation, prot. and inspection	33.6	14.2	
Environment and housing	147.0	682.9	829.9
Parks, recreation and nat. resources	118.8	162.7	
Sewerage	27.8	321.4	
Housing and urban renewal	0.4	105.0	
Sanitation, other than sewerage	—	93.8	
Government administration	143.7	267.3	411.0
Financial administration	72.3	91.9	
General control	61.2	135.5	
General public buildings	10.2	39.9	
Interest on debt	137.4	177.2	314.6
Other	90.1	208.3	298.4
Intergovernmental expenditure, Total	2,825.6	5.5	28.9[a]
To federal government	28.9	—	28.9
To state government	—	5.5	—
To local governments	2,796.7	[b]	—
Trust funds and utilities expenditure, Total	745.5	426.4	1,171.9
Utilities	—	379.6	379.6
Insurance trust funds	745.5	46.8	792.3
Employe retirement	177.8	46.8	
Unemployment compensation	564.2	—	
Other	2.5	—	
Net surplus (deficit), Total	362.4	(59.1)	284.9
General Surplus (deficit)	(56.3)	3.1	161.0
Trust funds and utilities surplus (deficit)	418.8	(62.2)	124.2

Source: Derived from tables 5 and 13 in U.S. Department of Commerce, Bureau of the Census, *Government Finances in 1980–81.* Surplus and deficits shown in last three lines calculated by authors using method described in Appendix B.

Note: Totals may not add, due to rounding.

lected from three "own sources": tax collections (including property, sales, and income taxes), charges (including tuition for education and fees for hospital services), and miscellaneous (including fines, interest, and sales of property). A fourth general revenue source is intergovernmental aid. Expenditures from the general account are divided into eight "direct general" expenditure functions and a ninth·general expenditure function, intergovernmental expenditure. Direct general expenditures include education (including state universities and local primary, secondary, and trade schools), social services (including public welfare and health and hospitals), transportation, public safety (including police, fire, and corrections), environment and housing (including sanitation, sewerage, and public housing as well as parks and recreation), government administration, interest on debt, and other expenditures. In all cases, expenditures, by function, include both capital outlay and current operating costs (such as wages and salaries and interest on debt).

The trust fund and utility account includes revenues and expenditures of locally owned public utilities (publicly owned water, electric, and gas utilities) and revenues and expenditures of the insurance trust funds. In the Census Bureau accounts, revenues to the insurance trust funds are broken out in two ways: (1) by fund type and (2) by revenue source. In Wisconsin, there are two large fund types—the state and local employes' retirement fund and the unemployment compensation fund—and two smaller fund types— the worker's compensation fund and the life insurance fund. There are two revenue sources identified by the Census Bureau as well—contributions and earnings on investments. Trust funds receive contributions from employes (for employe retirement), from taxpayers (payroll taxes for unemployment comensation), and from governments (state, local, and federal). Earnings on the portions of the trust funds invested are primarily from the employes retirement fund.[3]

A historical review of total state and local revenues and expenditures is undertaken in the next section. The third section concentrates on columns 1 and 2 of table 3.1—the separation of the state and local government "system" into its two "subsystems." A fourth section compares Wisconsin revenue and expenditure trends to national averages. Surpluses and deficits are not discussed in the text, but are brought up in Appendix B.

The U.S. Constitution divides governmental authority between the federal government and the states and leaves to the states the power to design the pattern and fiscal role of local governments. Because of this, a state and its local governments are more properly thought of as a "system" than as two distinct entities. Even if it were appropriate to study state and local governments separately, the existence of "intergovernmental transfers," in the form of aid from state to local governments and from the federal government to state and local governments, makes it difficult to decipher the roles of state and local governments because the government delivering a good or service may not be the one that funded its purchase. (The term "good or service" is meant here to include cash benefits to individuals, such as cash assistance benefits.) Any attempt to divide the system into a local portion and a state portion must keep in mind this integrated nature of the two governments. Hence, this chapter will look at state and local government in Wisconsin in two ways: as one system, and as two systems, with expenditures analyzed by "level of delivery" and by "level of funding."

Throughout this chapter, expenditures and revenues will be shown as a "percentage of personal income." This measure is chosen for several reasons. First, this presentation gives a measure of the impact of state and local government expenditures and revenues on the state's economy. Second, presenting expenditure and revenue data as a percentage of personal income roughly corrects for both general economic growth in the economy and inflation. Since there is no state-level equivalent of GNP and no state-level Consumer Price Index, no other adequate denominator seems appropriate. Finally, presentation of expenditures and revenues as a percentage of personal income is the approach chosen by most of the authors in this area, including the Census Bureau. The Advisory Council on Intergovernmental Relations (ACIR 1982) has objected to the percentage of personal income approach, preferring instead to use "tax capacity" and "tax effort" measures. This approach, while innovative, is not as intuitive as the percentage of personal income approach. Also, this measure is applicable only to tax collections and not to expenditure data. Finally, few other authors have adopted the ACIR measure in similar analyses.

State and Local Government as One System

From 1960 to 1973, state and local government expenditures and revenues grew rapidly as a percentage of personal income. However, since 1973 there has been virtually no such growth. Figure 3.1 shows the dramatic contrast between the two periods. Total state and local revenue grew rapidly from 14.5% to 25.1% of state personal income from 1960 to 1973, but the growth in total revenue collections from 1973 to 1983 matched the growth in personal income. Hence, total state and local revenue was 25.4% of personal income in 1983. Similarly, total state and local expenditures, 14.6% of personal income in 1960, grew to 22.6% of personal income in 1973, and stood at 22.5% of personal income in 1983 (see figure 3.3).

The breakdown of revenues and expenditures into the general and trust fund and utility accounts helps to explain these changing trends in overall state and local finances.

General Revenues

State and local general revenue, 13.0% of state personal income in 1960, peaked at 23.1% of personal income in 1973, but fell to 21.4% of personal

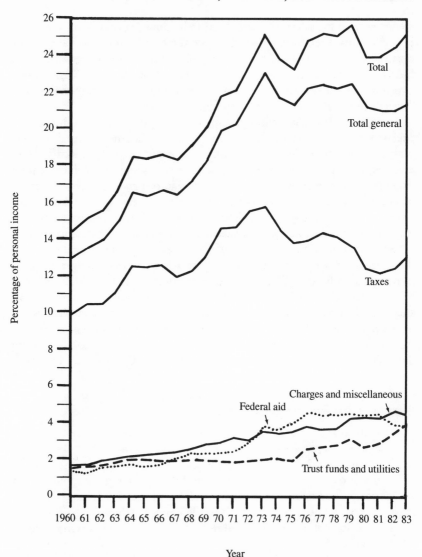

Fig. 3.1. Total state and local revenue, by type and as a percentage of personal income, 1960–83. Note: See Appendix A for a discussion of the sources of the data used for this figure.

income by 1983 (see figure 3.1). Both intergovernmental revenue and charges and miscellaneous revenue increased throughout the 1960–83 period, but the main source of state and local general revenue—tax collections—grew rapidly from 1960 to 1973 and was responsible for more than half of the increase in the share of personal income collected as general revenue in that period. After

1973, however, that growth abated and tax collections as a percentage of personal income fell back to the 1969 level. Despite the 2.6 percentage-point decline in the percentage of personal income collected from taxes after 1973, the general revenue share of personal income fell only 1.7 percentage points, suggesting that increases in federal aid and charges and miscellaneous revenue substituted for tax collections after 1973.

TAX COLLECTIONS. From 1960 to 1983, the share of personal income taken by state and local tax collections changed dramatically, both in scope and composition (see figure 3.1). Total tax collections by state and local governments in Wisconsin grew from 9.9% to 15.8% of personal income from 1960 to 1973. However, from 1973 to 1983 tax collections fell to 13.2% of personal income, about a third higher than the 1960 level.[4]

The property tax. The most significant change in the structure of Wisconsin state and local tax collections since 1960 has been the reduction of the relative importance of the property tax. In 1960, the property tax was Wisconsin's largest revenue source, accounting for 52.8% of total state and local tax collections. By 1981, however, that percentage had slipped to 34.0%. In 1977, for the first time in Wisconsin history, total income taxes collected exceeded property tax collections. In 1982, however, property taxes again overtook income tax collections.

When calculated as a percentage of personal income, property taxes declined only from 5.2% to 5.0% from 1960 to 1983 (see figure 3.2). However, property taxes had peaked at 6.5% of personal income in 1973. Most of the decline in the overall tax burden since 1973 has been the result of the decline in the property tax. Indeed, while all taxes, as a percentage of personal in-

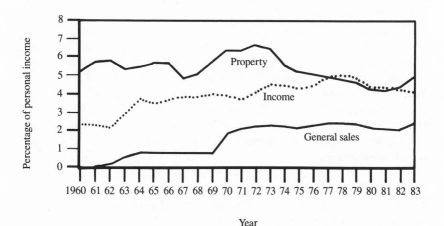

Fig. 3.2. Selected state and local tax collections, by type and as a percentage of personal income, 1960–83. Note: See Appendix A for a discussion of the sources of the data used for this figure.

come, declined 2.6 percentage points from 1973 to 1983, property taxes accounted for most—1.5 percentage points—of that decline.

The trend toward decreased reliance on property taxes appears to have been reversed after 1981. In 1982 and 1983, property taxes again became the largest source of tax collections in Wisconsin, increasing from 4.2% to 5.0% of personal income from 1981 to 1983. Figure 3.1 shows that this increase led a reversal in the decline in tax collections overall at the state and local levels, as tax collections rose by one percentage point from 1981 to 1983.

The general sales tax. When Wisconsin started collecting a general sales tax in 1962, only ten states were without a general sales tax. By 1970 the sales tax had become the third largest source of tax revenue for state and local governments in Wisconsin, and, by 1983, 17.9% of total tax revenue came in the form of general sales taxes.

The sales tax was created out of the movement to reduce property taxes in Wisconsin. At first glance, figure 3.2 seems to portray the success of slowing the growth in property taxes through sales tax increases. While the property tax burden was falling slightly from 5.2% to 5.0% of personal income from 1960 to 1983, the share of personal income collected in the form of general sales taxes grew from zero to 2.4% of personal income. Furthermore, as pointed out above, property taxes peaked in 1962—the year the general sales tax was implemented—but fell to only 37.7% of total taxes by 1983.

A closer inspection of the facts makes this conclusion less clear, however. The sales tax that first became effective in 1962 was a 3% "selective" sales tax—applicable only to specific items, mainly tangible personal property. The list of applicable items was expanded in 1963, but the biggest change occurred in 1970, when a "general" 4% sales tax took effect, applying to *all* items except those specifically excluded from the tax (mainly "necessities"). Aside from this major change in the tax in 1970, it is clear from figure 3.2 that there was little change, on a year-to-year basis, in the burden of the sales tax. Thus, property taxes were growing at the same time that the sales tax was growing, and the large fall in the property tax burden after 1973 was not financed by increases in sales taxes. Instead, these facts suggest that the sales tax increases from 1962 to 1970 more likely kept property taxes from growing faster than they otherwise would have and that, during the 1973–83 period, when the property tax burden fell, sales taxes were not increased to replace the lost revenue.

Income taxes. Aside from the sales tax, income taxes were the fastest growing tax in Wisconsin from 1960 to 1983, as they grew from 2.3% to 4.0% of personal income (see figure 3.2). The rate of growth in income tax collections was virtually uninterrupted from 1960 to 1978.

Until 1978, income taxes seem to have been rising at the same time that the property tax burden was falling. But when one compares the growth rates in the separate periods, this conclusion becomes less clear. In the 1960–73 period, income taxes (as a percentage of personal income) grew by 2.2 percentage points at the same time that sales taxes grew by 2.2 percentage points and property taxes increased by 1.3 percentage points. Conversely, in the 1973–78 period, both income and property taxes fell (as a percentage of personal income) and sales taxes increased only slightly.

Though inflationary bracket creep was a factor, the rapid increase in income tax collections was mostly deliberate, the direct result of six rate increases between 1962 and 1972, an unusual occurrence in Wisconsin, since from 1911 to 1962 tax rates were increased only twice.

Figure 3.2 shows a decline in the income tax burden after 1978. This decline seems to have led a similar decline in taxes overall, from 14.2% to 13.2% of personal income in the same period. Just as in the years before 1978, the changes were deliberate, the result of a one-time 16% income tax cut and a decrease in marginal tax rates in 1979 and the indexation of all tax brackets to the Consumer Price Index in 1981.

A critical point that cannot be ignored in a discussion of Wisconsin's income tax burden is the difference in growth rates of corporate and individual income taxes between 1960 and 1983. Corporate income taxes as a percentage of personal income remained essentially constant from 1960 (0.69%) to 1983 (0.66%). During that same time, however, individual income taxes grew from 1.6% to 3.4% of personal income.

Other taxes. Wisconsin in 1983 collected 13.8% of its tax revenues from four other sources: selective sales taxes (including motor vehicle, tobacco, alcohol, and utility fees), license fees (including motor vehicle, hunting, fishing, and corporate licenses), death and gift taxes, and other taxes.[5] The burden of these taxes did not change much from 1960 to 1973, but declined after 1973, accounting for more than one-fourth of the 2.6 percentage-point decline in the total tax burden over that period.

The largest tax category of the four—selective sales taxes—accounted for most of the fall in these tax categories. Of the 0.7 percentage-point decline in the share of personal income taken by these taxes, 0.5 percentage points of the decline (from 1.7% to 1.2% of personal income) came in the share of taxes collected from selective sales taxes.

CHARGES AND MISCELLANEOUS REVENUES. Charges and miscellaneous revenue sources grew in importance to state and local governments from 1960 to 1983. In 1960, charges and miscellaneous revenue accounted for only 13.0% of total state and local general revenue. By 1983, however, that figure had risen to 20.6%. Figure 3.1 shows that these changes helped to compensate for the fall in tax collections after 1973. Specifically, charges and miscellaneous revenue, 1.7% of personal income in 1960, grew to 3.5% of personal income by 1973 and 4.4% of personal income in 1983. This increase in charges and miscellaneous revenue offset the 2.6 percentage-point decline in tax collections from 1973 to 1983.

INTERGOVERNMENTAL REVENUE. Since state and local governments are treated as one system in this section, state-local intergovernmental transactions are not included as intergovernmental revenue here, but will be taken up below. Federal aid to state and local governments accounted for much of the growth in state and local general revenue from 1960 to 1983. Federal aid, as a percentage of personal income, grew from 1.4% to 3.8% from 1960 to 1983, making it the fastest-growing state and local general revenue source.

Increases in federal aid and in charges and miscellaneous revenue from 1973 to 1983 made it possible for state and local governments to reduce the tax burden on Wisconsin taxpayers after 1973, while maintaining nearly the same total level of revenue. However, figure 3.1 shows that the growth in federal aid leveled off in 1976. And, from 1981 to 1983, federal aid actually fell from 4.5% to 3.8% of personal income. Thus, federal aid, the second largest revenue source to state and local governments from 1973 to 1982, was exceeded by both charges and miscellaneous and trust fund and utility revenues by 1983.

General Expenditures

State and local general expenditures, 13.4% of personal income in 1960, grew to 21.1% of personal income in 1973 but fell to 20.0% of personal income by 1983 (see figure 3.3). All of the expenditure functions—except transportation—increased as a percentage of personal income from 1960 to 1973, with education and social services expenditures growing the fastest. From 1973 to 1983, three functions—education, transportation, and other— fell as a percentage of personal income, and more than offset a rise in expenditures on social services.

EDUCATION. Of all the goods and services provided by state and local governments in Wisconsin, education has the highest priority. In every year from 1960 to 1983, more than 30% of total state and local expenditures went toward education. And, over the twenty-four-year period considered here, education's share of the total state and local general expenditures rose from 31.8% to 38.4%. More pronounced, however, and shown in figure 3.3, education expenditures, as a percentage of personal income, rose from 4.6% in 1960 to 7.7% in 1983.

The general upward trend in education expenditures has not been steady, however. Figure 3.3 shows that while education expenditures more than doubled (from 4.6% to 9.6% of personal income) from 1960 to 1971, they slipped to 7.7% of personal income by 1983. While in 1983 education remained the highest priority item in state and local budgets and while it ac-

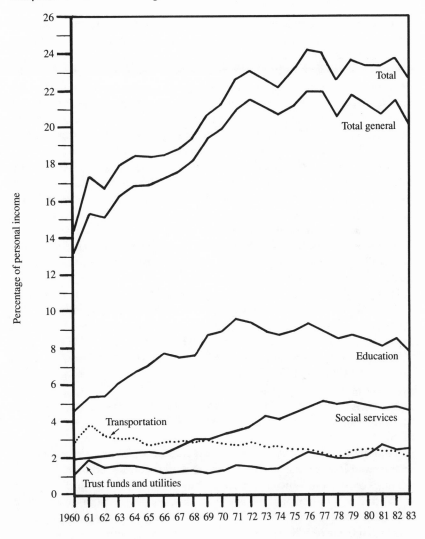

Fig. 3.3. Total state and local expenditures, by function and as a percentage of personal income, 1960–83. Note: See Appendix A for a discussion of the sources of the data used for this figure.

counted for more than half of the increase in total general expenditures from 1960 to 1973, it also accounted for all of the decline, relative to personal income, in state and local general expenditures from 1973 to 1983.

SOCIAL SERVICES.   In 1960, social services were the third highest priority item among those financed by state and local governments. But in 1968 social services expenditures surpassed transportation expenditures and became the second highest priority item for the first time (see figure 3.3). Social services expenditures, 13.7% of total state and local general expenditures in 1960, accounted for 22.3% of total general expenditures in 1983.

As a percentage of personal income, the growth in social services expenditures was even more striking. Only 2.0% of state personal income in 1960, they grew to 4.5% by 1983. Only education expenditures increased by a larger amount in the two decades covered here.

The largest portion of social services expenditures, public welfare, accounted for most of the growth in social services expenditures in Wisconsin. Only 1.0% of personal income in 1960, public welfare expenditures tripled to 3.0% of personal income in 1983.

Fourteen different income assistance programs are in effect in Wisconsin and account for the considerable growth in public welfare expenditures over the two decades covered here. Specifically, public welfare expenditures here include two federally enabled programs, AFDC (reaching 42,733 persons in 1962 but 264,924 persons in 1983), Medicaid (created in 1965 and reaching about 325,000 persons in 1978), and general assistance payments (to 7,368 persons in 1960 but to 16,457 persons in 1983).[6]

It is worth noting that the strong growth rate for social services expenditures continued only until 1977 (see figure 3.3), after which it leveled off to about 4.5% of personal income.

TRANSPORTATION.   Transportation expenditures played a decreasing role in state and local budgets throughout the period considered here. As a percentage of personal income, transportation expenditures declined from 3.0% to 2.0% of personal income from 1960 to 1983. Also, transportation expenditures, as a percentage of total expenditures of state and local governments, fell from 20.7% to 8.8% in that same time period.

OTHER EXPENDITURES.   State and local expenditure on the five other general expenditure functions rose from 3.7% to 5.7% of personal income from 1960 to 1983. Expenditures on environment and housing accounted for half that increase—from 0.9% to 1.9% of personal income from 1960 to 1983— but other functions also increased rapidly in the period studied here. Interest on debt, for instance, jumped from only 0.2% to 0.9% of state personal income, a figure that nearly equaled the expenditures on government administration in 1983.

Trust Fund and Utility Accounts

Though they account for a small share of total revenues and expenditures of state and local governments (see figures 3.1 and 3.3), the trust fund and utility accounts—since they grew so rapidly from 1960 to 1983—figure importantly in any discussion of state and local finances. For instance, the revenues of the trust funds and utilities more than doubled as a percentage of personal income in the 1960–83 period, from 1.5% to 4.0%, and grew from 9.7% to 15.7% of total state and local revenues in the same period.

TRUST FUNDS. Revenues in one of Wisconsin's trust funds (employe retirement) and one of that fund's revenue sources (earnings on investments) led the growth in trust fund revenues from 1960 to 1983. Employe retirement revenues grew significantly, from 0.6% to 2.1% of personal income from 1960 to 1983, but one revenue source of employe retirement funds—earnings on investments—accounted for all of that growth, and contributions to the employe retirement fund (from employes in this case) actually fell as a percentage of personal income over the 1960–83 period. Since the employe retirement fund is the biggest of the trust funds, the trends in total state and local trust fund revenues look similar. The 1.5 percentage-point increase in employe retirement fund revenues accounted for most of the 2.4 percentage-point increase in total trust fund revenues from 1960 to 1983.

The expenditures of the trust funds (cash payments to beneficiaries) also grew rapidly—from 0.7% to 1.4% of personal income—from 1960 to 1983.

It is worth noting that the trust fund accounts grew most rapidly from 1973 to 1983, at a time when general revenues and expenditures were falling as a percentage of personal income (see figures 3.1 and 3.3). From 1973 to 1983, earnings on investments tripled from 0.7% to 2.1% of personal income. This rapid increase led the increase in trust fund revenues, from 1.5% to 3.4% of personal income from 1973 to 1983. Similarly, trust fund expenditures doubled to 1.4% of personal income in 1983.

UTILITIES. Revenues of locally owned utilities increased slightly from 0.5% to 0.7% of personal income from 1960 to 1983, nearly matching expenditure growth from 0.6% to 1.0% of personal income in the same period. Nearly all of the growth occurred in the 1973–83 period.

State and Local Government as Two Subsystems

As suggested in the introduction, it is difficult to separate the state and local system into subsystems because of the integrated nature of the two governments. The difficulty arises because intergovernmental transfers cloud the meaning of "expenditures" by a government. Keeping this in mind, this section will first describe revenues of state and local governments by level, and then segregate the expenditures in two ways: (1) by level of delivery and (2) by level of funding.

Own-Source Revenues of State and Local Governments

In 1960, local governments in Wisconsin collected the majority of state and local revenues (see figure 3.4). By 1963, however, the state government's own-source revenue collections exceeded local government's own-source revenues for the first time, and by 1983 the state government's own-source revenue was nearly twice that of the local governments. This shift in the roles of state and local governments was caused by rapid increases in state revenues in the 1960–73 period and slow growth, as compared to personal income, in own-source revenue collections of local governments—especially after 1973.

TAX COLLECTIONS. The rapid increase in income taxes, the institution of the general sales tax, and the decline in the property tax burden in Wisconsin over the twenty-four years studied here altered dramatically the shares of tax revenues collected by state and local governments. Specifically, both state and local governments collected 5.0% of personal income in taxes in 1960 (see figure 3.4). By 1973 the state government was collecting a far greater share (9.7% as compared to 6.1%), and by 1983 the state government was collecting almost twice as much in tax revenues as the local governments were (8.4% as compared to 4.8%).

The primary impetus for reducing the property tax came from the state level in the 1960–83 period. Six property tax relief measures became effective at the state level over the two decades covered here: personal and general property tax relief in 1962–63, the Homestead Tax Credit in 1964, and the Farmland Preservation Credit, Home Improvements Tax Relief Program, and Machinery and Equipment Property Tax Exemption, all in 1977. State legislators substituted one form of revenue to local governments—state aid—for property tax collections.

In the 1960–83 period, the decline in tax collections was offset by growth in other revenue sources. Thus, in 1960 about 60% of state revenue and 50% of local revenue came from tax collections, but by 1983 the comparable figures had fallen to about 55% and 35%, respectively.

CHARGES AND MISCELLANEOUS REVENUE. State charges and miscellaneous revenue, 0.6% of personal income in 1960, were only 7.5% of state revenue in that year. By 1983, however, state charges and miscellaneous revenue had increased to 2.5% of personal income and 16.8% of total state revenue. Similarly, local charges and miscellaneous revenue grew from 1.1% to 2.0% of personal income and from 10.6% to 13.9% of total local revenue from 1960 to 1983. These figures suggest that state charges and miscellaneous revenue increased faster than did local charges and miscellaneous revenues.

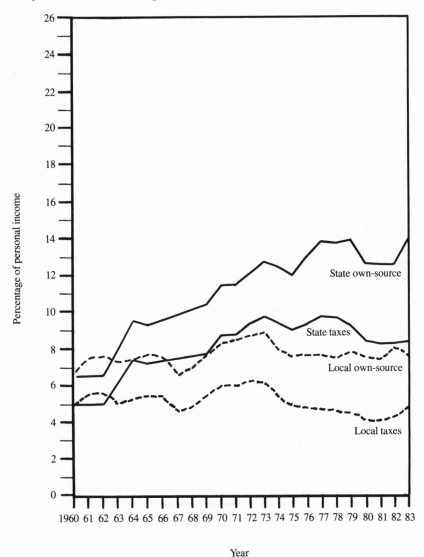

Fig. 3.4 Total own-source revenues and total tax collections, by government level and as a percentage of personal income, 1960–83. Note: See Appendix A for a discussion of the sources of the data used for this figure.

TRUST FUND AND UTILITY REVENUES. The state government administers most of the trust funds of state and local governments. The revenues to these accounts increased substantially, from 0.9% to 1.5% of personal income, from 1960 to 1973, and to 3.2% of personal income in 1983. The 1973–83 increase helped to outweigh decreases in tax collections, causing total revenues to level off at around 16% of personal income in the 1973–83 period.

Locally owned public utility revenues increased slightly, from 0.5% to 0.7% of personal income from 1960 to 1983, while locally administered trust funds remained at 0.2% of personal income throughout the period.

INTERGOVERNMENTAL TRANSFERS. An increasingly important source of revenue to local governments and expenditure by the state government in the 1960–83 period was state aid to localities (see figure 3.5, panel A). Intergovernmental revenues became the greatest source of revenue to local governments in 1963, and, in every year from 1960 to 1983, aid to local governments was the largest expenditure by the state government.

Both shared revenues and grants-in-aid increased significantly, from 3.7% to 6.4% of personal income, from 1960 to 1983 (see figure 3.5, panel A). In 1960 local intergovernmental revenue from the state government was 35% of local revenue. By 1983, it was the greatest single revenue source to local gov-

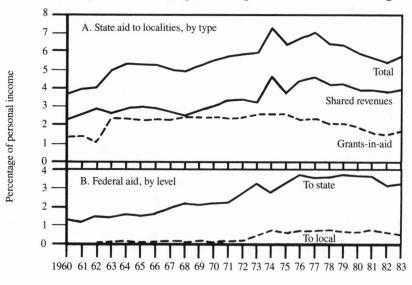

Fig. 3.5. Intergovernmental transfers, by type and as a percentage of personal income, 1960–83. Note: See Appendix A for a discussion of the sources of the data used for this figure.

ernments, accounting for over 40% of local revenue. At no point in the 1960–83 period did any other expenditure of the state government reach even half the level that intergovernmental expenditure reached.

Federal aid to both state and local governments increased rapidly over the 1960–83 period (see figure 3.5, panel B). The share of total state revenue collected as federal aid did not rise much until the early 1970s and the institution of general revenue sharing. By 1983, almost one-quarter of total state revenue came in the form of federal aid. Local governments also received increasing federal aid. From 1972 to 1974, with the institution of federal revenue sharing, federal aid to local governments grew by more than 500%.

Federal aid declined after 1981, however (see figure 3.5, panel B). At the state level, federal aid fell from 3.7% to 3.3% of personal income from 1981 to 1983. At the local level, the decline was from 0.8% to 0.6% of personal income.

The important points brought out by this discussion are that the portion of total local government revenue collected as intergovernmental revenues grew from 35.4% to 45.8% from 1960 to 1983, that the portion of state government revenues collected from the federal government grew from 17.1% to 22.0% in the same period, and that the portion of total state expenditures spent on aid to localities was never less than 40% in the twenty-four years covered here.

Expenditures, by Level of Delivery

While both state and local expenditures, by level of delivery, increased rapidly in the 1960–73 period, figure 3.6, panel A, shows that declining local expenditures caused the leveling off of combined state and local expenditures, as a percentage of personal income, after 1973. The state government, which delivered only 26.0% of total state and local expenditures in 1960, was delivering 37.8% of that total in 1983.

Level-of-delivery expenditures are the expenditures administered by the level of government on a particular good or service. Expenditures by level of delivery can be found in the first and second columns of table 3.1. Expenditures by level of delivery is the conventional division reported in the census accounts. As an example, it could be said that the state government "delivered" $990.5 million in education, while local governments "delivered" $2,560.1 million in education in 1981. This measure of expenditures takes no account of where the money to pay for goods and services came from.

EDUCATION. State delivery of education increased rapidly from 0.9% to 3.1% of personal income from 1960 to 1973. Locally delivered education expenditures also increased rapidly in the 1960–73 period—from 3.7% to 5.7% of personal income. From 1973 to 1983, however, state education ex-

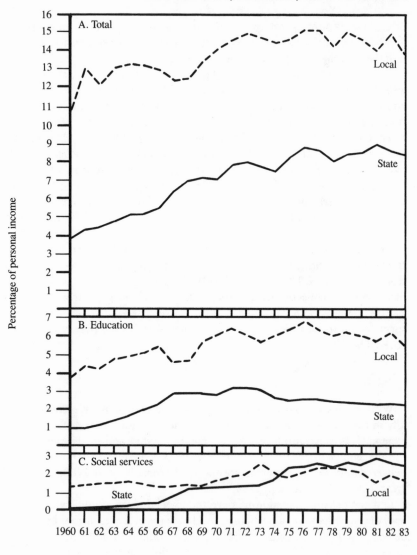

Year

Fig. 3.6. State and local direct expenditures, by level of delivery and as a percentage of personal income, 1960–83. Note: See Appendix A for a discussion of the sources of the data used for this figure.

penditures by level of delivery decreased to 2.2% of personal income, whereas local expenditures by level of delivery decreased only slightly, to 5.4% of personal income. These figures imply that the state delivered 20.2% of state and local education in 1960 and 35.5% in 1973, but only 29.1% in 1983.

The majority of state-delivered education is in higher education and the majority of locally delivered education is in primary and secondary education. However, the shifts in expenditures by level of delivery from 1960 to 1971 cannot be explained by changes in enrollment figures (see figure 3.6, panel B). Elementary and secondary enrollment rose from 710,000 to a peak of 999,900 in 1971.[7] However, local education enrollments declined in every year after 1971 and were at 784,800 in 1983. Local education expenditures, by level of delivery, began to decline after 1971, but then leveled off at nearly 6.0% of personal income after 1974. At the state level, however, education expenditures (by level of delivery) declined from 3.1% to 2.2% of personal income in the 1973–83 period, despite an 18.1% increase in enrollments at the University of Wisconsin (from 135,316 to 159,868) in the same period.

SOCIAL SERVICES. As mentioned earlier, social services expenditures increased rapidly in the 1960–83 period. Most of the increase came in the form of state-delivered social services (figure 3.6, panel C). There, expenditures increased from 0.4% to 2.6% of personal income from 1960 to 1983. Local social services expenditures increased from 1.6% to only 1.9% of personal income in the same period. However, local social services expenditures declined from 1973 to 1983.

The importance of the contrasting growth rates in social services expenditures by level is further understood when it is noted that all of the decrease in locally delivered expenditures and all of the increase in state-delivered expenditures from 1973 to 1983 can be explained by social services expenditures. This pronounced shift of roles for state and local governments as deliverers of social services is unique among the expenditure functions studied here.

The fastest-growing portion of state social services expenditures was public welfare, which increased from 0.1% to 1.9% of personal income from 1960 to 1983. In 1977, the state government relieved counties of the burden of sharing in the costs of AFDC and Medicaid. Health and hospital expenditures at the state level doubled from 0.3% to 0.6% of personal income in the same period.

OTHER GENERAL EXPENDITURES. State expenditures on transportation, public safety, environment and housing, government administration, interest on debt, and other general expenditures increased from 1.9% to 2.3% of personal income from 1960 to 1983, but total state general expenditures increased from 6.9% to 13.6% of personal income in the same period. Thus, these six functions accounted for 27% of total state general expenditures in 1960, but for only 17% in 1983.

Though expenditures by local governments in Wisconsin on these six functions fell from 48% to 43% of general expenditure, local expenditures in these areas were larger and did not decrease in importance as rapidly as did state expenditures in the same period.

Most of the trends described above are attributable to the decreased importance of transportation expenditures at both the state and local levels. Transportation expenditure, by level of delivery at the state level, fell by more than one-third, from 1.1% to 0.7% of personal income in the 1960–83 period, while local transportation expenditures fell by about a third, from 1.9% to 1.3% of personal income. In 1960, transportation was the largest expenditure function (other than intergovernmental) of state governments and the second most important expenditure function of local governments. By 1983, however, transportation expenditures were only 4.9% of state expenditures and 10.2% of local expenditures.

At both the state and local levels, expenditures on interest payments grew rapidly (from a negligible 0.01% to 0.4% of personal income) from 1960 to 1983. At the local level, expenditures on environment and housing more than doubled (as a percentage of personal income) in the 1960–83 period, so that, in 1983, these expenditures were higher than expenditures on transportation.

TRUST FUNDS AND UTILITIES. Since the state government administers most of the trust funds and local governments administer only a small employe retirement fund, the majority of trust fund revenues and expenditures are state-delivered. Expenditures from the state-administered trust funds increased from 0.6% to 0.7% of personal income from 1960 to 1973 but grew to 1.3% of personal income by 1983. The latter increase accounted for all of the increase in total state expenditures, by level of delivery, in the 1973–83 period.

Locally owned utility expenditures increased only slightly from 1960 to 1983, with most of the increase occurring after 1973.

Expenditures, by Level of Funding

The roles that state and local governments play in the provision of goods and services in Wisconsin can be determined not only by examining the delivery of services but by examining which level funds them. In this section, intergovernmental transfers are counted as an expenditure to the donating government and as *a reduction to expenditures* of the receiving government. Thus, expenditures here include the total amount spent by a level of government on a given good or service, either directly or by making intergovernmental transfers. (See Appendix C for a more detailed description of the method described here.) One may define expenditures by level of funding as the total expenditure on a given good or service out of that government level's own funds. There is no reason why intergovernmental transfers cannot be shown as positive and negative expenditures instead of intergovernmental revenues and expenditures. Moreover, since a great deal of the intergovernmental aids given by the state or federal governments are earmarked for a specific function, there is no reason why some intergovernmental revenues and expenditures cannot be allocated to specific functions. The result of this adjustment, of course, is that the expenditure numbers will no longer reflect level of delivery, but will reflect level-of-funding expenditures. Expenditures delivered by one level could be greater than, less than, or even equal to expenditures funded by that level.

In the delivery of state and local services, the state government took on an increasing role in the 1960–83 period, but state-delivered expenditures never exceeded local-delivered expenditures. From the perspective of level of funding, however, a much different picture emerges (see figure 3.7, panel A). Expenditures, by level of funding, at the local level exceeded expenditures at the state level only in the 1960–63 period. Rapid increases in federal and state aids caused a dramatic shift in the roles of local, state, and federal governments between 1960 and 1983. In 1960, local government expenditures by level of funding were 7.3% of personal income, while state and federal expenditures by level of funding were only 6.0% and 1.4% of personal income, respectively. By 1983, the local, state, and federal expenditures by level of funding were 7.7%, 11.0%, and 3.7% of personal income, respectively. Wisconsin followed national trends in these shifts. Nationwide, the state percentage of total state and local expenditures by level of funding increased from 46.8% in 1957 to 58.1% in 1983. In Wisconsin, the comparable figures were 46.0% and 60.5%, respectively.

There are now two very different answers one can give to the question, What was the role of state or local governments in the provision of goods and services in Wisconsin? One answer, by level of delivery, is that the state government delivered about 40% and the local governments about 60% of the state and local goods and services provided in Wisconsin in 1983. Another answer, by level of funding, is that the state government funded about 50%, the local governments about 35%, and the federal government about 15% of state and local goods and services provided in Wisconsin in 1983. Obviously these are two strikingly different interpretations—both of them useful—in describing the roles of state, local, and federal governments in the provision of state and local goods and services to Wisconsin taxpayers.

EDUCATION. In the two-decade period considered here, the state and federal governments undertook to replace local governments as the major source of funds for education expenditures in Wisconsin (see figure 3.7, panel

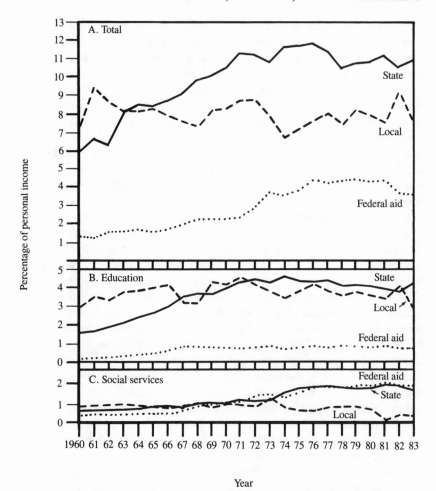

Year

Fig. 3.7. State and local expenditures, by level of funding and as a percentage of personal income, 1960–83. Note: See Appendix A for a discussion of the sources of the data used for this figure.

B). In 1960, local government expenditures by level of funding were almost twice state expenditures. But in all but one year, from 1972 to 1983, state expenditures by level of funding exceeded local expenditures. After 1973, expenditures on education at all levels of government fell as a percentage of personal income.

SOCIAL SERVICES AND OTHER EXPENDITURES. When one attempts to apply the level-of-funding approach to functions other than education, the answers become less certain. In this case, it is possible to give only upper and lower bounds on level-of-funding expenditures by the state, federal, and local governments. This problem occurs because not all intergovernmental aids are categorical.[8] Some aids are general in nature, not intended to go for any specific function, such as shared revenues from the state government and revenue sharing from the federal government. Aids that are general instead of categorical cannot be allocated to specific functions. Instead, in this chapter, general aids are put into a separate function called "general support" expenditures, that is, the amount of aid expended minus the amount received by a government but intended for no specific function. Because the level-of-funding expenditures calculated here will clearly be understated (overstated) to the extent that general support expenditures are positive (negative) for a government level, it can be said that the expenditure totals discussed here do not truly reflect the extent to which a government "funded" expenditures on a given function.

In 1983, for example, the state government gave $918.5 million in general support to the local governments in Wisconsin and the federal government gave $93.8 million of general revenue sharing to local governments. It is likely that a portion of this federal money was used to finance social services expenditures by both the local and state governments and that at least a portion of the state aids was used to finance local social services expenditures. Therefore, local social services expenditures by level of funding, shown in figure 3.7, panel C, are clearly an upper bound—the local governments in Wisconsin funded at most 0.4% of personal income, but likely funded less than that because of their use of general aids to finance these expenditures. Conversely, the federal government's expenditures by level of funding are clearly a lower bound. It is unclear, however, whether the figure cited for state governments is overstated or understated, because the state government both gave and received general support in 1983. Since no adequate way exists to allocate general support across the expenditure categories, it is possible only to alert the reader to the significance of the problem.[9]

The social services function exhibited the most interesting trends in total state and local expenditures by level of funding from 1960 to 1983.

The increase in social services expenditures at both the state and local levels and the increasing role of the state government as a provider of social services were highlighted earlier. However, a strikingly different picture now emerges (figure 3.7, panel C): an increasing role of the federal government, through federal aid, in funding state and local social services expenditures. In 1960, local government level-of-funding expenditures on social services exceeded both state and federal expenditures. By 1983, however, that order was reversed, as the federal government's expenditures by level of funding exceeded those of both the state and the local governments. These trends in the funding

of social services expenditures were unique. The social services function represented the only state and local function to be funded in 1983 primarily by an
outside source—the federal government.

Wisconsin state and local governments funded a lesser portion of social
services expenditures than did other states in the nation in 1983. The federal
government funded 36.2% of nationwide state and local social services expenditures in 1983, but 47.3% of such expenditures in Wisconsin.

The decreased level-of-delivery expenditures on transportation at both the
state and local levels can be traced to decreases in funding from the state and
federal governments. Local expenditures on transportation, by level of funding, were 1.2% of personal income in 1960 and 1.0% in 1983, while state
expenditures fell from 1.1% to 0.7% of personal income and expenditures by
the federal government fell from 0.7% to 0.3% of personal income in the
same period.

Wisconsin Compared to Other States

It has been demonstrated that Wisconsin's expenditures and revenues increased rapidly in the 1960–73 period, but that the growth in expenditures
and revenues (as a percentage of personal income) essentially ended after
1973. The comparisons to national averages displayed in table 3.2 show that
these trends changed Wisconsin's position relative to the national averages of
expenditures and revenues as a percentage of personal income.[10]

General Expenditures

Wisconsin's general expenditures as a percentage of personal income were
only slightly above the national average in 1960.[11] However, general expenditures in Wisconsin jumped from 103.1% in 1960 to 108.9% of the national
average in 1961 and remained consistently above the national average in most
years after 1961. In sixteen of the twenty-three years after 1961, expenditures
were between 8% and 14% higher than the national average.

From 1976 to 1983, Wisconsin's general expenditures as a percentage of the
national average have increased slightly. Recalling that Wisconsin's expenditures as a percentage of personal income decreased slightly in that period, this
comparison suggests that the national average of expenditures as a percentage
of personal income was falling at a faster rate. Figure 3.8 confirms this hypothesis, as it shows that the national average of general expenditures as a
percentage of personal income fell from 20.3% to 18.0% of personal income
in the 1976–83 period.

As the data in table 3.2 indicate, Wisconsin's position as a relatively high-
expenditure state can be explained by comparisons of expenditures in the

Table 3.2. Comparison of Wisconsin State and Local General Revenues and Expenditures to National Averages (based on percentage of personal income)

	Revenues				Expenditures				
Year	Total General	Total Taxes	Federal Aid	Charges & Misc.	Total General	Educa- tion	Social Services	High- ways	Other
1960	100.4%	110.0%	79.7%	91.7%	103.1%	99.4%	98.1%	127.7%	95.3%
1961	99.6	107.5	71.3	86.1	108.9	103.3	95.0	156.3	95.5
1962	99.0	104.5	82.6	88.0	104.7	101.3	96.0	135.8	95.5
1963	104.1	111.7	81.1	90.1	110.2	112.6	97.2	123.6	106.4
1964	119.7	130.6	86.6	101.6	119.9	123.8	107.0	119.8	121.7
1965	109.5	121.1	72.1	94.0	112.1	122.6	100.8	105.5	107.9
1966	107.8	119.4	71.3	94.3	111.6	124.1	96.8	118.9	98.2
1967	104.4	113.9	77.0	93.8	109.3	113.9	102.7	120.7	100.2
1968	105.9	113.5	84.0	97.2	110.8	114.7	105.6	124.5	101.8
1969	108.9	116.6	82.3	104.0	113.7	125.5	98.3	128.5	99.7
1970	113.9	125.8	81.0	99.6	113.4	126.0	84.4	121.5	110.8
1971	120.0	132.9	79.7	116.8	119.8	138.7	104.3	115.7	106.1
1972	112.1	123.1	82.3	101.5	111.1	124.1	94.3	125.5	99.8
1973	114.9	123.1	91.8	112.1	110.4	120.4	107.0	127.6	94.4
1974	111.0	118.6	93.3	103.5	110.1	120.4	106.3	135.5	91.8
1975	108.7	113.6	99.2	102.8	106.9	117.2	111.8	123.5	86.3
1976	112.7	112.0	104.1	126.1	108.0	120.1	113.9	127.5	84.4
1977	99.2	102.8	90.6	96.9	111.2	119.3	122.6	129.2	89.9
1978	108.6	112.3	99.8	106.7	106.8	116.4	119.7	119.3	84.5
1979	113.3	115.0	105.5	117.2	115.1	124.2	126.1	129.5	94.4
1980	108.2	108.5	105.2	110.7	111.7	121.4	121.3	124.1	91.5
1981	107.3	108.1	108.5	104.0	109.9	119.0	113.3	131.9	92.5
1982	111.6	113.4	109.3	109.2	122.4	131.8	118.5	145.3	108.6
1983	113.6	119.5	110.3	101.5	111.0	120.8	111.5	129.7	96.5

Source: Wisconsin Expenditure Commission (1986), and U.S Bureau of the Census, various years.

Note: Figures shown are Wisconsin's expenditures (revenues) as a percentage of personal income as a ratio to the United States' average expenditures (revenues) as a percentage of personal income.

areas of education, social services, and transportation; Wisconsin has consistently ranked lower in all other expenditure categories.

In 1983, Wisconsin's expenditure on education, as a percentage of personal income, was the tenth highest in the country and 120.8% of the national average. Most of the increase in education expenditures, relative to other states, occurred in the 1960–64 period, with Wisconsin between 15% and 25% higher than the national average in most years after 1964 (see table 3.2 and figure 3.8).

As social problems received increased national attention during the Great Society period, social services expenditures by all state and local governments

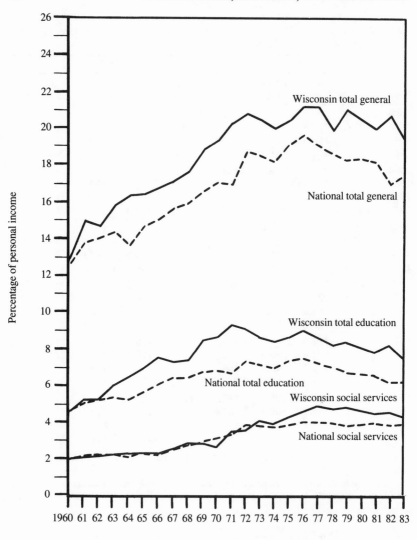

Fig. 3.8. Wisconsin state and local general expenditures, compared to national averages, as a percentage of personal income, 1960–83. (Source: Wisconsin figures taken from figure 3.3. National figures from table 3.2.)

increased. Wisconsin kept pace with these trends, remaining near the national average in the 1960–73 period. The increases in Wisconsin's relative position in social services expenditures occurred in the 1973–83 period (see table 3.2).

Despite a decline in transportation expenditures (as a percentage of personal income), Wisconsin has consistently ranked very high in transportation expenditures with little change in that position between 1960 and 1983 (see table 3.2).

General Revenues

Most of the growth (relative to the national average) in general revenues had occurred by 1971, when general revenues peaked at 120.0% of the national average. In the twelve years from 1972 to 1983, general revenues were between 8% and 14% higher than the national average in all but three years.

Specifically, Wisconsin increased taxes more rapidly than the rest of the United States in the 1960–71 period (from 110.0% to 132.9% of the national average), but since 1971 the decline in the tax burden has been slightly more rapid in Wisconsin than in the rest of the country (see table 3.2 and figure 3.9). Thus, Wisconsin's total tax collections as a percentage of personal income, the second highest in the country in 1971, had slipped to the fifth highest by 1983.

Wisconsin has earned its reputation as a high-tax state mostly because of its personal income tax burden. Not only was Wisconsin the first state in the United States to institute an income tax, in 1911, but in 1960 and 1978, Wisconsin ranked second in income taxes as a percentage of personal income. By 1983 Wisconsin's ranking in income tax collection had slipped to sixth in the nation.

Wisconsin's share of federal aid, only 79.7% of the national average in 1960, grew steadily throughout the 1960–83 period to 110.3% of the national average in 1983. Wisconsin also increased charges and miscellaneous revenue faster than other states in the 1960–83 period, exceeding the national average in all but one year after 1971.

Summary of Revenues and Expenditures, 1960–73

The period from 1960 to 1973 was a time of fiscal expansion and fiscal substitution in Wisconsin.

• State and local governments increased, from approximately 13% to 20%, expenditures as a percentage of personal income. Expenditures increased on nearly every function, with special concentration on education and social services.

• The increased expenditures were financed by increases in tax collec-

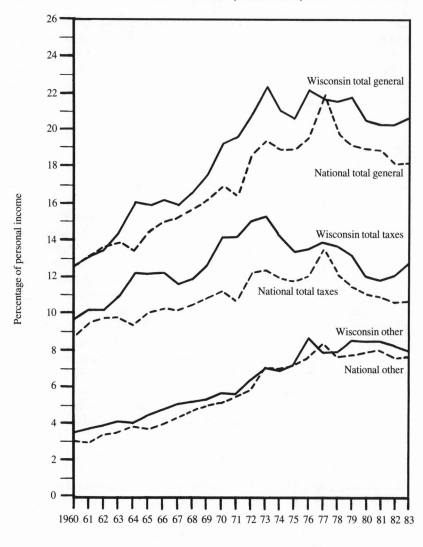

Fig. 3.9. Wisconsin state and local general revenues, compared to national averages, 1960–83. (Source: Wisconsin figures taken from figure 3.1. National figures from table 3.2.)

tions—particularly income and sales taxes—and in federal aid and charges and miscellaneous revenue.

• The state government expanded its role as a deliverer of state and local goods and services. Of all the functions, state delivery of both education and social services increased the most, as a percentage of personal income, during the period.

• The state and federal government increased their roles, relative to that of the local governments, as funders of state and local expenditures.

In the 1973–83 period, the revenues and expenditures of state and local governments in Wisconsin remained essentially constant (as a percentage of personal income). However, state and local governments undertook the following "substitutions" of revenue sources and expenditure functions:

• Other tax revenues, intergovernmental revenue, and charges and miscellaneous revenue were substituted for property tax revenue.

• Social services expenditures were substituted for declining (as a percentage of personal income) education expenditures.

• State delivery of social services expenditures continued to increase relative to local delivery.

• The federal government became the major funder of state and local social services expenditures and the state government became the major funder of state and local education expenditures.

Policy Implications

This chapter attempts to broaden understanding of current issues facing state budget strategists (1) by illustrating that the state budget is tightly linked with local and, to a much lesser extent, federal budgets; and (2) by reviewing outcomes of decisions made by earlier actors in the several interactive parts of the system.

That history highlights the growing role of the state as opposed to local governments. The state share of funds raised for state-local purposes rose from 41% in 1960 to 50% in 1983; and its share in the delivery of services went up from 26% to 38% in the same period. These changes followed from decisions by the state to assume responsibility for delivery of some services— notably social services—and from aggressive action to increase income and sales taxes. The state put contrary pressure on local property taxes by increasing revenue sharing on the one hand, and on the other hand, by increasing matching grants (which give incentive for local governments to spend more), by mandating standards for locally delivered services, and by promoting collective bargaining for local government employes.

One might say that the policy thrust of federal and state governments in the 1960s and 1970s was to overcome the bias to underspend in decentralized government. That bias exists because small jurisdictions must respond to competition for tax base and to the spill-out to nonresidents of benefits from local spending. However, the late 1970s and the 1980s saw policy strategists looking for ways to turn the bias around. Efforts to do this included limiting state income tax and local property tax rates or revenues. In Wisconsin, the sequence was income tax cuts in 1980, followed by a slowdown in state help for locals and consequent upward pressure on the property tax, which, in turn, sparked a new property tax revolt in 1987.

Another effort to control state-local finances is to legislate spending limits as opposed to tax limits. Two Wisconsin commissions in 1986 and 1987 have urged this strategy. The Expenditure Commission (1986) advocates targets that would move Wisconsin to the national average for the ratio of government expenditures to state personal income. The Wisconsin Local Property Tax Relief Commission (1987) proposes (1) a substantial cut in property tax revenues to be offset by an equivalent increase in state-collected sales taxes; (2) restricting the growth of local property tax revenues and local and state expenditures (including employe compensation) to the rate of growth in personal income; and (3) limiting state mandates and state aids to local governments and arbitrators' awards.

It is interesting to note that some efforts to reduce state-local taxing or spending have increased the role of state governments. Thus, California's Proposition 13 caused state taxes to fund 90% of local school budgets, and the state then assumed virtual control of the schools, including a say in the curricula, student testing, book selection, teacher salaries, and hiring practices. This illustrates the interrelationship of the several parts of the state-local system, wherein a change in one tax can alter not only spending but the location of power.

Appendix A. Statistical Sources and Accounting Methods

The source for all the data used in this chapter is the annual U.S. Bureau of the Census survey of governments. State and local data are published in the *Government Finances* series, but, when this publication did not present data in adequate detail, the *State Government Finances* series and *Retirement System Finances* series were used to obtain more detailed data. All expenditure totals can be found in the *Government Finances* series. The same publication was the source for all the local revenue data, but the *State Government Finances* series was used to obtain more detailed state revenue data.

To obtain level-of-funding expenditures, detail on intergovernmental transfers was obtained from all three publications. In some cases the transfers were obtained easily from tables on intergovernmental revenue and expenditure in both the *Government Finances* and *State Government Finances* series, but in other cases more detailed transfer data had to be obtained by other methods. The expenditure data, by function, in the *Government Finances* series include only *direct* expenditures on that function. However, the expenditure data, by function, presented in the *State Government Finances* series include intergovernmental expenditure. It was possible, therefore, to obtain more detailed state intergovernmental expenditure by function than was reported in the intergovernmental revenue and expenditure tables by simply comparing these figures. To obtain intergovernmental transfers for the insurance trust accounts, the *Retirement System Finances* series was used.

A more detailed description of sources and methods, as well as definitions of selected terms used in this chapter and underlying tables for figures 3.1–3.7 for the years 1960 to 1981, can be found in Lampman and McBride (1984). Tables for 1982 and 1983 can be obtained from the authors.

Appendix B. Deficits and Surpluses

One issue not considered in this chapter is deficits and surpluses. The Census Bureau does not report deficits and surpluses of either state or local governments, nor does it require revenues and expenditures to equate. For illustrative purposes, one may construct deficits and surpluses by comparing the revenues and expenditures of state and local governments. Table 3.B presents the results of that comparison.

Table 3.B shows that all funds of local governments in Wisconsin ran surpluses only seven times in the period considered here, all after 1972. In contrast, all funds of the state government were in surplus in nineteen of the twenty-four years covered here. A closer examination of the table shows that the surpluses of the trust funds were crucial, since the state general fund was in deficit eleven times between 1960 and 1983, but trust fund surpluses exceeded those deficits in all but five years.

Table 3.B shows that the general funds of state and local governments combined were in surplus only twelve times, while the trust funds and utilities were in surplus in twenty-two of the twenty-four years analyzed here. But the table also shows that eleven of the twelve general fund surpluses occurred after 1971. As a result, all funds combined were in surplus in every year after 1971, as contrasted to only three surpluses from 1960 to 1971.

A close examination of table 3.B shows that the sum of the state and local deficits or surpluses does not equal the "total" deficit or surplus. This apparent error is due to inconsistencies in the Census Bureau data in their presentation of intergovernmental transfers. Appendix C discusses this problem in more detail, but for the purposes of this appendix it is important to mention that the problem exists.

The results of the comparison between revenues and expenditures presented here does not match the deficits or surpluses of the state government reported elsewhere. However, the results parallel what is reported in the national income and product accounts (NIPA) for all state and local governments in the United States. Since the NIPA do not break out their accounts by state, the results presented here cannot be compared specifically, but the NIPA show that state and local governments nationwide ran surpluses twenty-one times in the 1960–83 period. As in the results we present, surpluses in the "social insurance funds" (including pension trust funds) figure greatly in the surpluses overall. The Commerce Department has pointed out the importance

Table 3.B. Deficits and Surpluses, 1960–83 (millions of dollars)

	State			Local			State & Local		
Year	General Funds	Trust Funds & Utilities	Total	General Funds	Trust Funds & Utilities	Total	General Funds	Trust Funds & Utilities	Total
1960	10.4	31.3	41.7	−28.9	−3.0	−31.9	−29.5	20.3	−9.2
1961	−22.7	2.7	−20.0	−109.4	−24.1	−133.5	−162.8	−29.3	−192.1
1962	−13.9	27.2	13.3	−41.3	−8.7	−50.0	−109.9	9.4	−100.5
1963	−50.3	29.6	−20.7	−60.9	−5.5	−66.4	−130.5	14.0	−116.5
1964	38.2	46.5	84.7	−34.0	−4.8	−38.8	−22.3	30.6	8.3
1965	8.3	62.4	70.7	−19.1	−0.8	−19.9	−51.9	51.2	−0.7
1966	−1.8	76.5	74.7	−25.6	6.7	−18.9	−61.1	71.2	10.1
1967	−21.5	88.7	67.2	−86.1	4.2	−81.9	−144.3	75.8	−68.5
1968	−86.1	93.0	6.9	−70.6	8.8	−61.8	−133.6	82.7	−50.9
1969	−88.1	110.9	22.8	−59.4	3.3	−56.1	−166.4	94.0	−72.4
1970	12.5	100.9	113.4	−38.1	6.4	−31.7	3.7	83.3	87.0
1971	−62.4	57.1	−5.3	−43.7	6.2	−37.5	−98.9	33.9	−65.0
1972	31.3	88.4	119.7	−42.6	8.1	−34.5	21.9	63.9	85.8
1973	176.2	143.4	319.6	91.2	8.4	99.6	378.4	110.1	488.5
1974	−45.5	169.4	123.9	335.7	6.2	341.9	235.1	133.9	369.0
1975	−63.8	48.3	−15.5	19.0	1.9	20.9	57.4	−2.8	54.6
1976	61.0	149.0	210.0	18.8	2.1	20.9	103.4	78.6	182.0
1977	139.7	336.9	476.6	79.3	9.9	89.2	160.9	180.4	341.3
1978	348.3	470.9	819.2	194.7	−21.1	173.6	561.1	267.8	828.9
1979	199.9	674.5	874.4	26.3	−41.8	−15.5	280.7	437.7	718.4
1980	21.6	491.6	513.2	−157.4	−28.1	−185.5	23.7	219.7	243.4
1981	−56.3	418.8	362.5	3.1	−62.2	−59.1	160.8	124.2	285.0
1982	94.4	544.1	638.5	−362.1	−22.6	−384.7	−182.8	521.4	338.7
1983	295.1	942.9	1,238.0	190.5	−140.0	50.5	723.0	803.0	1,525.9

Source: See Appendix B.

of including the social insurance funds in any study of state and local government finances, observing that social insurance funds are "included in the overall surplus because the surplus of these funds must be combined with the surplus of other funds to derive a measure of the fiscal impact of state and local governments on the economy. . . . However, for purposes of addressing the fiscal position of state and local governments, the social insurance fund surplus should be excluded because it is generally not available to finance capital spending or current operations. Accordingly, the two components are shown separately" ("State and Local Government Fiscal Position in 1978," *Survey of Current Business,* December 1978, 21).

Appendix C. Construction of Level-of-Funding Expenditures

This appendix briefly describes how calculations are made with the Census Bureau data to create expenditures by level of funding.

Table 3.C. State and Local Total Expenditures in Wisconsin, by Level of Delivery and by Level of Funding. Exhibit: 1960 and 1981 (millions of dollars)

	State	Local	Federal	Total
		1960		
Total direct expenditures				
by level of delivery	$329.6	$930.5	—	$1,260.1
Plus (less) intergov. transfers				
State to local	315.6	–315.6[a]		
State to federal	—		—	
Federal to state	–117.3		117.3	
Federal to local		–2.4	2.4	
Local to state	–16.0	16.0[a]		
Equals: Total expenditures				
by level of funding	$511.9	$628.5	$119.7	$1,260.1
		1981		
Total direct expenditures				
by level of delivery	$4,012.7	$6,236.1	—	$10,248.8
Plus (less) intergov. transfers				
State to local	2,796.7	–2,796.7[a]		
State to federal	28.9		–28.9	
Federal to state	–1,617.0		1,617.0	
Federal to local		–368.7	368.7	
Local to state	–271.5	271.5[a]		
Equals: Total expenditures				
by level of funding	$4,949.8	$3,342.2	$1,956.8	$10,248.8

Source: Lampman and McBride (1984).

[a]These figures are not the same as those reported by the Census Bureau. See text above.

Table 3.C presents both total level-of-delivery and level-of-funding expenditures of state and local governments for 1960 and 1981 as an example of the procedure used. The table shows that level-of-delivery expenditures are adjusted for intergovernmental transfers to compute expenditures by level of funding. The federal government gives aid to both state and local governments and aid is given by the state government to local governments. To adjust expenditures by level of delivery for these intergovernmental transfers, the aids are added to the expenditures of the donating government and subtracted from the expenditures of the recipient government to arrive at expenditures by level of funding. When expenditures are adjusted in this manner, the conclusion can be drawn that the state government funded $4.9 billion, local governments $3.3 billion, and the federal government $1.96 billion of expenditures in Wisconsin in 1981.

The example shown in table 3.C is for total state and local expenditures. The same calculation can be performed for individual expenditure functions as well, since many of the intergovernmental transfers are categorical, intended to be used for a specific expenditure function.

Four of the numbers in table 3.C are footnoted to point out that the numbers used

are not the same as those shown by the Census Bureau. For example, the figure reported by the Census Bureau as local intergovernmental revenue from state governments is $2,548.7 million, not the $2,796.7 million shown in table 3.C. Though it is
unclear why these inconsistencies exist, there is a reason to believe that the state numbers are more accurate. The Census Bureau compiled the local government data by a
survey of local governments. For this reason, the Census Bureau states that the "state
government data are not subject to sampling; consequently, state-local aggregates
shown here for individual states are more reliable (on a standard error basis) than the
local government estimates they include" (*Government Finances in 1980,* 11). Concluding that the state data are of a higher quality, we forced local intergovernmental
transfer data into equality with state intergovernmental data.

It is worth noting that the Advisory Council on Intergovernmental Relations
(ACIR), in reporting its "expenditures, from own funds," uses essentially the same
procedures and data used here. The only difference is that they force equality with the
local intergovernmental data instead of the state intergovernmental data. Since the
ACIR began presenting complete data on a state-by-state basis only in recent years, the
presentation in this chapter covers a greater period of time.

NOTES

1. The purpose of these graphs is to present the large amount of data available on
state and local government finances in Wisconsin between 1960 and 1983 in a simple
manner. Complete data for the years 1960 to 1983 are available from the authors. Data
for the years 1960 to 1981, as well as more detailed decriptions of methodology and
definitions, can be found in Lampman and McBride (1984).

2. Perhaps the major contribution that can be claimed for this chapter is its useful-
ness for the reader as an introduction to the detailed data in the *Government Finances*
census, as published by the U.S. Bureau of the Census. All the data cited in this chapter
are found in census publications. The Bureau of Economic Analysis, in the national
income and product accounts (NIPA), and the Bureau of the Census, in its *Government
Finances* census, compile data on state and local government finances and both are
often used to study intergovernmental finance. The census, however, provides the
most detailed state-by-state breakdown of state and local government finances.
Accordingly, census data used here are discussed in Appendix A.

3. The insurance trust funds accumulate funds for future payments and earn on the
investments made with these funds.

4. For a historical background on Wisconsin's tax structure and its overall progressivity and regressivity, see Wisconsin Department of Revenue (1979). According to
that study, there was little change in the pattern of tax burden by income level between
1959 and 1979.

5. The numbers cited here are not shown in any figure. The source of the 1960–81
data (and for similar data cited later but also not in a figure) is Lampman and McBride
(1984). Data for years after 1981 are available from the authors.

6. A study prepared for the Wisconsin State Legislature identified the fourteen different programs in operation in Wisconsin in 1978. For a more detailed discussion, see
Donoghue (1979), 284–86.

7. See the *Wisconsin Blue Book,* the statistics on education section, various years.

8. The problem described here does not apply to education expenditures by level of funding, because general aids cannot be used to finance education expenditures.

9. Note that this problem of classification of general aids does not apply to total expenditures by level of funding, because general support expenditures are added into these totals. The measurement problem above applies only to functional breakdowns.

10. The sources for the national comparisons in this section are the U.S. Census Bureau *Government Finances* annual reports, the Advisory Council on Intergovernmental Relations's annual reports, and Wisconsin Expenditure Commission (1986). The latter uses essentially the same methodology as used here, but concentrates on national comparisons. It came to our attention after we completed this chapter, and we suggest that the reader use it as a companion piece.

11. The national averages discussed here and used to construct table 3.2 and figure 3.8 were constructed by taking expenditures or revenues, summed over the fifty states, as a percentage of total national personal income. The figures are not the arithmetic average of each state's personal income figures.

4

A Demographic Portrait of Wisconsin's People

PAUL R. VOSS

A fundamental element in establishing policies and setting priorities is the understanding of the population to be served by these activities. What are the apparent needs of various segments of the population based on an examination of their social and economic characteristics? What changes in these characteristics have occurred in recent years? What do these recent changes suggest are the likely needs of the population over the next few years?

The purpose of this chapter is to describe contemporary, and in some cases projected, demographic characteristics of the people of Wisconsin, and to suggest ways in which these factors are linked to broader issues of state planning and public policy.

Population Growth in Wisconsin

For the 1980s, Wisconsin clearly seems headed for an era of slow growth—slower certainly than has been experienced in any recent decade (see table 4.1). Census figures indicate that the population of Wisconsin increased by 6.5% between 1970 and 1980 to a 1980 figure of 4,705,642 people. Estimates for the period since 1980 suggest that there has been a considerable decline in the rate of growth, the result of a recent increase in the net flow of migrants from the state, and it now appears that Wisconsin will add no more than 4–5% (perhaps 200,000 persons) to its population during the decade of the 1980s.

The slow growth projected for Wisconsin's total population places the state well below the fast-growing states in the West and South. Figure 4.1 shows the 1980–85 estimated percentage change in population for each state. While the population increase for the entire United States during this period

Table 4.1. Population Growth and Source of Growth in Wisconsin, 1910–90

Date	Total Population (1)	Percentage Increase During the Preceding Decade		Change during the Preceding Decade			Percentage of U.S. Population in Wisconsin
		Wis. (2)	U.S. (3)	Total Population (4)	Natural Increase (5)	Net Migration (6)	(7)
1990 (April 1)	4,900,000	4.1	9.6	194,358	333,000	–138,642	1.97
1980 (April 1)	4,705,642	6.5	11.4	287,821	277,672	10,149	2.08
1970 (April 1)	4,417,821	11.8	13.4	466,044	459,561	6,483	2.17
1960 (April 1)	3,951,777	15.1	18.5	517,202	566,718	–49,516	2.20
1950 (April 1)	3,434,575	9.5	14.5	296,988	366,506	–69,518	2.27
1940 (April 1)	3,137,587	6.8	7.3	198,581	226,516	–27,935	2.37
1930 (April 1)	2,939,006	11.7	16.2	306,939	297,550	9,389	2.39
1920 (January 1)	2,632,067	12.8	15.0	298,207	268,161	30,046	2.48
1910 (April 15)	2,333,860	—	—	—	—	—	2.53

Sources: Column 1, 1910–80, is from U.S. Bureau of the Census, *1980 Census of Population,* PC80-1-A1, "United States Summary," table 8. The 1980 number reflects a small correction to the enumeration reported after the final numbers were published. Column 3, 1920–80, is from the same publication, table 3. The 1990 figure was derived from U.S. Bureau of the Census (1984), *Current Population Reports* Series P-25, no. 952, "Projections of the Population of the United States, by Age, Sex, and Race: 1983 to 2080," tables 1 and 2, part B, Middle Series. Column 4 is derived from column 1. Column 5, births minus deaths, 1920–80, is from the *Wisconsin Public Health Statistics* for each year. Births and deaths have been recomputed to a 1 April to 30 March basis to match census dates. Column 6 is derived as the difference between total population change and natural increase. Net migration is the estimated difference between the (unobserved) numbers of in-migrants and out-migrants. Column 7, 1910–80, is from U.S. Bureau of the Census, *1980 Census of Population,* table 10. 1990 figures estimated by author (except for U.S. figure in column 3).

was 5.4%, some of the southern states and many of the western states have experienced a moderate to large increase in their populations—continuing a pattern firmly established in the 1970s. Recent estimates suggest that during the first half of the 1980s, fully 91% of the nation's total population increase of 12 million persons accrued to the South and West. Wisconsin's pattern of slow growth during this period is shared by most other midwestern and northeastern states.[1] This figure reveals the demographic basis for various Northeast and Midwest coalitions working on issues of state-federal relations that affect economic development, including the issue of an equitable rate of return of federal program tax dollars to these states.

Components of State Growth

The demographic explanation for Wisconsin's population change is found in the trends in the state's births, deaths, and migration. Figure 4.2 shows

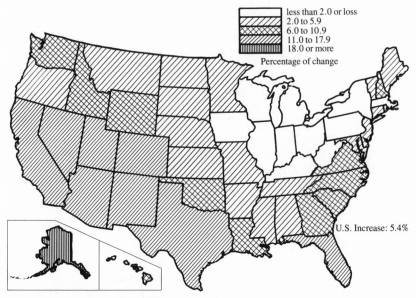

Fig. 4.1. Percentage change in population, by state, 1980–85. (Source: U.S. Bureau of the Census, 1986. Current Population Reports Series P. 26, No. 85–52–C. "Provisional Estimates of the Population of Counties: July 1, 1986.")

trends in the annual number of these events from 1920 to 1985. The top line represents the annual number of births during this period and the middle line illustrates the annual number of deaths. The shaded area between these lines represents natural increase (the difference between births and deaths) each year. An extraordinary feature of this chart is the high number of births—and the accompanying large natural increase—in the 1950s and early 1960s. However, the significance of the post–World War II baby boom lies not only in its large numbers, but also in its size in relation to the generations both before and after it. From 1947 through 1966 (years in which the number of resident live births in Wisconsin was consistently in excess of 80,000), some 1.8 million babies were born—57% more than were born during the previous twenty years and about 26% more than during the twenty years to follow. In 1973 the number of births dropped to a level of just below 63,000 before beginning to rise again. The upturn in the number of births in the 1970s is attributed by demographers to be the expected outcome, "an echo," of the fertility of the large baby-boom generation of the 1950s. Many demographers anticipate that this trend will continue through the middle of this decade, despite the apparent downturn in births witnessed in Wisconsin during the early 1980s. Sandwiched by two much smaller generations, that of the depression era of the 1930s and the "baby bust" of the 1970s, the baby boom's influ-

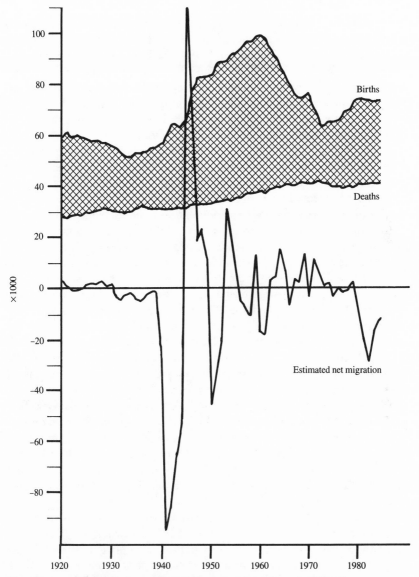

Fig. 4.2. Annual births, deaths, and estimated net migration, Wisconsin, 1920–85.
(Sources: Births and deaths, Wisconsin Department of Health and Social Services. Various
years. *Public Health Statistics*. Net migration numbers derived by author.)

ence on society is disproportionately strong. Just as the last three decades were riddled with the problems of first educating and then employing the baby-boom generation, the 1980s and 1990s will be marked by such imposing questions as how to provide meaningful jobs, necessary retraining programs, and promotional opportunities for a baby-boom generation in its middle age. Success in such activities will assist in minimizing the flow of baby boomers from the state as competition increases for the limited middle- and upper-level supervisory and managerial positions in the labor force.

Migration is the other determinant of Wisconsin's population growth pattern. Table 4.1 shows net migration figures for Wisconsin by decade since 1910. (Net migration is the balance of all people entering and leaving the state.) During the early part of this century and again in recent decades, the state witnessed net additions to its population resulting from migration patterns. Migration losses peaked during the 1940s and recent gains reached a maximum in the 1970s. Both trends are related, at least in part, to mobilization patterns of the armed forces. Some of the large numbers of men and women pressed into service in the 1940s did not return to the state following the end of World War II—thus pushing up for that decade the net losses due to migration. On the other hand, the 1970s witnessed the demobilization from a war begun in the 1960s. While some young men and women surely chose not to return to Wisconsin, those who left in the 1960s and did return in the early 1970s raised the net migration contribution of growth for the state. Indeed, figure 4.2, which shows estimated annual net migration, suggests that the early 1970s were years of net in-migration, while the trend in the late 1970s shifted to a small net out-migration. Although some of the year-to-year fluctuation in the migration numbers in this figure arises from errors in the estimation procedure, the numbers suggest that even in decades when the aggregated intercensal numbers (shown in table 4.1) were significantly negative, there were individual years which experienced net in-migration.[2] These numbers also reveal the dramatic increase in net out-migration which dominated the state's migration pattern in the early 1980s.[3]

It is clear now why Wisconsin is growing slowly in the 1980s. Although there are more births than deaths, these additions by natural increase are currently reduced by losses due to migration. One obvious key to human resources in Wisconsin in the future is what happens to the trend in migration, and more will be said about this in a separate section. It is useful here, however, to point out that the *net* flows of migrants to and from the state (shown in table 4.1) have traditionally remained small enough that their impact on state growth has been modest: sometimes augmenting natural increase and sometimes subtracting from the natural increase component. And this has meant that, since early in this century, Wisconsin's growth rates have consistently been below those for the nation (compare columns 2 and 3 in table 4.1). As a consequence, the proportion of the nation's total population residing in Wisconsin has fallen persistently and by 1990 will dip below the 2% mark (column 7, table 4.1).

The projected slow growth trend for Wisconsin's total population does not, of course, necessarily hold true for all segments of the population. This point is taken up in the next few sections as some of the variation in growth patterns is discussed.

Population Change by Race

The nonwhite population in Wisconsin, for example, is growing more rapidly than the white population (columns 2-4, table 4.2). The same statement can be made for the United States as a whole, but for the nation the growth differential is due mainly to racial differences in birthrates. The difference between the national and Wisconsin growth trends, on the other hand, is heightened because of the racial differential that exists in net migration flows. During the past decade, Wisconsin witnessed a net outflow of whites and a net inflow of blacks.[4] This difference is projected to continue through the decade of the 1980s.

The distribution of majority and minority populations in Wisconsin in 1980 is also presented in table 4.2. Over 94% of Wisconsin's 1980 population was white, while the black population made up just under 4% or about 183,000 persons. Hispanics constituted about 63,000 persons or 1.3% of the total population. Unfortunately, Census Bureau procedural changes make it impossible to calculate rates of increase for the last ten years among Hispanics. In addition, the rates of growth among the "all other" race category in the 1970s are affected by enumeration problems, resulting in an artificially high implied net migration for "other" races between 1970 and 1980. Nevertheless, even after bringing this latter rate into reasonable alignment with other racial categories for the 1980s, nonwhite growth, while numerically small, will exceed the growth rate for whites.

The Changing Age Profile of the Population

Although total population change is one of the driving forces behind other changes in the economy, including the demand for goods and services, much of the ongoing restructuring of the institutions of society relates to the changing proportions of the population in specific age groups. And these changing proportions, in turn, reflect past fluctuations in the components of population change discussed above. The most notable of these has been the decline in fertility which occurred in the 1930s, the baby boom that followed World War II, and the subsequent drop in the birthrate during the 1960s and 1970s

Table 4.2. Wisconsin Population by Race and Spanish Origin: 1970–90

		Race			Spanish
	All Races (1)	Whites (2)	Blacks (3)	All Other (4)	Origin (5)
Population					
1970	4,417,821	4,258,959	128,224	30,548	(a)
1980b	4,705,642	4,443,035	182,592	80,140	62,972
1990	4,900,000	4,563,000	243,000	94,000	125,000
Percentage change					
1970–80	6.5	4.3	42.4	162.3	(a)
1980–90	4.1	2.7	33.1	17.3	98.5
Natural increase					
1970–80	277,672	239,349	32,226	6,115c	(a)
1980–90	333,000	280,000	43,000	10,000	19,000
Net migration					
1970–80	10,149	−55,273	22,142	43,477	(a)
1980–90b	−138,642	−160,035	17,408	3,860	43,000
Percentage of total population					
1970	100.0	96.4	2.9	0.7	(2)
1980	100.0	94.4	3.9	1.7	1.3
1990	100.0	93.1	5.0	1.9	2.5

Sources: Population, 1970, is from U.S Bureau of the Census, 1973, *1970 Census of Population*, vol. 1, "Characteristics of the Population," part 51, Wisconsin, table 17; 1980 is from *1980 Census of Population*, vol. 1, chap. B, "General Population Characteristics," part 51, Wisconsin, tables 15 and 16; 1990 figures are estimated by the author. Natural increase for 1970 and 1980 are from *Wisconsin Public Health Statistics* for the years presented. Births and deaths have been recomputed to a 1 April to 30 March basis to match census dates; 1980–90 figures are estimated by the author.

aThe Spanish-origin population for 1970 is not available in a form consistent with the 1980 count.

bThe data for racial subgroups do not incorporate some marginal corrections made to the 1980 total count after publication of counts by race. As a consequence, the figures shown for racial subgroups do not add to the corrected total given in column 1.

cThis figure includes a few births and deaths reported as "race unknown."

(again, see figure 4.2). Each of these major rises and falls set into motion some relatively predictable permutations in the changing population age profile of the state.

The age-sex profile of the population of Wisconsin, shown as a "population pyramid" in figure 4.3, clearly reveals the postwar crescendo in childbearing. Members of the large baby-boom generation, now in their twenties and thirties, stand in marked contrast to the smaller generation of persons in their forties and fifties—the latter group reflecting the low birthrates of the Great Depression. Changes in the age-sex structure between 1980 and 2000, also shown in figure 4.3, reveal the dramatic growth in store for the state of persons between the ages of 35 and 54.

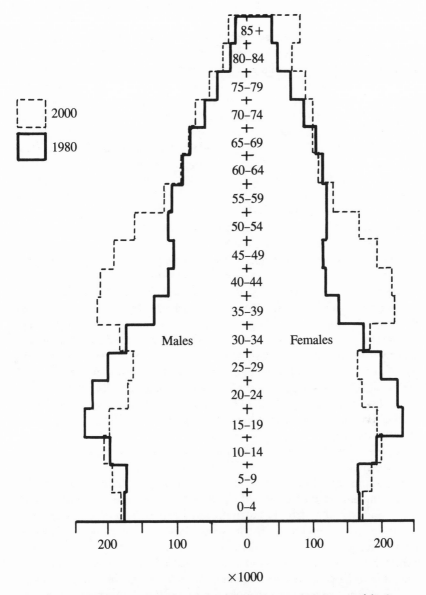

2000

1980

85+
+
80–84
+
75–79
+
70–74
+
65–69
+
60–64
+
55–59
+
50–54
+
45–49
+
40–44
+
35–39
+
Males   30–34   Females
+
25–29
+
20–24
+
15–19
+
10–14
+
5–9
+
0–4

200   100   0   100   200

×1000

Fig. 4.3. Wisconsin's age composition, 1980 and 2000. (Sources: U.S. Bureau of the Census, 1980 Census of Population, PC80-1-B51, "General Population Characteristics: Wisconsin," Table 18, issued August 1982; *Wisconsin Population Projections 1980–2010,* Wisconsin Department of Administration, 1983.)

The concentration of the population in certain ages previews a number of unavoidable changes that will affect not only school and college enrollments and the demand for particular kinds of housing, but also other economic and government programs. This is illustrated in figure 4.4, which shows the number of children under age five and elderly persons 65 and over in Wisconsin from 1920 to 1980 with projections to 2000. In 1940 there were about 250,000 people in each of these age groups, and in 1960 both the number of young children and the number of elderly had increased to more than 400,000. However, since that time, growth trends have diverged such that by 2000 it is estimated that there will be 350,000 children in the state under age five (about the same number as in 1950) but 700,000 elderly persons—twice the number of young children. In 1980, 12% of Wisconsin's population was 65 and over, and by 2000 it is projected to be over 13%. Since both youth and elderly have unique needs with respect to societal resources, it is critical that agencies and institutions serving these age groups anticipate and appropriately adjust their programs as these demographic trends unfold.

Perhaps the clearest view of how the changing age structure will affect the economy in Wisconsin in the 1980s is summarized in figure 4.5, which shows the projected population change for various age categories in the state between 1980 and 1990. Again, the total population increase during this decade is likely to be very modest, as shown in the first bar of this figure. However, the low growth pattern is not applicable to most of the age groups. By 1990 there will be 5.9% fewer children 5–17 years of age and 19.1% fewer young adults 18–24 years of age. Both of these age categories encompass traditional student groups. On the other hand, there will be an increase in other age groups, among them a 32.2% rise in the number of older middle-aged Wisconsin adults—the group usually at the peak of its productivity and earnings potential. There will be over a 29.0% increase in the proportion of young adults age 25–44 (many of them prospective homeowners) and a 16.3% increase in the number of elderly (heavy consumers of health care). These data signal clearly that manufactured products, public services, regulatory activities, and other facilities and activities that have an impact on specific age groups in the population will be reshaped by the demographic trends of the 1980s. And this point has not been lost on those in the marketing and advertising communities. The housing industry, the insurance industry, public health care facilities, schools, the criminal justice system, entertainment, public welfare, and the character of the labor force will all be affected by these demographic changes. For labor market economists these data suggest an impending labor shortage of entry-level workers. While such a situation may create difficulties for those industries that depend on constant turnover of young unskilled workers (e.g., fast-food restaurants), age distribution effects on the economy over the next decade are generally viewed as salutary.

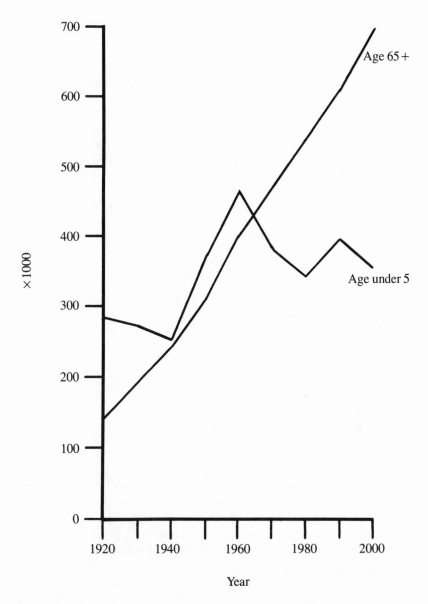

Fig. 4.4. Young children and older adults in Wisconsin, 1920 to 2000. (Sources: 1920 through 1980, U.S. Bureau of the Census, various years. *Census of Population*. 1990 and 2000, Wisconsin Department of Administration, 1983, *Wisconsin Population Projections 1980–2010.*)

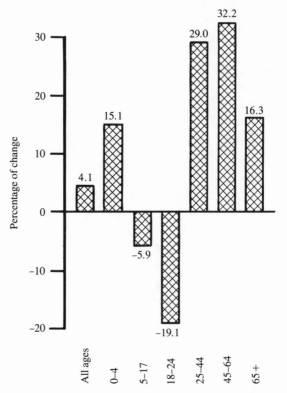

Fig. 4.5. Projected population change for selected age groups, Wisconsin, 1980 to 1990. (Source: Wisconsin Department of Administration, 1983, *Wisconsin Population Projections 1980–2010.* "All Ages" number derived by author.)

Wisconsin's economy will share the same fortunes as the U.S. economy as it responds to the changing age composition of the population. Unemployment should ease downward, labor costs are likely to rise relative to the costs of capital, and, as the capital/worker ratio increases, productivity should rise and inflation should likely be kept at bay. These demographic pressures arising from the changing age composition of the population are precisely the reverse of those which prevailed during much of the 1970s.

Geographic Differences in Growth

The sharp decline in births since 1960 brought with it a drop in the rate of population growth for the state and, in the process, revealed migration comings and goings as the principal determinants of local area population growth and decline. As a consequence, individual communities are subject to greater

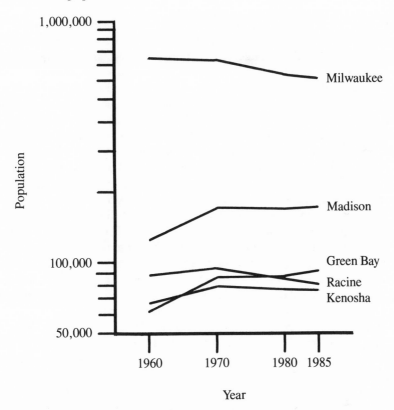

Fig. 4.6. Central city population trends, five largest Wisconsin cities: 1960–85. (Sources: 1960 through 1980, U.S. Bureau of the Census, various years, *Census of Population;* 1985, Wisconsin Department of Administration, 1985, *Official Population Estimates for 1985.*)

year-to-year variation in growth as migration responds to the buffeting of economic good times and bad. Figure 4.6 shows the 1960–85 population trends for the five largest cities in Wisconsin. During this period only the cities of Madison and Green Bay increased in population—and even here the gains have been nominal in recent years. The other cities have declined in population since 1970, due primarily to the excess of departing migrants over arriving ones. For Milwaukee, the loss was substantial: 81,000 persons or more than 11% of the population at the start of the decade. The decline was so large, relative to gains in surrounding suburban counties, that between 1970 and 1980 the entire four-county metropolitan area recorded population decline.

Although urban population decline is not necessarily the prelude to economic stagnation that it is widely thought to be, it does severely strain traditional mechanisms of metropolitan finance. The demographic forces behind this trend are now well documented. In-migration from rural areas to the city has slackened, but the out-migration continues, particularly of middle-class families. Jobs have left the central city for suburban shopping centers and newer industrial areas. The result is a reduction in the absolute number of workers, especially those in the higher income levels, which in turn results in a loss in the tax base. In many central cities the population that is left behind includes a high proportion of alienated, unemployed minorities and other lower-income citizens who often have—and herein lies the unfortunate irony—a greater need for the high-cost services and support structures of the city than do those who left. The entire demographic process has tended to produce a segregation of the population, not only by race but also by age, and by other characteristics common among those who are financially and social- ly unable to change their residential environment. The likelihood of soon reversing this process through substantial urban resettlement seems small, although there are hints in the most recent population estimates for Milwau- kee City—confirmed to some extent by a recent special census and the voices of some planners and developers in the city—that Milwaukee's population is showing some buoyancy in the 1980s relative to recent past trends.

An unanticipated counterpoint to the trend in the 1970s of metropolitan decline was the "rural renaissance"—the revival or acceleration of population growth in rural areas, including many areas very remote from metropolitan regions. The character of this demographic turnaround for Wisconsin was for the northern and western areas of the state to shift between the 1950s and 1970s away from widespread population decline, while the southeastern area began to witness a steady diminishing of its growth. As part of this transfor- mation, less populated areas began to increase in population, and the more densely populated areas experienced declining growth or actual population losses. The trend marked the end of the rush of population to large metro- politan cities, which had characterized the decades of the 1950s and 1960s, and the renewal of growth in low-density rural areas.

In Wisconsin, turnaround growth particularly affected several northern lake counties (Oneida, Vilas, Sawyer, Washburn, and Burnett) and some of the central sand counties (Adams, Marquette, and Waushara). As a group, these counties witnessed especially high growth rates due to high rates of net in-migration during the 1970s. It is useful to point out in this context a point that is too easily overlooked. These high rates of net migration did not neces- sarily imply large movements of people. For the most part, these counties witnessed net additions to their population averaging fewer than 500 persons per year, although such additions to sparsely populated areas did have sub- stantial impacts on local economies and environments.

The components of population change for the state's 72 counties, summa- rized in figure 4.7, show the emergence of the population turnaround in

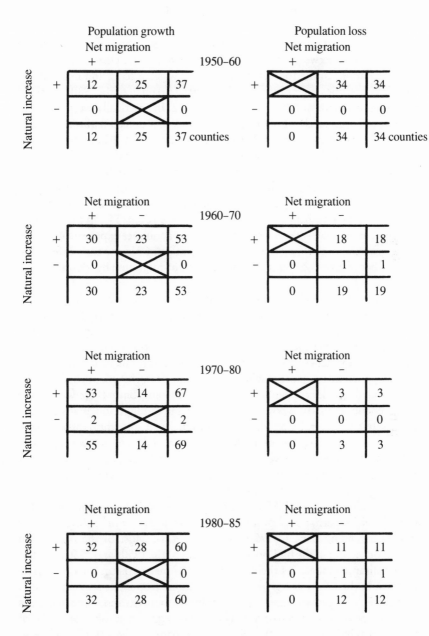

Fig. 4.7. Number of Wisconsin counties experiencing different combinations of components of change 1950–60, 1960–70, 1970–80, and 1980–85. (Source: Based on U.S. Bureau of the Census, various years, *Census of Population;* and Wisconsin Department of Administration, 1985, *Official Population Estimates for 1985.*)

Wisconsin from the 1950s to the 1970s and the relaxation of these trends in the early 1980s. Between 1950 and 1960 nearly half (34) of the state's counties lost population. In the following decade this was cut to 19 and in the 1970s only three counties lost population. During the first half of the 1980s the trend has reversed and the number has increased to 12. In practically every case, this is the result exclusively of net migration losses that exceed natural decrease. Only two instances of natural decrease (an excess of deaths over births) occur.[5] The complement of this trend is shown in the shift toward more dispersed and widespread growth, from 37 counties with population increase in the 1950s to 69 counties in the 1970s. The number of counties witnessing net in-migration during this period more than quadrupled, from 12 to 55. And once again, the numbers for 1980–85 represent a reversal from the trend established in the 1950–80 period. The number of counties experiencing population growth has declined from 69 in the 1970s to 60 in the early 1980s, and the number of growing counties showing net out-migration has doubled from 14 to 28.

The reasons for the acceleration of rural population growth in the 1970s were many, including lower out-migration, the spillover effect from metropolitan areas into adjacent nonmetropolitan areas, better transportation and highways (which permit access to wider markets), a preference for the amenities of rural existence, the search for leisure or retirement life-styles, economic opportunities in areas where small manufacturing plants had opened or expanded, and less dependence on earned income. Since there were many factors encouraging rural population growth and in-migration, many demographers felt this trend was likely to continue well into the 1980s. Recent trends, however, suggest that the migration differences favoring nonmetropolitan growth have weakened considerably. In fact, it is very difficult at this point to foresee how rural/urban migration patterns will shape Wisconsin's economic development in the 1980s.

The trends of the early 1980s—the full five-year period spanning April 1980 to April 1985—perhaps are best viewed alongside the six preceding five-year periods extending back to 1950 (see figure 4.8). Most of the population growth occurring in the high-growth decades of the 1950s and 1960s went to metropolitan counties. As the growth rates in metropolitan areas began to diminish in the 1960s, the growth rates in nonmetropolitan areas increased. By the 1970s the growth rate differential between metro and nonmetro areas clearly favored the nonmetropolitan counties—again, a graphic depiction of the "rural renaissance." In the 1980s, accompanying the overall decline in population growth, rates for both the metro and nonmetro sectors are less than half those that prevailed just a few years earlier. The differential still favors nonmetropolitan counties—in contrast to national figures, which show metropolitan counties once again to be growing more rapidly than nonmetropolitan counties.

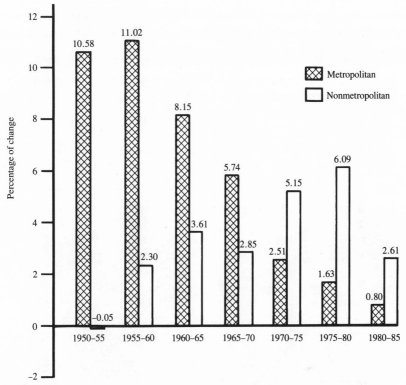

Fig. 4.8. Percentage population change for five-year periods 1950 to 1985 in Wisconsin metropolitan and nonmetropolitan areas (1980 metropolitan definition). (Source: Derived by author.)

The drop in metropolitan growth since the late 1970s has some interesting features. As mentioned above, Milwaukee County's rate of decline has subsided, so the trend is clearly not being driven by change in the state's most populous county. Growth in most of the state's smaller metropolitan areas currently reveals a mixed pattern of change relative to the 1970s. Several in the northern part of the state are growing more rapidly; those in the southeastern corner of the state, more slowly. The most dramatic change in metropolitan growth since the 1970s is to be found in the three suburban counties of the Milwaukee metropolitan area, where growth has fallen off substantially. Waukesha, Washington, and Ozaukee counties have shifted from strong net in-migration counties in recent decades to net out-migration in the early 1980s.[6]

The drop in nonmetropolitan growth in the 1980s (a trend that Wisconsin shares with most other states) cannot be traced to any particular group of counties. Growth is dramatically down in the environmentally blessed recreational counties in the northern part of the state. But growth is also down in the predominantly agricultural counties as well as in those nonmetropolitan counties employing a substantial proportion of the work force in manufacturing jobs (see Kale and Voss 1986).

Figure 4.9 shows just how pervasive the slowdown in growth in the 1980s has been. The vast majority of counties are showing slower growth than in either of the five-year periods in the 1970s.

Migration

In the discussion of table 4.1, the point was made that Wisconsin's population growth for most of this century has not been radically altered by the

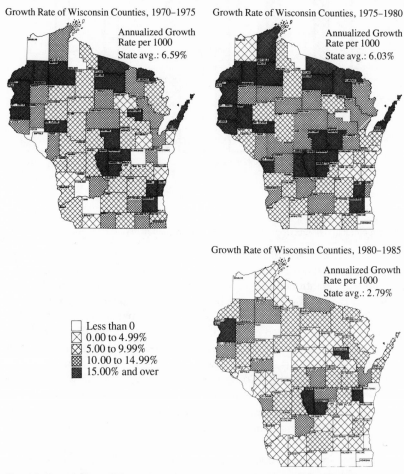

Fig. 4.9. Growth rates of Wisconsin counties: 1970–75, 1975–80, and 1980–85. (Source: Derived by author.)

migration component of population change. There have been identifiable brief periods of dramatic net in- or out-migration, but over the long haul, most of the state's growth in recent decades has been through natural increase.

The early 1980s represent a marked departure from this general pattern. Current estimates place the net loss due to migration patterns between 1980 and 1985 at approximately 100,000 persons. Certainly no recent five-year period has posted a net migration loss of this magnitude. Figure 4.2 shows that net out-migration increased substantially in the years 1980–83, suggesting its strong association with the severe loss of employment in many of the state's manufacturing industries during the 1982 recession. The level of net out-migration has likely subsided during the 1984–85 period, but the total loss over the full five-year period remains uncharacteristically large.

Table 4.3 suggests that the loss was predominantly among those persons of working age. Additions to the elderly have remained relatively invariant during the past fifteen years. The overall downturn in growth is largely the result of weakened growth only among those under the age of 65. This again provides at least indirect corroboration for the notion that the growth trend has been dominated by the trend in employment.[7]

The relatively small net migration numbers estimated for years prior to 1980 conceal a very important aspect of migration which frequently goes overlooked: small net numbers are often the outcome of very large flows of persons migrating in opposite directions. Results from recent censuses serve to illustrate this point. Table 4.4 shows the migration flows into and away from Wisconsin for the intervals 1955–60, 1965–70, and 1975–80. The data are derived from census tabulations based on a question in the decennial enumerations which asks about residence five years earlier. In each instance, the net number of migrants (in minus out) is very small relative to the total number of persons arriving and departing.

A second illustration of large cross flows yielding small net numbers is drawn from the distribution by age of Wisconsin's in-migrants and out-migrants during the period 1975–80 (see figure 4.10). During this five-year

Table 4.3. Wisconsin Population Change by Age Group, 1970–1985

Period	Growth of Population Under Age 65	Growth of Population Age 65 and Over	Total
1970–75	108,641	39,279	147,920
1975–80	85,613	54,288	139,901
1980–85	18,049	48,059	66,108

Source: Numbers estimated by Demographic Services Center, Wisconsin Department of Administration.

Table 4.4. Migration of Persons Five Years Old and Over between Wisconsin and Other States
        for Three Five-Year Periods

Period	In-Migrants	Out-Migrants	In + Out	In − Out
1955–60[a]	198,759	228,328	427,087	−29,569
1965–70	306,215	297,238	603,453	8,977
1975–80	290,020	327,998	618,018	−37,978

Sources: For 1955–60, U.S. Bureau of the Census, 1963, *1960 Census of Population,*
PC(2)-2B, "Mobility for States and State Economic Areas"; for 1965–70, U.S Bureau of the
Census, 1977, *Current Population Reports,* P-25, no. 701, "Gross Migration by County: 1965
to 1970"; for 1975–80, U.S Bureau of the Census, 1984, *1980 Census of Population,* Supplementary Report, PC80-S1-17, "Gross Migration for Counties: 1975 to 1980."
    [a]Numbers in this row are not adjusted for missing data on the question concerning resi-
dence five years earlier. Adjusted numbers for in- and out-migrants would likely be 6–8%
higher.

period, the state was a net recipient of young children and a net exporter of
adults. However, except for ages 20–24 and 25–29, the two migration curves
are rarely very far apart. Indeed, the curves are nearly coincidental for ages 30
through 54, even though 86,232 persons in these ages moved to Wisconsin
from another state while 90,775 moved away. There is nothing in the dynamics of interstate migration that requires this outcome of a small net number
arising as the difference between migration cross flows, although it is a common enough occurrence.

The small net impact on Wisconsin's population arising from migration
does not mean, of course, that the issue of migration is of little concern. On
the contrary, considerable interest has recently centered on who arrives in or
leaves Wisconsin as measured by the migrants' levels of education, their occupational skills, the extent of their dependence on state resources, and the
income that they generate (or otherwise would have generated) for the state.
These questions, while not new, have recently been the focus of heated
debate.

Data from the 1980 census covering migration patterns for the period
1975–80 reveal that Wisconsin is experiencing a net loss of some of its best-
educated, most highly skilled and well-paid workers through out-migration.
Again, the net numbers are admittedly small when compared with the total
volume of flows in and out, which yield the net result. This fact notwithstanding, attracting people back to the state or otherwise stemming the net loss of
such individuals is high on the agenda for several public interest groups and
state legislators. Three recent debates centering on these issues can be cited.

INHERITANCE TAX REFORM. Recognizing Wisconsin's net loss through
migration of its older residents (see figure 4.10), individual citizens, educa-
tors, business leaders, and selected state legislators have long been calling for
the relaxation or elimination of the state's inheritance tax. The idea that a

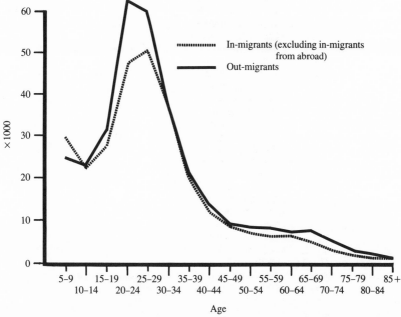

Fig. 4.10. In-migrants from other states and out-migration to other states, by age (for persons five years and over in 1980), Wisconsin 1975–80. (Source: U.S. Bureau of the Census, 1984, County-to-County Migration Flows, machine readable file.)

relatively progressive inheritance tax structure is a possible contributing factor in the decision to leave the state for some of Wisconsin's more affluent older residents finds support in surveys of tax accountants, trust attorneys, and recent out-migrants themselves. However, this latter evidence can be criticized for methodological flaws and has often led to highly selective and one-sided interpretations.[8] In 1984, I used a statistical model to isolate the influence of state death tax levels on the interstate migration patterns of the elderly, net of other known or suspected influences such as climate, cost-of-living and quality-of-life factors, differences in population size of states, and the distances separating them. The data were unable to reveal any relationship suggesting that elderly individuals respond to their state's death tax levels in deciding to leave and establish residence elsewhere (Voss, Tordella, and Manchin 1984). The results of this large statistical study notwithstanding, there does appear in some of my subsequent analyses that out-migration rates among Wisconsin's older residents do increase in direct relationship to estimates of net worth. This may reflect some migration influence of a progressive inheritance tax, but it likely also reflects the greater ability of persons of high net worth to live out their postretirement years in areas having more

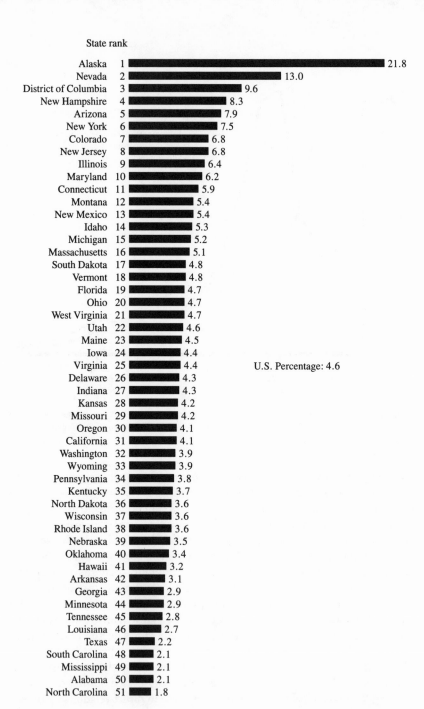

State rank

State	Rank	Value
Alaska	1	21.8
Nevada	2	13.0
District of Columbia	3	9.6
New Hampshire	4	8.3
Arizona	5	7.9
New York	6	7.5
Colorado	7	6.8
New Jersey	8	6.8
Illinois	9	6.4
Maryland	10	6.2
Connecticut	11	5.9
Montana	12	5.4
New Mexico	13	5.4
Idaho	14	5.3
Michigan	15	5.2
Massachusetts	16	5.1
South Dakota	17	4.8
Vermont	18	4.8
Florida	19	4.7
Ohio	20	4.7
West Virginia	21	4.7
Utah	22	4.6
Maine	23	4.5
Iowa	24	4.4
Virginia	25	4.4
Delaware	26	4.3
Indiana	27	4.3
Kansas	28	4.2
Missouri	29	4.2
Oregon	30	4.1
California	31	4.1
Washington	32	3.9
Wyoming	33	3.9
Pennsylvania	34	3.8
Kentucky	35	3.7
North Dakota	36	3.6
Wisconsin	37	3.6
Rhode Island	38	3.6
Nebraska	39	3.5
Oklahoma	40	3.4
Hawaii	41	3.2
Arkansas	42	3.1
Georgia	43	2.9
Minnesota	44	2.9
Tennessee	45	2.8
Louisiana	46	2.7
Texas	47	2.2
South Carolina	48	2.1
Mississippi	49	2.1
Alabama	50	2.1
North Carolina	51	1.8

U.S. Percentage: 4.6

Fig. 4.11. Percentage of 1975 population age 55 and over out-migrating between 1975 and 1980. (Source: U.S. Bureau of the Census, 1980, Public Use Microdata Sample, machine readable files.

90

temperate climates than Wisconsin. Perhaps the most interesting feature of the out-migration of Wisconsin's elderly residents is how small it actually is. Indeed, the evidence is compelling that Wisconsin does very well relative to other states in retaining its older citizens. This is shown in figure 4.11. Very few states in the "frost belt" have rates of out-migration of elderly lower than Wisconsin's 1975–80 rate of 3.6%.

WISCONSIN'S "BRAIN DRAIN." Table 4.5 shows the migration of persons to and from Wisconsin, between 1975 and 1980, by level of education for persons age 25 and over in 1980. Several of the state's citizens have pointed to these numbers or similar data as a sign that Wisconsin is experiencing a "brain drain"—an alarming net loss of its educational capital (Drilias 1985). However, while the data clearly do signal a net loss of more highly educated persons, the use of emotive expressions such as "brain drain" very likely is exaggerating the importance of what may also be viewed as a relatively small net migration difference.

By focusing only on the loss of college-educated adults, recognition of the fact that nearly 55,000 college-educated adults over the age of 25 moved *to* Wisconsin during the 1975–80 period is easily missed. Moreover, it can be argued that the net loss of 15,000 college-educated adults is hardly large enough to deserve much of the attention it has been given. The production of college graduates in the state over a five-year period exceeds this level by a factor of roughly seven, which means that a loss of this magnitude can be sustained even while continuing to increase substantially the overall educational capital in the state and provide meaningful employment for Wisconsin's college graduates. Furthermore, just as with the migration exchanges of Wisconsin's elderly, which reveal strong retention but low attraction, there is evidence in detailed migration rates that Wisconsin is among the top third of states in the ability to retain college graduates. The net loss results largely from Wisconsin's inability to attract more college-educated in-migrants to the state during the 1975–80 period.[9]

WISCONSIN AS A "WELFARE MAGNET." A third concern of persons worried about Wisconsin's migration numbers focuses on the apparent net in-migration of low-income households, persons receiving public assistance in-

Table 4.5. Migration by Educational Level of Persons 25 and Over, Wisconsin, 1975–80

Level of Education	In-Migrants	Out-Migrants	Net Migrants
Not a high school graduate	26,175	24,410	1,765
High school graduate	50,588	52,710	−2,122
Some college	32,217	38,828	−6,611
College graduate	54,620	69,896	−15,249

Source: Derived from the U.S. Census Bureau's County-to-County Flows File Summary Tape.

come, and mothers receiving AFDC payments. Acknowledging Wisconsin's relatively high AFDC benefit levels, particularly in comparison to Illinois, a major effort was mounted as the 1986–88 state budget was pieced together to severely limit the governor's proposed 3% cost-of-living increase in AFDC payments. Once again, however, a careful examination of the migration data from the 1980 census suggests that there is little statistical evidence—at least for the 1975–80 period—to back up the anecdotal accounts which constitute the basis for the argument (Voss 1985). The flow of low-income in-migrants from northeastern Illinois to southeastern Wisconsin and the smaller flow in the opposite direction can be shown to result simply from the difference in the size of the origin groups in the two states. This is illustrated by the numbers in table 4.6. The probability of an AFDC mother living in northeastern Illinois moving to southeastern Wisconsin is no greater than that of an AFDC mother in southeastern Wisconsin moving to northeastern Illinois. The migration flows for 1975–80 can be explained by a purely demographic account without any need to invoke an argument based on individual motivations and differential benefit levels.

In a study commissioned by Governor Anthony Earl's Expenditure Commission, actual applicants for AFDC in Wisconsin were surveyed regarding their reasons for moving to the state. This study confirmed the small migration influence implied by the earlier census analysis. The authors of the Expenditure Commission report, among whom I was one, concluded that perhaps 3% of applicants for AFDC during any given period may represent migrants who have moved to Wisconsin and were motivated, in part, by the potential for higher benefits in the state (Wisconsin Expenditure Commission 1986).

Table 4.6. Migration between Southeastern Wisconsin and Northeastern Illinois as a Percentage of the Relevant Origin "Pool"

	Wisconsin	Illinois
1. 1980 Population	2,394,971	7,740,505
2. 1980 population below poverty	185,458	843,429
3. 1980 census estimate of AFDC household heads[a]	22,580	86,620
4. Total out-migrants to the other area	21,600	34,960
5. Below poverty out-migrants to the other area	1,800	5,600
6. AFDC out-migrants to the other area[a]	200	600
7. % of total "pool" migrated to other area (row 4)/(row 1)	0.9%	0.5%
8. % of poverty "pool" migrated to other area (row 5)/(row 2)	1.0%	0.7%
9. % of AFDC "pool" migrated to other area (row 6)/(row 3)	0.9%	0.7%

[a]This estimate is based on the number of female-headed families with children under the age of 18 in 1980 who reported receiving income in the form of public assistance in 1979. Comparison with the state's AFDC caseload for April 1980 suggests that the estimate is low. However, under the assumption of no difference in the extent of underestimation between Wisconsin and Illinois, the percentages in row 9 will maintain their same relative difference.

Consequences of Slow Growth

The implications of slow growth for the state are both good and bad. Slow growth could eventually mean a decline in the number of representatives in Congress (as it did for ten states in reapportionment of the 98th Congress following the 1980 census[10]). For the business community slow growth means less growth in sales and gross income if products do not stimulate new demand. Slow population growth for the state results in part from population decline in some areas where the cost of social services, like education and fire protection, are likely to remain high despite attritions from the tax base.

On the other hand, slow growth generates less demand for higher-cost public sector services that usually accompany rapid population growth. Low population growth reduces the pressure on suburban sprawl, which causes the serious and almost always irreversible loss of farmland.

This chapter has touched on only a few of the demographic changes that are affecting the economic and political future of the state. The demographic processes that underlie these shifts are generally understood well enough that it is possible to foresee at least some of their medium-term implications. Policy is sometimes made without the benefit of the demographic "early warnings" that can enable policymakers to anticipate the effects of population change and adjust the course of economic development. Fortunately, however, there exists in this state a very large resource of demographic expertise. There also exists a willingness on the part of state agencies and legislative staffs to involve demographic judgment and insight in the policy process. Monitoring demographic trends requires periodic analysis of what has changed and what the change means. Demographic change usually proceeds slowly, but on a massive scale.

The downturn in the economy in the early 1980s was part of a deep national recession, and its effect on Wisconsin's population might, in fact, have been anticipated better than it was. As it turned out, this particular recession had a significant impact on the state's economy and saw the Wisconsin unemployment rate reach higher levels than the national rate.

Is the second half of the 1980s likely to repeat the events of the first half? Probably not. The late 1980s will not see the same sort of pressure on the entry-level positions in the labor force as was the case in the late 1970s and early 1980s as the baby-boom generation matured to working age. Moreover, the current public-private partnership efforts to improve the state's climate for economic development can be expected to have some payoffs. This should serve both to retain existing businesses and to attract new businesses to the state—thus depressing the out-migration from the state and encouraging a rise in in-migration. Wisconsin is likely to experience slow growth over the next five years, but the growth rates are almost certain to be higher than they were in the early 1980s.

NOTES

1. The decade of the 1970s was also a period which saw most (89.9%) of the nation's population growth focused on the South and West. During these years, however, Wisconsin's growth was buoyed up by two factors. First, the industry mix in the state was such that Wisconsin's economic performance sustained population growth in many of the state's manufacturing counties. Second, fed by rural-bound migrants from the upper Midwest's largest metropolitan cities, many nonmetropolitan counties witnessed strong population growth. This combination, at a time of weakening growth among many states in the Midwest and Northeast, led the *Wall Street Journal* to dub Wisconsin the "Star of the Snowbelt" in the 1970s. It should be noted that in spite of the slow growth for the state between 1980 and 1985, recent estimates by the Census Bureau reveal that Wisconsin's rate of population increase exceeded that of its neighboring states in the East North Central Division. During this five-year period, Ohio and Michigan lost population, and Indiana and Illinois grew at rates considerably below that for Wisconsin.

2. For the period under examination here, net migration has been a modest contributor to the state's growth, generally constituting well under 25% of total population change for decades prior to 1980. Since annual net migration estimates are computed as the difference between total population change and natural increase, they are based on a current population estimate. Hence, all estimation errors get heaped on the net migration estimates. A small percentage error in the population estimate can result in a very large error in net migration estimate, and, as a consequence, the annual net migration numbers plotted in figure 4.2 show considerable year-to-year fluctuation. Nevertheless, major events are revealed with clarity, such as the beginning and end of both World War II and the Korean War.

3. Components of growth for the three five-year periods from 1970 to 1985 are shown below. These figures show the modest upturn in natural increase occasioned by the baby-boom "echo," discussed above. In addition, the figures clearly show the strength of net migration in the early 1970s, the reversal to a very small net out-migration in the late 1970s, and the dramatic increase in net out-migration in the early 1980s.

	1970–75	1975–80	1980–85
Births	339,051	342,959	368,899
Deaths	205,213	199,125	202,710
Natural increase	133,838	143,834	166,189
Net migration	14,082	–3,933	–100,081

Source: Estimated by the Demographic Services Center, Wisconsin Department of Administration.

4. The net migration numbers given for the period 1970–80 in table 4.2 are based on estimates of net migration. Actual in- and out-migration numbers for the second half of the decade are available from the 1980 census (for persons aged 5 years and over in 1980).

	All Races	Whites	Blacks	Spanish Origin
In-migrants	319,421	282,485	20,528	10,761
Out-migrants	327,998	308,178	11,934	6,781
Net migration	–8,577	–25,693	8,594	3,980

Source: U.S. Bureau of the Census, *1980 Census of Population,* Supplementary Report, PC80-S1-17, "Gross Migration for Counties: 1975 to 1980" (issued March 1984).

5. In each instance (the 1960s and 1980s) this county is the same (Iron County) and results from the county's older population composition. Decades of out-migration of young persons have left behind an older resident population (resulting in relatively higher death rates) and have created a deficit of young adults (resulting in relatively lower birthrates).

6. A similar pattern of downturn in suburban growth in the early 1980s is apparent in many of the larger metropolitan areas of the Midwest.

7. The correlation between the rate of change in the population under age 65 and the rate of change in employment among the state's counties for the period 1980 to 1985 is a modest 0.43. Before calculating the correlation coefficient, the data for three multicounty metropolitan areas were combined on the assumption that in metropolitan areas the county groups constitute a single labor market area. These metro areas are Milwaukee (Milwaukee, Ozaukee, Washington, and Waukesha counties), Eau Claire (Eau Claire and Chippewa counties), and Appleton-Oshkosh-Neenah (Calumet, Outagamie, and Winnebago counties). There are several reasons why the correlation is not higher. First, there is evidence in the labor mobility literature to confirm what otherwise is common sense: Not everyone moves immediately upon becoming unemployed. Unemployment Compensation benefits, the hope of being rehired, having a spouse who is employed, the difficulty of selling a home in a depressed housing market, the presence of family and other relatives in the area—all of these are reasons why loss of a job doesn't always translate into migration. For this reason, one might not expect the correlation to be very high. Second, the employment numbers used here were taken from the state's Unemployment Compensation data base (maintained by the Department of Industry, Labor and Human Relations). This data base does not include all forms of employment data. For example, small proprietorships generally are not covered. In addition, the data are geocoded to the address of the employer rather than to place of residence of the workers, a fact that would be expected to weaken the relationship between change in employment (based on place of work) and change in population (based on place of residence). Finally, the low correlation is a reminder that demographic change is indeed a complex phenomenon. Attempts to reduce such change to one or two simple explanations are always going to come up short.

8. For an extended report on this topic and references to other work in the state, see Voss, Tordella, and Manchin (1984).

9. This conclusion is based on the results of a recent master's thesis carried out by David Landry (1987).

10. The 98th Congress was the first in which reapportionment based on the 1980 census took effect. Some seventeen seats shifted as a result of reapportionment. Eleven states gained representatives: Arizona 1, California 2, Colorado 1, Florida 4, Nevada 1, New Mexico 1, Oregon 1, Tennessee 1, Texas 3, Utah 1, and Washington 1. Ten states lost representatives: Illinois 2, Indiana 1, Massachusetts 1, Michigan 1, Missouri 1, New Jersey 1, New York 5, Ohio 2, Pennsylvania 2, and South Dakota 1.

5

Targeting Economic Development in Wisconsin

PETER K. EISINGER

Stimulating the growth of employment, earnings, and the tax base through public efforts to expand the private sector has now become a universal preoccupation of state government. No state in the 1980s was without an elaborate array of direct and indirect subsidies to capital for the purpose of what is broadly defined as economic development. Although politicians who govern economically healthy states are prone to exaggerate the effects of state policy,[1] few observers would argue that the various stimulative efforts that states employ are unimportant. Even if subnational economies are largely boosted or buffeted by great international and national forces over which state governments have little influence, state policies nevertheless provide some leverage to capitalize on rising trends or counteract declining ones. In this chapter I shall briefly review the performance of the Wisconsin economy since the early 1970s, discuss the state's current efforts to encourage stable and productive growth, and suggest ways that might increase the effectiveness of state economic development policy.

The Wisconsin Economy

Compared to its Great Lakes neighbors, Wisconsin's economic performance in the 1970s was strong enough to earn the state the *Wall Street Journal's* admiration as the "star of the snowbelt." For most of that decade the state's unemployment rate not only remained below the national average but also below that of Illinois, Michigan, Ohio, and Indiana (Wisconsin Strategic Development Commission 1985a, 20).

Other measures suggest the unusual level of Wisconsin's economic vitality in this decade. Personal income growth between 1967 and 1979 outstripped that in both the nation at large and in Wisconsin's sister states, although in absolute terms per capita income was higher in Illinois, Ohio, and Michigan in 1979 (Wisconsin Strategic Development Commission 1985a, 21). And the rate of capital investment in the state between 1967 and 1977 (new capital expenditures grew by more than 134%) was higher than the national average of 125% and the East North Central regional figure of 106% (U.S. Bureau of the Census 1979, 117). High capital expenditures in industries such as food processing, printing, paper-making, fabricated metal products, and machinery were accompanied by growth in manufacturing employment. Between 1967 and 1977 the number of manufacturing jobs, which then accounted for 30% of all Wisconsin nonagricultural jobs, grew by 5.8%. In the rest of the East North Central states, manufacturing employment dropped by almost 3% over the same period, while in the nation at large the manufacturing sector was increasing by only 2% (U.S. Bureau of the Census 1979, 116). Wisconsin's export-related employment, a measure of the state's ability to attract outside dollars to its economy, grew by 228% between 1972 and 1981, far surpassing the regional growth rate of 117% and falling just short of the national figure of 238% (U.S. Bureau of the Census 1979, 116; and 1986, 591).

The state's relative boom ended with the recession of the early 1980s. Employment growth came to a virtual standstill: in 1984 there were only 3,000 more nonagricultural jobs in the Wisconsin economy than there had been in 1980 (U.S. Department of Labor 1986, 76). Manufacturing was particularly hard hit, especially in the heavy industrial sectors that had been the state's strength, as job losses amounted to more than 134,000 in the first two years of the decade. Wisconsin's rate of job loss outpaced the national decline in this sector, as demand for heavy machinery nationally and in the export market slackened. Other indicators of business growth revealed signs of economic rigor mortis: the rate of new business incorporations actually fell by 3% between 1980 and 1983, though it was rising both nationally and in the Great Lakes region. The pace of business failures, once below that of other midwestern states, rose above the regional average (U.S. Bureau of the Census 1986, 571–72).

Yet by the middle of the 1980s the grim news from the economic front began to abate amid growing signs of the state's regenerative powers. Service sector jobs, particularly in retail trade, personal business services, and finance, insurance, and real estate led the general expansion. Even the manufacturing sector grew by a few thousand jobs between 1984 and 1986, and the state's long-range economic forecast predicts that manufacturing, which employed about a quarter of all workers in 1985, will still do so in 1995 (Wisconsin Department of Development 1987a, 27). (Less than 20% of all jobs nationally are currently in the manufacturing sector.) The state unemployment rate once again fell below the national average (U.S. Department of Labor 1986, 76).

This brief economic history provides the basis for two important observations that must bear on any economic development strategy. One is that the state economy clearly possesses the resources to outperform both the regional and national economies in certain crucial respects. A key task for state economic development policymakers, therefore, is to identify and nurture the particular elements that provide a Wisconsin advantage. A second observation is that Wisconsin's unusual degree of dependence on manufacturing employment in traditional industries renders the state particularly vulnerable to fluctuations in certain trade, credit, and consumption patterns. Thus, a second task for economic development officials is to ferret out new markets for state producers, encourage entirely new industries of the future, and foster new businesses that promise to fill unique market niches, all of which may provide countercyclical opportunities in periods of general recession.

Economic Development Policy in Wisconsin

The administration of Democratic Governor Anthony Earl (1983–86) represents the crucial watershed period in the history of Wisconsin's economic development policy. A pivotal event in these years was the establishment of the Wisconsin Strategic Development Commission (SDC) in 1984, but several innovative policy initiatives had preceded this step.

Prior to the Earl years, Wisconsin's economic development tools were limited to a comparatively sparse array: tax exemptions for business; industrial revenue bond and tax increment financing programs; and a Community Development Finance Corporation, which was capitalized by private investors in return for a state tax credit, for the purpose of investing in small businesses identified by community development corporations (National Association of State Development Agencies 1983). Propelled by the sharp decline in the early 1980s of the Wisconsin economy, as well as by growing and voluble discontent among businesspeople over the quality of the state's "business climate," the Earl administration began to experiment with programs designed to bring the state's policy efforts to encourage economic development into line with those of its competitors.

Earl first appointed a Marketing Wisconsin Task Force to respond to charges that the state's industrial marketing program was fragmented and underfunded. (Wisconsin's Department of Development was spending $82,000 a year on industrial promotion, compared to nearly $600,000 in Illinois, $1.5 million in Michigan, and $8 million in Ohio.) The task force recommended the formation of a public/private body, funded by equal contributions of $500,000 each from the business community and the state legislature, to recruit industry and to advertise the virtues of the state on a full-time basis. Forward Wisconsin was duly incorporated in early 1984 and funded at the recommended level.

Other initiatives in the period immediately prior to the establishment of the Wisconsin Strategic Development Commission included the creation of the Wisconsin Technology Development Fund, a program of matching grants to business and university partnerships for new product development, and the Customized Labor Training Fund to support job training programs tailored to particular businesses. In 1983 the legislature also renamed the Wisconsin Housing Finance Authority as the Wisconsin Housing and Economic Development Authority (WHEDA) and permitted it to establish economic development programs. The most active of these, the Small Enterprise Economic Development program, is funded through the issuance of bonds and notes. It is a small program: through 1985 it had made only forty loans averaging slightly over half a million dollars (Wisconsin Department of Development 1986).

To plan ways of strengthening the Wisconsin economy over the long term and to explore additional initiatives, the governor established the Wisconsin Strategic Development Commission by executive order in the spring of 1984. Composed of business leaders, labor officials, state bureaucrats, and state legislators (including Republican Tommy Thompson, who defeated Earl for the governorship two years later), the SDC commissioned more than fifty research papers and held public hearings all over the state over an eighteen-month period. In August 1985 the commission released its final report, a comprehensive package of recommendations for stimulating economic growth in the state through public and private efforts in partnership.

Wisconsin was one of approximately twenty states that engaged in a strategic planning exercise in the early 1980s. Although details of the various state plans varied widely, they had in common an effort to assess strengths and weaknesses of their respective state economies and recommendations for a coordinated set of policy initiatives that would enable local firms and entrepreneurs to capitalize upon, stimulate, or anticipate new or growing markets. The Wisconsin plan offered an analysis of the growth prospects of industries important to the Wisconsin economy, a discussion of emerging jobs in the small-business and high-technology sectors, and a comparison of the state's taxing and spending patterns in relation to a sample of other states in the region and beyond.

On the basis of its analysis, the SDC made a series of nearly one hundred specific recommendations for action. Rather than offering a coherent strategy for action, the report sought to focus public and private efforts in partnership in several broad areas: the small-business and entrepreneurial sector, the chief source of new jobs in the state economy; the university system, an underused resource for technology transfer and basic product development; and the tax and regulatory systems, which many still regarded as more burdensome to business than those in competitor states. In response to the release of the report, the governor called a special session of the legislature in the fall of 1985 to consider legislation on economic development.

Having just cut the personal income tax by $171 million in response to a preliminary report of the SDC, the legislature approached the full set of final recommendations with only a modest degree of enthusiasm. The special session produced a bill authorizing the creation of a Strategic Planning Council to provide long-term guidance on economic development issues (members had not yet been appointed two years later). In addition, Wisconsin Act 53 directed the State of Wisconsin Investment Board (SWIB), responsible for the management of the state's $15 billion pension fund, to report every two years its plans for investing in Wisconsin businesses. In its budget bill earlier that year, the legislature had authorized SWIB to place up to 2% of its funds in venture capital investments, though no provision restricting these to Wisconsin undertakings was imposed. In a later special session in the spring of 1986, the legislature took further steps to address an apparent venture capital shortage in the state by allowing the Wisconsin Housing and Economic Development Authority, which raises its capital through the issuance of bonds and notes, to establish a small seed capital fund. Finally, the state lawmakers removed several minor tax irritants about which business groups had long complained. Other recommendations of the SDC, many of which called for studies, regulatory modifications, and coordinating actions, were implemented by the governor or the relevant state agencies without the need for legislative action (see Wisconsin Department of Administration 1987; and Wisconsin Department of Development 1987b).

Tommy Thompson's victory over Tony Earl in the 1986 gubernatorial elections did not end the state's interest in the SDC recommendations. The legislature, still dominated by the Democrats, and the new governor continued to work slowly through the list. The Wisconsin Technology Development Fund and the Customized Labor Training Fund were consolidated under the Wisconsin Development Finance Board, and their combined appropriations were raised from $1 million to $21 million over the 1987–89 biennium. The legislature further reduced the personal income tax and began to phase out the state's inheritance tax. In March 1987 the governor established an Advisory Committee on Business Incentives to explore the cost of tax exemptions, tax credits, and capital subsidies and to develop guidelines for their use. Its report, issued in September 1987, proposed a set of criteria that linked the granting of incentives to the cost per job, the ratio of public expenditures or foregone revenue to capital investment, the multiplier effect, and other similar standards (Wisconsin Department of Development 1987c). Finally, at the urging of the governor, the legislature began a major campaign of highway and bridge rehabilitation, justified predominantly on economic development grounds.

A number of observers of Wisconsin politics in the late 1980s, including those in the administration, the Department of Development, and on both sides of the party aisle in the legislature agree that the Strategic Development Commission report continues in the late 1980s to play a role as a framework for action. It serves as a device for highlighting economic development as an abiding concern, and it provides a checklist of action arranged in no particular priority that functions as a periodic spur to action by one policy advocate or another. Certainly its work encouraged Forward Wisconsin, the state's quasi-public economic development marketing corporation, to develop a list of targeted industries on which to concentrate its efforts to retain and recruit business.

At the same time much of Wisconsin's economic development energy is consumed by efforts to keep or attract individual major industrial employers, a throwback to the old days of trying to compete with other states for footloose firms. Potentially costly and less certain to produce new jobs than less glamorous programs directed at encouraging small-business formation and technological innovation (Birch, 1979; Birch and MacCracken, 1984), these have been condemned by opponents from both parties in Wisconsin as a form of "corporate welfare" (*Wisconsin State Journal,* 17 February 1987). Governor Earl had undertaken a substantial, but unsuccessful, campaign to attract the General Motors Saturn plant in 1985, a pattern that has been repeated by the attempts to keep the American Motors Corporation in business in Wisconsin and then, under Governor Thompson, to persuade General Motors to expand its truck manufacturing facilities in the state. A similar, ultimately unsuccessful, effort was made to attract Sematech, a joint government/business research organization specializing in semiconductor research.

Although the Thompson administration argued that economic development is not a matter of trying "to hit a home run" (*Wisconsin State Journal,* 9 May 1987), the political incentives for making the effort to attract a major industrial concern remain powerful. Some officials in fact seem to conceive economic development as a reactive process, responding to relocation opportunities on a case-by-case basis, thus rejecting the notion that development is best pursued strategically, that is, by reference to goals, by concentrating resources on growth industries, and by planning over the long term.

At the end of the 1980s it could be said that to some extent the state's economic development efforts lacked coherence and vision. Although Governor Thompson continued to assert that economic development remained his highest priority, the momentum generated by the Strategic Development Commission had slowed, and few people in state politics, either in or out of the administration, seemed to have an economic development agenda. Yet the continuing research efforts of the professional policy analysts of the Department of Development, as well as the Strategic Development Commission report itself, suggest a way to revitalize this policy area.

Targeting Economic Development Policy

Even the most diverse state approach to encouraging business and employment growth must confront the problem of eliciting maximum effect from limited resources. One answer to the problem is to pursue a careful targeting strategy. Targeting involves focusing or concentrating resources. There are at least two general ways in which targeting might guide Wisconsin's economic development. One of these involves focusing resources on types of businesses, sectors, or industries that either currently play a major role in the state's economy and whose loss would be crippling or promise great, possibly countercyclical, growth. A second way in which resources may be targeted is to concentrate them on geographic areas in distress.

Targeting is a term that is politically fraught, for it suggests that prosperous regions within the state and successful industries not included on the target list must subsidize the economic development of others. Those firms and areas receiving help also pose a threat to nonsubsidized competitors within the state. Two responses are possible to these claims. One is that an uneven pattern of subsidy already exists: some firms and industries are assisted while others are not. Although in Wisconsin all enjoy certain of the state's various tax exemptions, the pattern of access to other forms of public assistance is more random than rational. The second response is to make clear that a targeting strategy need not preclude exceptions when a clear opportunity arises to help a firm in a nontargeted industry or nontargeted area whose growth or survival will pay clear dividends in economic development.

Wisconsin's economic development could be targeted in at least four specific ways that emphasize different industrial or sectoral targets or different regions. Few radical adjustments to current policy are necessary: both the rationale and some of the mechanisms already exist. What is required is an effort to continue on the course begun in the strategic development planning exercise, that is, to think about, organize, and administer policy as a coherent, long-range enterprise that is sensitive to market conditions faced by Wisconsin producers and entrepreneurs. The four ways to target policy include focusing on (1) "mature" manufacturing industries, (2) small-business formation and expansion, (3) new industries of the future, and (4) intrastate regional disparities.

Targeting Mature Industries

A long-range economic forecast issued by the state Department of Development in the summer of 1987 predicts that the manufacturing sector in Wisconsin will generate 38,000 new jobs by 1995, a growth rate since 1985 of 7.4% (Wisconsin Department of Development 1987e). Compared to the increase of only 2,400 manufacturing jobs in the previous ten years, this represents a substantial rebound. Growth is projected to occur mostly in the production of durable goods, particularly in nonelectrical machinery, fabricated metals, and electrical equipment. These are all "mature" industries, that is, manufacturing activities historically present in the Wisconsin economy that typically grew on the basis of well-established technologies. Mature industries, a term used with some imprecision in public policy discussions, are usually distinguished from industries in the broad service sector and those in high technology.[2] Although mature industries may eventually come to use or adapt sophisticated technology in their operations, they typically do not lead in the production of such technology or its hardware. However specifically they are defined, the loss of industries long present in the manufacturing sector would represent a serious blow to the economic health of the state. It is in the clear interests of the state to identify these industries and focus assistance on them as long as they continue to serve identifiable markets.

Opportunities for targeting mature industries in Wisconsin are also highlighted in a study conducted by the Department of Development for the State of Wisconsin Investment Board (SWIB), in which the object was to identify industries in need of capital and that also promised employment growth. The list of industries is designed to serve as a guide to SWIB investments. Of the top twenty-five industries on the list, five are mature industries: paper mills, farm and garden machinery, commercial printing, construction machinery, and electrical industrial equipment. These industries employ nearly 90,000 people in the state or 17% of all manufacturing employment (Wisconsin Department of Development 1987b, 37, 41).

Yet another research effort identified industries that generated higher job growth in Wisconsin than in the national economy over the 1976–83 period. The top twenty-five industries on this list, deemed likely job generators in the future, include nine mature industries, among them several concerned with the processing of wood products and food (Wisconsin Strategic Development Commission 1985a, 72). As the Strategic Development Commission report observed about the likely job generators, "The industries that fall into this category are the true winners in Wisconsin" (73).

Several states, including Pennsylvania, Ohio, and Massachusetts, have developed a mature-industries policy. Massachusetts's efforts serve as the most coherent model. The state established an Industrial Services Program in 1985 to oversee several initiatives addressed to industries such as textiles, machinery, shoemaking, and fishing. These efforts included expanded state financing for plant modernization, a program to assist troubled firms by providing assistance in reorganizing or high-risk financing through an economic stabilization fund, and reemployment assistance and benefits for displaced workers. Another element of the mature-industries program, known as the Massachusetts Social Compact, seeks to cushion the trauma of plant closings by calling for companies to agree to provide voluntary prenotification to workers in case of a shutdown in return for access to various sorts of state economic development financial assistance (see Ferguson and Ladd 1986).

Targeting Small Firms

As Birch and others[3] have discovered using national data sets, Wisconsin state government researchers have found that small businesses dominate the job-generation process in the state. In a study issued late in 1984 the Department of Development reported that businesses with fewer than twenty employes produced 60% of all new jobs in the state between 1969 and 1976 through both expansion and new business births. Businesses with twenty-one to one hundred employes accounted for another 17% (Wisconsin Department of Development 1984, 6). Despite the high risks of business failure among small firms, devoting substantial economic development resources to encouraging small-business formation and growth promises high employment benefits.

The state is already committed to fostering small business, and it maintains an array of programs to do so. An active Small Business Development Center program, funded mainly by the U.S. Small Business Administration but administered by the university system, offers assistance in matching inventors with manufacturing firms, provides evaluations for inventors regarding the feasibility and marketability of new product ideas, conducts technical evaluations of new products, and offers evaluations of opportunities for small-business ventures. In addition, the Department of Development administers at least five separate small-business programs, including export information and assistance, a bureau of minority business, and a small-business ombudsman and permit center. Other programs are administered through the Vocational, Technical and Adult Education system and the University Extension.

Several problems are apparent. One is that the state's efforts are fragmented. There is no centralized bureau in charge of small-business assistance and no sense of how these various programs might be coordinated. A second is that several types of programs are missing. Business incubators, for example, publicly supported in at least eighteen states, exist in Wisconsin only as private ventures. Seed capital programs for early-stage financing are also missing, although observers agree that expansion-stage venture capital has increased in recent years (Wisconsin Department of Development 1987d, 6). A third problem is that criteria are lacking for targeting businesses within the large and diverse small-business sector.

Each of these problems may be easily and inexpensively remedied. Centralized coordination requires administrative adjustments. Incubator and seed capital programs are not costly, and a targeting mechanism already exists in the Department of Development's mandate to report to SWIB every other year on types of investments that will have the greatest likelihood of enhancing the state's economic development.

Targeting New Industries

Although employment growth projections in the high-technology sector are unfavorable for all but a few states (Browne 1983), it is still possible for most states to identify a comparative advantage in one of these industries of the future. Wisconsin has a modest advantage vis-à-vis other states as a location for biotechnology concerns. The biotechnology industry is in its infancy, both in terms of the range and applications of its scientific achievements and in terms of its organizational character. In 1985, for example, there were only sixty-five biotechnology firms in the state, all but a few of which were very small operations. Nevertheless, many observers are convinced that the field promises enormous employment dividends in the next several decades.

The state's attraction for biotechnology operations consists not only of an industrial and agricultural economy that provides both a market and a research matrix for biotechnology developments, but also of a university system with excellent facilities and faculty in this broad emerging area. Genetic engineering promises to play an increasingly important role in agriculture (Wisconsin traces 22% of its jobs to this sector directly or indirectly) and forestry, as well as in brewing, food processing, and pharmaceuticals. Nevertheless, the policy response on the part of the state to biotechnology as a component of a targeted economic development policy has been slow.

The University of Wisconsin at Madison established a Biotechnology Center in 1984 with substantial state assistance to coordinate research on the campus and communicate its results to industry. In the spring of 1987 the center led the way in establishing a biopulping consortium that brought eleven paper companies—each of which pledged to contribute $75,000 over a five-year period—together with university researchers to focus on issues of technology transfer. Governor Thompson also established a Biotechnology Council to advise his office, to serve as a liaison between the state and private firms in the industry, and to advertise the virtues of locating a biotechnology enterprise in Wisconsin. These efforts represent a modest attempt to emulate similar technology transfer consortia in other states, such as Pennsylvania's Ben Franklin program, Ohio's Thomas Edison program, and New York's Centers of Excellence, among others. These latter programs are all funded both by their respective states and by industrial participants at a much more generous level than the Wisconsin program, and all are more broad-ranging in their technological interests. Early reports suggest that these centers, which focus on areas such as laser applications in manufacturing, advanced ceramics, high-technology welding, robotics, and computer-assisted manufacturing and design, are indeed producing new products and processes and helping to stimulate local employment by spinning off new firms (Dimancescu and Botkin 1986). Wisconsin has yet to commit to technology-transfer programs of this scale.

Geographic Targeting

Regional disparities in economic performance within the state are sharp. A study by the Department of Development divided Wisconsin into nine regions and found widely varying levels of prosperity (Wisconsin Department of Development 1987a). Unemployment rates in 1985, for example, ranged from 10% in the northwestern region to 6.2% in the counties of the southwest. The state mean was 7.2%. Per capita income in the southeast was more than 50% greater than than in the northwest.

Testimony presented before the state legislature's Committee on Ways and Means by University of Wisconsin economist Donald Nichols suggests that the pattern of prosperity, as measured by personal income growth rates, is an inverse function of the extent to which a region's income is earned in the manufacture of durable goods (Nichols 1987). As the economic base of a region depends more on firms that trace their fortunes to the troubled steel industry, its vulnerability increases to international competition and the rise of substitute materials used in place of steel. The Department of Development study of regional economies points out in addition that areas of the state particularly dependent on farming are highly vulnerable to fluctuations in demand for agricultural products. The conclusion that may be drawn from both analyses of regional disparities is that economic diversification is a key to stable growth.

These findings have two broad policy implications. State initiatives to revitalize mature industries and foster small-business growth and formation should concentrate disproportionately on less prosperous areas. This may be done either through the creation of special incentives for firms that form or locate in distressed counties (a state-level version of urban enterprise zones) or simply by allocating a greater percentage of funding for various state economic development programs to low-growth areas. Judging by the early experience with urban enterprise zones, as well as that of the European regional growth policies, the first option is likely to meet with only modest success. The second option has been tried only in a few states. Pennsylvania concentrates industrial development financing in distressed counties, and Massachusetts seeks to distribute its resources to areas and communities in the state that have not enjoyed the benefits of the Boston economic boom.

Conclusions

Most people involved with policy to promote economic development agree that there is no "silver bullet" that will at once permit a state to solve intrastate development disparities and promote stable and productive employment and tax base growth. Little agreement exists on what works and what does not. In any event, state economic development policy, which tends to operate at the margins of great economic forces, is generally a congeries of small, often overlapping, programs pursued on a broad front. Nevertheless, to concede all this is not to suggest that it does not matter whether or not the resources a state devotes to economic development are used efficiently.

There are, as we have seen, clear rationales for targeting small business and new industries as growth generators. Early evidence supports the notion that state intervention can bridge critical capital gaps in the business-formation and technology-transfer process and thus make a difference in a state's development experience.

Targeting mature industries and distressed areas makes sense as a prophylactic strategy, for displaced workers, declining industries, and regional pockets of poverty represent a drain on state resources. A four-pronged targeting strategy, in short, will reduce the probability that the state's economic development resources will be dissipated either by random application or by reactive efforts to attract or retain economically viable industries that exploit uncertainty about their choice of location to leverage public assistance.

NOTES

The author wishes to thank John Portz and John F. Witte for their careful reading and helpful comments on an earlier draft.

1. Governor Michael Dukakis of Massachusetts based much of his campaign for the Democratic nomination for the presidency on the claim that his policies resulted in the "Massachusetts Miracle." Heavy defense spending and the concentration of universities in the Boston area contributed at least as much to the region's economic resurgence as the state's array of imaginative economic development policies.

2. The high-technology sector has been defined as those industries with a higher than average effort devoted to R&D and a higher than average proportion of their work force in scientific and technical professions (see Riche et al. 1983).

3. See, particularly, Armington and Odle (1982).

6

Wisconsin Income Tax Reform

JOHN F. WITTE

In the year 1985 the state of Wisconsin dramatically altered its income tax system. In this chapter I discuss the general problem of tax reform and criteria for evaluating tax policy, describe and evaluate the changes in the Wisconsin law, briefly sketch how the reform was accomplished politically, and conclude with a suggested agenda for the future.

The General Problem of Tax Reform

Income tax reform is a very curious area of public policy in that there is general agreement on the criteria on which policy changes should be judged and often a broad political consensus on the rough format for reform; but yet significant and lasting tax reform is rarely accomplished at either the federal or state levels. Indeed, the normal historical pattern of tax policy is in a direction counter to reform principles. I have argued elsewhere (see Witte 1985, 1986) that this failure (specifically at the federal level) is an indication of inherent problems of policy making in a representative democracy. The pleasant argument of this chapter is that the Wisconsin case demonstrates that radical reform is not impossible.

Although emphasis varies, there is basic agreement on the criteria for judging tax reform. The criteria generally follow standard textbook principles that have been discussed at least as far back as Adam Smith.[1] The list includes horizontal and vertical equity, administrative efficiency, economic efficiency, and simplicity. At the simplest level, horizontal equity means equal taxation of equal incomes; vertical equity means that those with higher incomes should bear a heavier "burden" of taxation; administrative efficiency means that the ratio of administrative costs to revenue collections should be minimized; economic efficiency means that the tax system should have as little effect as possible on the pure market allocation of resources; and simplicity means simplicity.

Since World War II, there has also been remarkable agreement among both academic tax experts and practitioners on the basic contours of a "reformed" tax system. The guidelines were first formalized in detail by Henry Simons in *Personal Income Taxation* (1938). Conceptualizing an accretion definition of income as all consumption plus additions to wealth in a specified period, he proposed a very broad base for an income tax. That meant few, if any, exclusions, exemptions, deductions, tax credits, or special rates or timing of tax payments. Given that broad base, the appropriate rate structure could be defined politically (although Simons himself argued for an unspecified degree of progressivity).

For current tax systems, with much narrower bases than he envisioned, this has meant that tax reform proposals should broaden the base through repeals of exclusions, deductions, and so forth. This base-broadening would then allow a reduction in marginal rates, again producing an effective rate pattern that was to be determined politically. In the last decade, most reform proposals have also included a reduction in the number of brackets, some embracing a single flat tax. The rationale given for the reduction in brackets is simplicity, but since from the tax preparer's perspective the number of brackets is inconsequential, this aspect of reform proposals should really be evaluated on vertical equity grounds.

Given the stakes involved in tax politics, the breadth of agreement among relevant elites on both the criteria and the broad outlines for reform is remarkable. At the federal level in 1984 and 1985, we witnessed liberal tax reform economists and Democratic politicians roundly applauding a conservative Republican Treasury Department tax reform proposal as revolutionary. Although the bill ultimately enacted in 1986 was not nearly as comprehensive as the initial proposals and overall may have further complicated the tax code, the number of special provisions either eliminated or reduced makes the bill the most radical reform measure passed in the seventy-year history of the modern income tax.

However, in the past major tax reforms have soon been followed by sharp transitions that undo the reforms and often make the situation worse than when the cycle began. This is what happened in the period from 1976 to 1981. Thus, the key questions are, What are the major obstacles to lasting tax reform? and How was Wisconsin able to accomplish the reforms it enacted? The first question can be considered in general terms; the latter requires a more concise description of the Wisconsin case.

There are two answers to why tax reform is so elusive despite the apparent consensus on relevant criteria and the direction of reforms. First, the theoretical criteria and structure of reforms are not so simple when applied to actual tax systems. For example, horizontal equity does not lead to a simple solution when considerations of differing economic circumstance and need are taken into account. Medical and casualty deductions are meant to protect against differing levels of expenditure that are beyond the control of individuals. Should we equally tax the same gross income of two families who differ radically in annual medical expenses or uninsured casualty losses? Dependents and family size pose similarly difficult choices. Should single taxpayers without dependents be treated the same as couples with large families?

Similar arguments emerge over vertical equity and economic efficiency. There are philosophical disagreements over the appropriate degree of vertical equity and even what is meant by it. For example, does a proportional tax represent vertical equity because it extracts a higher absolute amount from the wealthy, compared to the poor? Liberal proponents of a progressive system have long argued no, but the case is "uneasy."[2]

There are both empirical and normative problems with the criterion of economic efficiency. Empirically there is constant debate over the effects on market allocations, investment, and labor incentive for different tax systems. Although analysis has become more refined in recent years, no one can describe these effects with much certainty in real economic systems that are so far from pure market models. In addition, however, even if we could specify the consequences of various policy choices with any accuracy, there remains the problem of the trade-off between efficiency and macroeconomic expansion and equity considerations. We are no closer to resolving those debates than we were when Adam Smith laid the groundwork for modern economics and tax theory.

The confusion in applying reform criteria would be greatly mitigated if all the pieces of a reformed tax system could be brought together. Elimination of most, rather than just a select few, special tax provisions would provide a sense of fairness that would offset the claims of need that provide the rationale for special treatment. At the same time, one could argue that overall horizontal equity would increase because taxable income would be much more standard across income groups. Also, with a radical reform, many special provisions would be completely eliminated, and far fewer individuals would itemize deductions (perhaps no one if all deductions were eliminated). The result would be much greater simplicity and higher administrative efficiency.[3] Finally, both because lower rates would be in effect and because less investment income would be diverted to tax-sheltered activity, one could at least argue—even if not conclusively prove—that efficiency in the allocation of resources, aggregate investment, and labor incentives would all be increased. Thus, to deal with conflicting tax reform principles requires a radical enough change that the negative aspects of reform are overwhelmed by major restructuring along the lines Henry Simons suggested.

The second reason why major tax reform efforts have been so elusive is that when operating under normal conditions, it is extremely difficult for a fragmented, pluralistic power system to generate the political momentum necessary to provide the guarantees for radical reform that allow such reform to take place. Partial reform movements become bogged down as bargaining proceeds on a provision-by-provision basis, with each special interest trying to minimize losses, often by pointing at other groups who (they claim) will not suffer as much. Politicians may gain considerable credibility by participating in a radical overhaul of a system that as a whole few citizens have kind words for. However, they stand to gain little in a modest trimming process and may well lose considerably as intense minorities protest their losses. When faced with piecemeal reforms, a better political strategy may be to support those special interests critical to one's district while hoping to gain some residual benefit from the reform label, or (more likely), the tax reduction that has always accompanied tax reform.

What this argument suggests is that enactment of radical tax reform, at either the state or federal level, requires a certain critical mass of changes. The reform must be radical enough that elected politicians can support the bill on general reform grounds and thus overcome the particularistic arguments of individual special interests. If the reform is broad and if most, if not all, provisions reduce special benefits, it will be harder for any specific interests to argue that they were singled out unfairly.

The state of Wisconsin in 1985 was able to produce such a radical reform, although some changes in the new tax code do not follow pure reform principles. In evaluating these changes I will consider the effects of major provision changes on simplification, base-broadening, vertical and horizontal equity, and economic efficiency. Since there is no independent measure of administrative efficiency that can be applied to evaluate legislative changes before they take effect, it will be assumed that simplification of the system will pay some unspecifiable dividends in administrative savings.

Evaluation of the 1985 Wisconsin Tax Reform Legislation

The problem of tax reform at the state level is compounded by the federal income tax. Because people are required to file federal income taxes, simplification is dependent on how closely the state system resembles the federal system. The ultimate in simplicity is to take the federal system, using the federal computation for adjusted gross and taxable income, and then apply the requisite state tax rates. State laws would automatically be adjusted on a same-year basis as federal laws change. The difficulty with this approach, and other degrees of "federalization," is that the state system is locked into the federal code, regardless of the character of that law relative to other reform criteria. Thus one could have a simple state tax system with all the attendant inequities of the present federal system.

The reforms enacted in Wisconsin were significantly influenced by the federal system, although several other factors were also important. Some of the groundwork and general directions for reform were set through tax revisions enacted in 1979 and a new marital property law. A number of provisions in the 1979 legislation set patterns that were carried through in 1985. That law reduced the number of brackets from eleven to eight and dropped the top rate from 11.9% to 10.0%. In addition, state and local taxes were eliminated as itemized deductions; property taxes were treated as credits; capital gains and the standard deduction were federalized; and partial indexing was enacted. Marital property reform was important because it mandated an end to income-splitting, which was previously required for joint returns.

However, even with these prior changes, the 1985 tax system remained very complex. The individual long form was seventy lines, requiring ten adjustments to federal income, and requiring that income be split between spouses, with separate computations for each. The Department of Revenue reported a 14% error rate on returns, compared to 8% at the federal level.

Evaluating tax legislation in terms of reform criteria is as difficult as trying to clearly state the criteria. Simplification and base-broadening are potentially the easiest characteristics on which to judge changes. The remaining criteria of horizontal and vertical equity and economic efficiency are inherently more difficult. I will begin by describing the major changes in the 1985 legislation, focusing on their effects on simplification and changes in the tax base.

Simplification and Base-Broadening

Table 6.1 presents the major 1985 changes in the Wisconsin tax code. The table is divided into (1) adjustments to income; (2) deductions; (3) credits; (4) changes in other provisions; and (5) rate and bracket changes. Each change is evaluated on whether it simplified tax reporting and broadened the tax base. A number of complicating factors entered into making these determinations. Judgments were based on the existing tax system as it would have taken effect following marital property reform. In terms of simplicity, the federal system had to be taken into account. For example, it may be as simple to calculate a tax credit as to subtract a deduction from income. If the federal system relies on deductions, however, the state taxpayer must make a further computation and thus the change is more complex. On the other hand, fully repealing a provision, even if it remains in the federal system, is considered simpler because no entry is required at all. Those provisions listed as neutral substitute one set of calculations for a comparable set.

Table 6.1. Comparison of Current and Prior Law and Effects on the Tax Base and Simplification for Provisions Altered by the 1985 Tax Reform

Modifications	Previous Law	New Law	Simplicity	Base-Broadening
Adjustments to Income				
1. Social security benefits	Not taxed	Federalized—partially taxable	Yes	Yes
2. Federal civil service retirement	First $1,600 not taxed	Federalized—fully taxable	Yes	Yes
3. Disability income under RR act	Not taxed	Federalized—fully taxable	Yes	Yes
4. U.S. military pay	Exclusion of $1,000	Federalized—fully taxable	Yes	Yes
5. Award to crime victims	Not taxed	Fully taxed	Yes	Yes
6. Payments for well contamination	Not taxed	Fully taxed	Yes	Yes
7. Incentive stock options	Fully taxable at time option exercised	Federalized—income accrues when sold; income taxed as capital gains	Yes	No
8. Foreign earned income	Exclusion of $15,000	Federalized—exclusion of $80,000 foreign income	Yes	No
9. All-savers certificates interest	Fully taxed	Federalized—not taxable	Yes	No
10. Reinvested dividends	Fully taxed	Federalized—not taxable	Yes	No
11. Farm losses	No restrictions on farm loss income	Limited offsets based on nonfarm income	No	Yes
12. Business deductions for travel and entertainment	Federalized—fully deductible	Limitations imposed for deductions for meals, entertainment, and travel	No	Yes
13. Depreciation	Federalized—ACRS	Disallow ACRS and substitute pre-1981 schedules for rental property and farming income with high nonfarm income	No	Yes
14. Capital gains	Federalized—exclude 60% long-term	Add a 100% exclusion for qualified Wis. small businesses	No	No
15. Adoption expenses	Excludable if amount exceeds 5% AGI	Added to medical deduction and eligible for itemized credits	Neutral	No

(*continued on following page*)

Table 6.1. Comparison of Current and Prior Law and Effects on the Tax Base and
Simplification for Provisions Altered by the 1985 Tax Reform (*continued*)

Modifications	Previous Law	New Law	Simplicity	Base-Broadening
Deductions				
16. Standard deduction	$2,300 singles; $3,400 married	Sliding scale inverse with income; range from $5,200 to $0 for singles, and $7,200 to $0 for couples	Neutral	No
17. Low-income allowance	Maximum of $5,700 including standard deduction	Repealed	Yes	No
18. Casualty losses	Deductible	Repealed	Yes	Yes
19. Political contributions	Partially deductible	Repealed	Yes	Yes
20. Misc. deductions	Deductible	Repealed	Yes	Yes
21. Mortgage interest	Deductible	Changed to 5% credit in excess of standard deduction	No	Yes
22. Investment interest, including credit card and consumer loans	Deductible	Changed to 5% credit for first $1,200 in excess of standard deduction	No	Yes
23. Charitable contributions	Deductible	Changed to 5% credit in excess of standard deduction	No	Yes
24. Medical expenses	Deductible	Changed to 5% credit in excess of standard deduction	No	Yes
Credits				
25. Personal exemption credit	$20 taxpayer, spouse, dependents; $25 over 65; $20 added for head of household	Replaced with dependent credit of $50 and $25 credit for over-65 taxpayer	Yes	Yes
26. Property tax/rent credit	10% for homeowners and renters	Reduced for 1986, then repealed	Yes	Yes
27. Earned income credit	30% of federal credit (nonrefundable)	Repealed	Yes	Yes
28. Child-care credit	30% of federal credit (nonrefundable)	Repealed	Yes	Yes
29. Research and research facilities credit	5% on noncapital expenses (nonrefundable)	Repealed for individuals, retained for corporations	Yes	Yes
30. Community development finance authority credit	75% of stock or interest purchase	Repealed for individuals, retained for corporations	Yes	Yes

(*continued on following page*)

Table 6.1. Comparison of Current and Prior Law and Effects on the Tax Base and
Simplification for Provisions Altered by the 1985 Tax Reform (*continued*)

Modifications	Previous Law	New Law	Simplicity	Base-Broadening
31. Second-earner credit	1.5% of lower-income spouse (1986 only, none prior)	2.5% of lower-income spouse	Neutral	No
32. Employe stock ownership plans credit	None	5% credit on interest paid by employes to purchase stock (1986 to 1988 only)	No	No
Other Provisions				
33. Minimum tax	Add-on 5% on tax preference income and deductions in excess of $10,000	Use 55% of federal tax liability	Yes	Yes
34. Indexing	Based on CPI, ranging from −3% to +7%	Suspend for 1986, restore in 1987 with automatic suspension for budget shortfall	Neutral	Neutral
35. Net operating loss and credit carry foward	Five-year carry forward on unused operating loss, fuel and electricity credits; seven years on unused research credits	Increase all to fifteen years	Yes	Yes
36. Rates and brackets	Eight brackets with rates from 3.4% to 10.0%	Four brackets with rates from 5.0% to 7.9%	Neutral	NA

The definition of base-broadening used in this chapter is a change, holding other provisions constant, that will yield added revenue. This definition applies in the most straightforward manner to adjustments in income and deductions. Such adjustments reduce gross or taxable income. In a very narrow sense, tax credits do not affect the base on which the tax is levied because they reduce computed taxes. However, viewed more broadly, credits are specialized provisions providing tax benefits for specific types of spending or personal or household status. Although they tend to favor the less well-off rather than the rich more than deductions, they have the same politically attractive property of reducing taxes. Further, one of the unique features of the Wisconsin legislation is a switch from itemized deductions to an itemized credit system. Thus, for consideration here, credits will also be analyzed for their base-broadening effects. Also, because of their impact on the tax base I have included the standard deduction, the low-income allowance, and personal exemption credits in the analysis, although in some studies they are not included as reductions from the base.[4]

The most serious problem with determining the revenue effects of specific provisions is that in reality the changes are not being made with all other provisions held constant. For example, changes in itemized deductions are affected by changes in the standard deduction. If the latter is increased, fewer taxpayers will itemize, and the amount of revenue lost by raising the standard deduction will automatically decline. In addition, if the standard deduction is increased over prior limits, that change will lose revenue, offsetting gains from revising itemized deductions. Thus, while most of the changes in deduction provisions appear to broaden the base, as a package, changes in itemized and standard deductions could either gain or lose revenue.

These complications aside, by any judgment, the 1985 legislation dramatically simplified the Wisconsin tax code and probably broadened the base as well. In terms of simplification, twenty-two of the thirty-six major changes simplified the code, nine made it more complex, and five were neutral. The end result will be a thirty-six-line tax return (as tentatively drafted), which will become even simpler as several temporary provisions are phased out. In the process, eight special provisions were federalized; six were repealed immediately; two were repealed for individuals (remaining for corporations); and the property tax credit was to be repealed in 1987. The changes in the rates, the creation of the sliding-scale standard deduction, the increase in the second-earner credit, and changes in indexing are neutral in terms of complexity from the perspective of the taxpayer because they require the same level of computations, use similar tables, or have no effect on filing procedures.

As indicated in table 6.1, of the nine changes that add complexity, four are changes from deductions to credits for mortgage interest (21), investment and consumer interest (22), charitable contributions (23), and medical expenses (24). These require a new calculation from the federal form and thus add complexity. However, because of the creation of the sliding scale–standard deduction, which declines with increasing income, the Department of Revenue estimates that the percentage of taxpayers itemizing will decline from the current level of 20% to approximately 11%. Three additional provisions, while more complex than existing law, also broaden the base: the limited-loss provision for farm income when there is high nonfarm income (11, hobby farming); limitations on business deductions for travel and entertainment (12); and the stiffer depreciation rules (13). Of the two remaining provisions that add complexity, one was meant to improve the business climate by allowing capital gains exclusions for new (not more than five years old), small companies (less than two hundred employes and not listed on a major stock exchange) that have at least 50% of their payroll and property in Wisconsin (14); the other, employe-stock-ownership-interest (ESOP), is very minor and temporary (32).

Marks for the bill in terms of base-broadening are equally high on a provision-by-provision basis. Of the thirty-five changes in table 6.1 that affect the base, twenty-two broaden the base, twelve narrow it, and one, the indexing change, is neutral. Of the provisions that narrow the base, only two, the special capital gains exclusion for Wisconsin businesses (14) and the ESOP provision (32), also add complexity. Four of the provisions sacrifice a broader base in order to federalize and thus simplify (7, 8, 9, 10). An additional provision, computation of the state minimum tax (33), switched from a unique state-defined minimum to 55% of federal tax liability. Since the federal definition is more lenient than the previous state definition, this change loses revenue overall (although some taxpayers will pay more).

The second-wage-earner credit (31), which was increased from 1.5% to 2.5%, was included to partially offset the considerable penalty that two-earner families with relatively high incomes suffered under the marital property reform. Even with this addition and the new rates, families with two middle-to-high incomes will be penalized in relation to the 1985 system.[5] Another relatively minor, revenue-losing provision was designed to aid businesses by increasing loss carry-forward and fuel and research credits (35). These benefits to business were more than offset by the tighter restrictions on business travel and entertainment. The latter was estimated to raise revenue from corporations by $3.4 million over the biennium, while the former was estimated to lose $2.7 million (Lang 1985, 9).

The remaining provisions that narrowed the base were the changes in the standard deduction and the low-income allowance. Because under previous law the low-income allowance added to the standard deduction for low-income filers, I have considered the repeal of the allowance along with the changes in the standard deduction as joint revenue losers. The new, sliding-scale standard deduction provides a higher deduction for low-income taxpayers and also loses considerable revenue in the aggregate when compared to the old standard deduction / low-income allowance. Some of this loss is picked up by the much lower cost of the remaining itemized deductions, which have been changed to tax credits. Three deductions—for casualty losses, political contributions, and miscellaneous—were repealed outright. A Revenue Department estimate based on the 1983 tax model computed the old system of itemized deductions as costing approximately $115 million and the new system of credits as costing only $40 million. Unfortunately, at this time, effects on the base of the total shift from itemized deductions with the old standard deduction and allowance to itemized credits with the sliding-scale standard deduction are not available.

Although on a provision-by-provision basis the new law appears to broaden the tax base, the definition of what the base is has changed, and an estimate of aggregate revenue cost for the various parts of the code is not available. In terms of changes in adjustments to income, an estimate of all the changes except the partial taxability of social security (which was not available in the tax model) indicated that the adjusted gross income (AGI) of the average taxpayer would increase slightly, from $18,659 to $18,678 in 1983 dollars. This would be slightly less with the partial taxation of social security, but the revenue gain would not be that great because only half of benefits are taxed for recipients with high non–social security income. The major effort "above the line" (i.e., prior to deductions and tax credits) was to federalize for simplicity's sake. In so doing, a number of provisions lost revenue. Of the changes in "adjustments to income" affecting primarily individuals in table 6.1, seven changes expanded the base and six narrowed it. The result is modest change in aggregate AGI, but a much simpler system.

For the remainder of the code, as stated above, the effects on aggregate reductions from the base are uncertain and the "base" itself has changed. In the past we could have made comparisons between taxable incomes (AGI minus standard or itemized deductions), but that comparison is now meaningless. What is clear is that there will be fewer categories of deductions to contend with and fewer taxpayers utilizing itemized deductions, and that a major tax policy tool has been invented with the sliding-scale standard deduction.

Because the standard deduction will now account for much more of the deductible income and affects so many taxpayers, it will clearly become at least as important as the rate structure in terms of future manipulation of the tax system. In one sense the state has shifted from adjusting the system through numerous small levers to relying more heavily on one large lever. The advantages of this lever are that it can produce substantial shifts in aggregate revenue and can have considerable effect on distribution by simply varying the level and rate of decline of the deduction. Although proposed changes in the new standard deduction will be politically very sensitive, they will not be as directly tied to specific interest groups as was the case under the old system. This should facilitate changes, particularly if the need to increase revenues should arise.

Horizontal and Vertical Equity and Economic Efficiency

Judging legislative changes on horizontal and vertical equity or economic efficiency grounds is difficult because of the inherent difficulties with these concepts and because of the problems of measuring the effects in any systematic fashion. We can, of course, look at the overall distributive effects of the changes to judge the impact in terms of vertical equity. Those distributive effects are depicted in figures 6.1 and 6.2.

Effective rates declined for all income groups as a result of the 1985 bill. The aggregate revenue reduction was $275 million over the biennium, with

$171 million in permanent ongoing provision changes. The one-time 1986 property tax credit accounts for almost all the difference. Seventy-three percent of individual taxpayers will have lower taxes, 20% will have their taxes unchanged, and 7% will have an increase.

As is apparent in figures 6.1 and 6.2, the effects of the permanent reductions are not evenly distributed. Figure 6.1 portrays the reduction by income group as a percentage of taxes paid. It is clear that in these terms, the income group from $5,000 to $10,000 and those earning over $200,000 do much better than the average reduction of 7.97%. The lowest income group (below $5,000) actually pays slightly higher taxes owing in part to changes in the property tax/rent credit, low-income allowance, and repeals of the civil service retirement exclusion and the earned income credit. However, the small amounts of taxes paid in this group make any changes based on percentages of taxes paid very sensitive to slight shifts. Indeed, because adjustments to income increase the adjusted gross income for this group, their effective rate actually drops from 0.75% to 0.69% even though the group pays more than under prior law.

The same conclusions emerge from figure 6.2, which indicates the effective rates between previous law and the law after tax reform and marital property

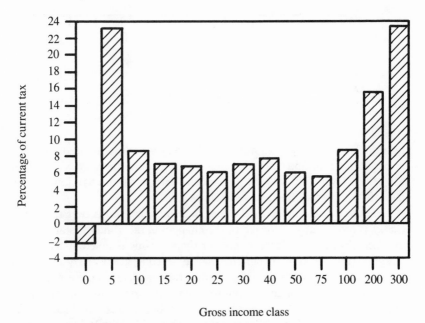

Gross income class

Fig. 6.1. Tax reduction as a percentage of current tax, by adjusted gross income class ($1000s). (Source: Legislative Fiscal Bureau, memorandum to the state legislature, 9 July 1985.)

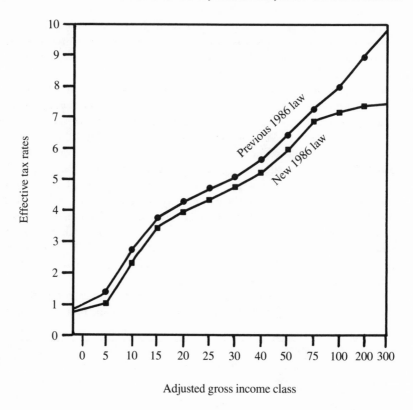

Fig. 6.2. Effective tax rates by adjusted gross income class ($1000s). (Source: Legislative Fiscal Bureau, memorandum to the State Legislature, 9 July 1985.)

reform. The rate drop is slight for the lowest group, then essentially constant at between 0.3% and 0.4% for those with incomes between $10,000 and $100,000. Over $100,000 the gap widens until, for those 850 joint returns over $300,000, the effective rate declines 2.1%.

The relative advantage of the very high income groups over the middle classes is most sharply affected by the changes in rates and the standard and itemized deductions. Because most of their income is taxed at the highest marginal rate, the major benefit for the high-income groups is the drop in the top tax rate from 10.0% to 7.9%. On the other hand, the benefits to the large middle classes are limited by compressing the marginal rates and raising the first bracket rate to 5%, combined with the sliding standard deduction that is lower than previously for joint returns with over $45,500 AGI (and itemized credits will be less valuable than the deductions were). As incomes rise above $100,000, the top rate effect again begins to create a relative advantage.

Several factors affect these distributional estimates. First, they are based on the 1983 tax sample, and income distributions could have changed slightly.[6] Second, and of much more consequence, the estimates do not take into consideration the *federal offset,* which is gained as a result of state income tax deductibility on federal returns. Given progressive marginal federal rates, with a 49% rate for joint returns above $113,860 of taxable income, this offset disproportionately benefits those at the upper income levels. What this means for analysis of this law is the reverse. The actual cuts in the effective rates are considerably smaller for those at the upper levels after we incorporate the federal offset. For example, for those over $300,000 the real effective rate reduction is close to 1%, not 2.1%. Thus, figures 6.1 and 6.2 overstate the actual effective tax savings and the amounts of effective rate reductions, particularly at the upper end of the distribution. That of course may change dramatically with the impending changes in the federal law.

How one judges these distributional results depends more on preference and philosophy than anything else. As a class the rich do better than poor or middle classes, even after we adjust downward for the federal offset. How much better, and how one views this change, depend on one's perspective on the problem. For example, taxpayers reporting more than $100,000 on joint returns account for only 0.7% of the total joint returns. Thus, a very small group of people (10,367 returns) receives disproportionate breaks totaling $23.9 million. On the other hand, under prior law this same group was paying $163.9 million in taxes, or 9.8% of the total revenue raised on joint returns. This will drop to $140 million, which is still 9.1% of the total for 0.7% of the taxpayers. If, as has been indicated to me in interviews described below, lowering the top rate was the political pinwheel that allowed this reform bill to move, even the most diehard liberal may view the cost in terms of progressivity as worth the price.

The problem of judging the results of this legislation in terms of horizontal equity turns on a different issue. If one adopts a relatively singular view that horizontal equity can be really judged only in terms of taxpayers of equal incomes paying equal amounts, or, more precisely, being able to reduce their taxes by equal amounts, then the bill is clearly a positive step. The above-the-line adjustments in income at the very worst provide at least as inclusive an income base as prior law and probably a slightly broader base. There is still plenty of room for action, given the large number of income exclusion categories that remain at both the federal and state level; however, relative to prior law the changes are at least neutral in terms of equalizing the treatment of different sources of income.

Although the above-the-line calculations are not a major improvement on horizontal equity, the changes in itemized and standard deductions clearly improve the situation. The advantage of a standard deduction, beyond its simplicity, is that it is impervious to expenditures that lead to special treatment. That this change introduces a sliding scale so the standard deduction is no longer constant for all income groups should be judged on grounds of vertical, not horizontal, equity. This reform therefore produced obvious gains in horizontal equity, but the rub comes when one ponders what the standard of horizontal equity should be. As discussed earlier, many deductions, exclusions, and exemptions are meant to stimulate desired activity or to take into account expenditures that affect the economic power of individuals. Thus, if one adopts a more complex theory of horizontal equity that includes need and rewarding citizens for desirable actions, such as giving to charity, this, and any other tax reform along base-broadening lines, is clouded.[7]

Finally, how does this legislation affect economic efficiency? The answer is that no one knows. There are provisions intended to stimulate economic development, such as the privileged capital gains provisions for small Wisconsin companies. But such provisions may misallocate investment funds or reduce growth by discouraging large out-of-state companies from bringing resources to the state. Who knows? The loss carryover provisions and research and fuel credits will aid business, but do we want to aid businesses that lose money? The tougher rules for business deductions may require separate books for state and federal expenditures and will surely lead to incessant carping and threats by businesses. But will they cut back activity or will the executives be impressed by the reform effort and the lower top rate? Finally, will the rate reductions encourage wealthy individuals to remain and invest in the state, or will the adverse effects of the limitation on deductible investment interest ($1,200), the tighter farm provisions, and depreciation changes on real estate turn them away?

In terms of business and investment incentives, the bill sends mixed messages. But perhaps more important is the extent to which this tax bill highlights how little we know about how tax changes affect business behavior, and how desired economic goals are often contradictory. We want large, usually national, corporations to remain and expand in the state, but we also want to nurture small state businesses. We want to uphold economic efficiency in industry to ensure survival, but we also want to preserve the employment base of marginal businesses. We want high-income taxpayers to invest in businesses in the state, but not to run hobby farms or work the tax-sheltered real estate market. Finally, we want business to feel welcome, but we object to the three-martini lunch and the hunting lodges while approving tax-deductible tickets to Green Bay Packers games.[8] Although simplified economic models and isolated empirical studies may provide insights into the economic efficiency of some provision changes, it is seemingly impossible to assess an overall effect on economic efficiency for a large tax bill with a multitude of interrelated modifications.

The Politics of Tax Reform

Factors Affecting Tax Reform

A number of factors were instrumental in the successful enactment of Wisconsin's income tax reform. The origin and driving force behind the reform effort was the executive branch, with a progressive governor who viewed tax reform as a major agenda item from the beginning of his term. The Department of Revenue played a major role beginning with an initial meeting with Governor Anthony S. Earl in December 1983. The vehicle for developing proposals was a Strategic Development Commission (SDC), which was formed by the governor to study and recommend changes on a wide range of economic development issues. One of their major subcommittees dealt with the issue, working closely with Department of Revenue staff.

Both the governor and the commission were sensitive to the well-publicized dissatisfaction of the business community. A survey was commissioned to assess business attitudes. Although the survey made no attempt to randomly sample business and instead worked from organizational lists, it was well publicized and often referred to by the Governor's Office and the commission. It found that although the actual business taxes in the state were competitive with or lower than those in neighboring states, the perceptions of the businessmen surveyed were that the state was a high-tax state that was hostile to business. They particularly cited the high personal tax rates as a problem.

The various interests of this set of political actors shaped the commission's recommendations and the governor's legislative proposal. The governor was interested in reform principles, wanted to lower taxes, and wished to improve the state's image with business. The Department of Revenue wanted to simplify the income tax and reduce the heavy reliance of the revenue system on income taxes, thus lowering the state's relative ranking among states in income tax use. The business community was also interested in lowering income taxes but focused more on bringing down the top personal rate.

The final two factors that were important in enacting the tax reform were the fiscal situation, which permitted a tax cut, and the use of the budget process to enact the legislation. After a spending cut and temporarily increased taxes to solve an impending deficit early in the Earl administration, revenue totals had turned around and a surplus was projected for the upcoming biennium.[9] The governor, having had considerable legislative experience, understood his powers in the budget process and timed proposals to be part of that process.

The Legislative Process

After more than a year of deliberation, in which the Department of Revenue staff supplied the SDC with a series of papers discussing tax reform criteria, a decision was reached in the commission to present a general outline for tax reform that was radical in nature. During deliberations there was considerable disagreement among members of the SDC over whether the bill should simply cut taxes across the board or whether the tax cut should be a part of a major reform package. The governor clearly indicated that tax reduction had to be tied to tax reform, and in December 1984, the commission made a very strong recommendation that included many of the major components of the final reform bill. Based on a proposal prepared by the Department of Revenue, they recommended that, excepting federal bond interest, adjusted gross income be federalized; a sliding-scale standard deduction be created that ranged from $6,800 to $4,000 for married couples and $4,900 to $2,500 for single taxpayers; all itemized deductions be removed; credits for dependents be raised to $50, but with no credit for the taxpayer or spouse, and no extra credit for the elderly; and the eight brackets be reduced to three with rates of 5%, 7%, and 8%.

Governor Earl got what he wanted from the commission and his proposal closely followed the commission's recommendations. The only major changes from the commission's report were to add a $50 credit for the elderly, increase the upper limits of the standard deduction to $5,200 for singles and $7,200 for couples; make state and local bond interest taxable (to federalize, the commission had made this nontaxable); and reduce the SDC's proposed 3% credit for second-wage-earner income to 2.5%. The measure was introduced on 25 January 1985 as part of the governor's budget proposal.

Both proposals were very radical. In all, sixteen income exclusions, deductions, and credits were to be disallowed. While retaining deductions for business and farms, all personal itemized deductions were to be excluded. This permitted a sliding-scale standard deduction with a considerable floor of $2,500 and $4,000. In addition, the property tax, earned income, child care, community development, and research credits were to be repealed.

The governor's proposal was made with an eye to the bargaining process ahead in the legislature. Secretary of Revenue Michael Ley later described this process succinctly in a speech before the National Tax Association:

> What we kept in mind during the development of this plan is that if nothing else, the budget process is a bargaining process between the executive branch and the legislative branch. The first rule of effective bargaining is to ask for more than you can get. The next most important rule is to not offer even the slightest hint of concession until you are absolutely sure that you have retained as much as you could. (Ley, June 1985)[10]

Under the Wisconsin budget system, even though a Ways and Means Committee had been created for the first time in this legislature, the bill went directly to the Joint Finance Committee (see chapter 2). From the beginning it was clear that the "pure approach," which repealed all deductions, would not pass. The Speaker of the assembly and the senate majority leader had been on the SDC and had voted against the proposal for that reason. The Joint Finance Committee acquired the necessary votes for passage by adding in deductions for charitable giving (over 1% AGI), medical expenses (over 5% AGI), and mortgage interest for a principal residence only but with a $8,000 cap. To partially pay for those provisions, they lowered the sliding-scale standard deduction to zero. They also created four brackets and lowered the top rate "below 8%," which for numerous people interviewed was an important psychological barrier, to 7.9%. However, the pressure for wider deductions did not let up as they passed the bill to the Democratic caucuses.

The assembly caucus reached an impasse on the matter of deductions. First, liberals tried to add tougher provisions on business deductions, depreciation, and farm losses for those with high nonfarm income. The caucus rejected these provisions because they would have complicated above-the-line income and because of their antibusiness tone. The intense pressure from specific lobbies continued and fueled the general sentiment favoring further broadening of the deductions that the finance committee had allowed. But key assembly Democrats, including the Speaker, resisted. They were strong supporters of the governor, who was holding firm for no deductions and threatening to veto any across-the-board reduction without major reform characteristics. Furthermore, the caucus had agreed early in its deliberations to hold the line on the rate reductions set by the Joint Finance Committee and they had also agreed to not allow any amendment, on either taxes or spending, which did not contain a means for funding the expenditure. Since rates could not be raised, that meant that no added deductions could be funded without an offset elsewhere.

The impasse was broken in the caucus when Representative Dismas Becker brought forward a plan developed with the assistance of the Legislative Fiscal Bureau that switched to the itemized credit system, while adding consumer credit and adoption expenses, lifting the cap on mortgage interest, and dropping the floor on charitable giving. The switch to credits made this change revenue neutral in comparison with the Joint Finance Committee bill, while also broadening the benefits that were included. The compromise satisfied the general sentiment that a broader set of deductions had to be included, but also had advantages favored by reformers and liberals. For reform-minded legislators, it simplified the code by increasing the number of taxpayers using the standard deduction. And for liberals, the switch to credits from deductions was viewed as progressive in that credits proportionately benefit the poor more than the rich.

Although a number of senators were involved in assembly discussions from the beginning, the senate also had an independent role. The senate caucus added a number of complicating provisions, which represented an agreement to accept both liberal and conservative amendments. On the conservative, probusiness side, this is where the changes in capital gains, the lower minimum tax (but at 30% of the federal rate, not the 55% finally enacted), and employe-stock-ownership plan interest credit were first approved. Several liberal issues, partly resurrected from the rejected assembly proposals, were also enacted. Those that made it through the conference committee were the restrictions on business travel and entertainment, changes in the Asset Cost Recovery System for rental and farm property (an attempt was made to scrap it entirely), and the limitations on losses for farm families with high nonfarm income.

A conference committee of six members worked out the differences, adopting in compromised form the provisions listed above from the senate bill, but accepting the rest of the above-the-line decisions and the itemized credits from the assembly version. Consistent with normal budget procedures, when the final budget, including tax revision, was brought before both houses, the Democrats adopted a unit rule to vote against any amendments. Thus the bill passed unamended, and really without Republican involvement except on the Joint Finance Committee where they were in a significant minority.

Tax Reform and the Budget Process

Although a number of issues are raised by Wisconsin's power-oriented budget process (see chapter 2), there is no question that that system facilitated the passage of tax reform. "Open" tax legislation, where amendments are offered without restriction by all legislators and decided in open forums, produces abhorrent tax policy. Politicians who are besieged by intense lobbying from specific groups have little choice but to make a public effort on their behalf. Some of these efforts are successful and over the years the code is cluttered with a maze of special-purpose provisions. During reform periods these same groups clamor for protection of the provisions they have won. This makes it extremely difficult to hold together any major program of change. And without a broad program of reform that widely distributes losses, but therefore also widely distributes gains, there is considerable political risk in abandoning intense constituencies. Open politics makes it more difficult to hold a program together and to resist the inevitable pressures of factions.

The Wisconsin budget process does not, to say the least, provide such an open forum. It begins with a strong bias in favor of a governor's program. A governor represents a broader set of constituencies than a senator or representative and thus can more easily deflect special pleadings. He also has the opportunity to fashion a sweeping program, before and somewhat out of the intense light of the legislative process.

Legislative decision making during the budget process is also centralized. To be successful a governor can concentrate first on a small number of key decision makers on the Joint Finance Committee and then on the majority party caucuses. If the governor has a working majority in each house, he can restrict most of his bargaining to his own party. Because the Joint Finance Committee utilizes work groups to consider changes and because caucuses are at least partially closed and amendments can be restricted, it is easier to fend off the inevitable special-purpose amendments. The unit rule, which provides unanimity in opposition to floor amendments once the budget bill reaches the floor, eliminates the same type of additions at that stage. Finally, if provisions added by the legislature are perceived by the governor as particularly damaging to his program, he can exercise the line-item veto and work to have it sustained.

Everyone I interviewed, from both parties, agreed that passage of this reform bill was made possible by this centralized process. Many of the general arguments in chapter 2 still apply and were often voiced, particularly by Republicans. What probably pushes this case as a positive example of a power-oriented budget process is that there appeared to be widespread consensus on the basic building blocks of this reform package: a simpler system, lower top rates, and an income tax reduction. Thus, in this case, the process facilitated the most radical changes in our tax system since its inception in 1911.

Conclusion and Recommendations

The tax reform of 1985 not only changed the system in a very positive direction based on comprehensive tax base principles, but also suggests a future path to what would be an ideal state income tax system. Reforms of state systems are limited by the federal code. If a state system is to remain simple, it must be coordinated with the federal system. Under this legislation, Wisconsin has made a major stride toward federalizing adjusted gross income. Although there are obvious disadvantages in that the system becomes tied to federal decisions, any major deviations produce complex filing problems that affect all taxpayers.

Unless the federal system becomes intolerable in terms of above-the-line exclusions, and it is currently moving in the opposite direction, Wisconsin should continue to eliminate special provisions that fail to match that base. The first task will be to bring the Wisconsin system in line with the 1986 tax reform act. The most important aspects of that tax bill from the point of view of federalizing Wisconsin's individual income tax are (1) raising the floor for medical and miscellaneous deductions; (2) tightening business and investment expense deductions; (3) fully taxing unemployment compensation and dividends; (4) repealing the second-earner deduction; (5) eliminating the deduction for consumer interest; (6) limiting the deduction of investment interest to net investment income; (7) repealing income averaging; and (8) eliminating special treatment of capital gains income. The state should follow the example of the federal tax code in all of these cases except the elimination of the two-earner deduction, which must be retained to offset the effects of changes in filing described above (see p. 117). Each of these provisions (and a number of others in the 1986 act) serves to broaden the base and eliminate or reduce the benefits from special provisions. Federalizing thus serves the dual purpose of simplifying and base-broadening.

In addition, the state should carefully evaluate provisions in the 1985 state reform for capital gains treatment of new, small Wisconsin businesses, the treatment of nonfarm income losses, and the differential treatment of real estate depreciation and limits on business deductions. The political mileage gained by these deviations seem hardly worth the confusion. The guiding principle should be to federalize AGI to the maximum extent possible, and particularly not to deviate for primarily symbolic reasons, which is often the case when the amount of revenue is small.

Below the line the target should be to repeal all tax credits except the personal exemption. This would effectively eliminate itemized deductions of all kinds and allow the system to be adjusted by changing the rates for the sliding-scale standard deduction, the amount of the personal exemption, and the tax rates themselves. These are simple levers, but refined enough to obtain whatever mix of revenue and incidence is dictated by prevailing political attitudes. Realizing such a system will be difficult politically, but the 1985 act provided momentum in this direction. Finish the job and Wisconsin's tax system may again be a model for the nation.

NOTES

The author would like to thank Yeang Eng Braun, Robert Lang, Priscilla Boroniec, and Ron Shanovich for comments on an earlier draft of this chapter; Mark Rom for research assistance; Elizabeth Uhr for editorial assistance; and those individuals too numerous to name who agreed to share their knowledge of the 1985 tax reform process.

1. See Groves (1970) for an excellent treatment of the historical development of tax philosophy.

2. The reference is to a well-known book exploring the philosophical and economic debate over vertical equity. See Blum and Kalven (1952).

3. I have argued elsewhere (Witte 1985) that all previous federal legislation that has

borne the stamp of "tax reform" has ultimately, if not immediately, produced a more complex tax code. The basic reason is that provisions are rarely eliminated; rather, they are "tightened" to prevent abuse. The tightening almost always adds a further layer of complexity to the code. In addition, when the winds change and tax reform is no longer politically popular, the provisions are often expanded, grafting yet another set of complex rules onto the reformed provisions.

4. For example, the government's official list of "tax expenditures" does not list exemptions or standard deductions (see U.S Office of Management and Budget, *Special Analysis G.,* various years).

5. Depending on how the joint return rates are structured, combining the income of two taxpayers will normally benefit those family units in which one wage earner earns considerably more than the other. The income is "averaged" and the family falls into a lower marginal bracket than the higher-paid spouse would be in. Because bracket widths are wider for joint returns than for single returns, if there are two high incomes, the family is at a disadvantage relative to the one-earner case. Depending on how the single and joint brackets and rates are defined, the two-earner family may well pay more tax than if each filed separately. For example, under the rates adopted for 1986 in response to the combined income requirement under marital property reform (before the current legislation was passed), a couple with taxable income of $70,000 would have paid $6,499.80 before credits, whereas two single people, each with $35,000 in taxable income, would have paid $2,754.50 each or a combined tax of $5,509 before credits.

6. Because the distributional effects are relative, the lag in the data base is relatively inconsequential, particularly in a period of low inflation. Of course, when changes are made that affect income not included in the tax model, such as taxing social security, or when radical, compounded changes are introduced, such as the shift of itemized deductions to credits in conjunction with the provision for a sliding-scale standard deduction, old data and an outdated model create serious problems. For this reason the state is foregoing a scheduled 1985 update in the tax sample so that it will have data for the 1986 tax year.

7. Henry Simons was characteristically blunt in his choice of a narrow definition of horizontal equity. He realized the merit of some of the arguments for need considerations but also argued that once the process of special exceptions begins there is no way to draw a line between those that are in and those that are out. Thus all exceptions are ruled out and one ignores special pleadings. My personal bias is the same as his, but arriving at that position has been made easier for me by observing the explosion in tax expenditures that occurred after his death. See Simons (1938) and Witte (1985, chap. 3).

8. Early in the debate over restrictions on business entertainment, an indignant legislator shockingly inquired, did the proposed amendment mean that tickets to the Packers games purchased by businesses would no longer be deductible? The answer was yes, but the retreat, demonstrating once again that all things must be kept in perspective, was swift.

9. As it turned out that projection was wrong, and beginning in the fall of 1985, revenue projections again went down. Early in 1986 emergency spending cuts were again necessary.

10. Because Secretary Ley was involved with the legislature, the speech was actually given by Assistant Secretary John Laabs.

PART TWO

HUMAN NEED AND HUMAN SERVICES

7

Poverty and Income Transfers in Wisconsin

SHELDON DANZIGER AND ANN NICHOLS-CASEBOLT

The 1935 Social Security Act established a nationwide system of income transfers to provide income support to assist individuals in times of economic crisis, such as unemployment, or when personal situations, such as old age or loss of the major breadwinner, threatened economic security. Over the fifty years since the passage of that act, coverage and benefit levels in most of its original programs expanded and a variety of new income support programs were added. By 1983 over 40% of all U.S. households received some form of government cash transfer, and total expenditures reached $221 billion.

How effective have these programs been in reducing poverty? This chapter addresses that question in relation to Wisconsin's income transfer system. It begins by describing the major programs established by the Social Security Act and the program parameters over which Wisconsin has control. Then it compares these parameters to those in other states and analyzes the anti-poverty effectiveness of income transfers. We show that poverty is lower in Wisconsin than in the United States as a whole and that income support programs reduce poverty to a greater extent here than in a typical state. However, poverty rates and the impact of transfers vary dramatically by demographic group—the elderly benefit the most and female-headed families with children the least. We explore this issue and suggest policy options.

Income Transfer Programs

There are two major categories of income transfer programs: social insurance and public assistance (welfare). While both have as their goal the provision of income security, the groups they serve, their level of benefits, and their operating rules differ significantly.

In social insurance programs, eligibility and benefit levels depend on past contributions and some identifiable problem such as old age, death of a spouse, disability, or unemployment. Benefits are paid as a matter of earned right and not financial need. The four major benefit programs in this category are the Old Age, Survivors, and Disability Insurance program (OASDI), commonly referred to as social security, Unemployment Compensation, Workers' Compensation, and Medicare.

Social security, the largest, pays benefits to insured workers who are retired or disabled and to their eligible dependents and survivors. The benefit amount is related to past earnings and is established by federal law. In 1979, about $2.36 billion in social security payments went to 760,000 Wisconsin beneficiaries (table 7.1).[1] In that year about 70% of the recipients were retirees, 20% were disabled, and 10% were survivors. Medicare, the nation-

Table 7.1. Income Transfer Beneficiaries and Expenditures in Wisconsin, Selected Programs, 1969 and 1979

	1969		1979	
	Bene-ficiaries (thousands)	Annual expenditures (millions of 1979 dollars)[a]	Bene-ficiaries (thousands)	Annual expenditures (millions of 1979 dollars)
Social insurance				
Cash benefits				
Social security	576.7	$1,232.6	760.0	$2,361.0
Unemployment Compensation	76.0	79.2	198.0	217.0
Workers' Compensation	NA	1.3	NA	1.9
In-kind benefits				
Medicare	469.0	275.2	602.0	605.0
All social insurance		1,588.3		3,184.9
Public assistance (welfare)				
Cash benefits				
Aid to Families with Dependent Children	77.1	129.3	201.4	288.0
Supplemental Security Income[b]	25.9	63.3	67.5	110.7
General relief	6.8	21.8	NA	16.0
In-kind benefits				
Medicaid	NA	287.7	420.0	559.0
Food stamps	89.0[c]	11.1	185.0	47.2
All welfare		513.2		1,020.9

Sources: *Statistical Abstract of the United States,* 1970, 1971, 1980, 1981; data from the Wisconsin Department of Industry, Labor, and Human Relations.
Note: NA = not available.
[a]The Consumer Price Index was 60.5 in 1969 and 119.8 in 1979, with 1977 at 100.0.
[b]Prior to 1975, Old-Age Assistance, Aid to the Blind, Aid to the Totally and Permanently Disabled.
[c]Includes food stamps and commodities.

wide program that finances medical care costs for the aged and certain disabled persons, was the second largest program in Wisconsin in 1979, serving about 600,000 at a cost of $605 million.

Unemployment Compensation provides temporary wage-related benefits to unemployed workers, and Workers' Compensation provides benefits for temporary or permanent work-related injury, disease, or death. Although guided by federal law, states generally determine eligibility requirements and benefit amounts for these programs. And as we show below, Wisconsin's participation rates and benefits are among the highest in the nation.

These social insurance programs accounted for 75% of the income transfer expenditures received by Wisconsin residents in both 1969 and 1979. Most of the 1969–79 increase in these expenditures resulted from legislated increases in social security benefit levels. To a lesser extent, higher unemployment rates (4.5% in 1979, up from 3.3% in 1969) and expanded eligibility coverage and benefit extensions in Unemployment Compensation caused increases in both the number of beneficiaries and expenditures. Higher medical-care costs and expansion of Medicare benefits to disabled social security beneficiaries also added to this growth.

Eligibility for welfare is conditional upon financial need as measured by current income and assets and is not contingent upon past earnings or contributions. Welfare provides a minimum standard of living rather than a replacement of lost earnings.

Welfare programs accounted for only a quarter of income transfer expenditures in each year, but are the most controversial programs, for several reasons. First, with the exception of food stamps, these welfare programs are all financed by state as well as federal funds, and benefit levels are established by the state legislature. The special case of Supplemental Security Income is described later. (Two social insurance programs involve state monies— Unemployment Compensation and Workers' Compensation. Nationally, welfare costs to states in 1979 were almost twice those of social insurance programs. See chapter 3 in this volume for a picture of the trends in financing human services.) Second, the growth rate in the number of welfare beneficiaries has been more rapid than in the number of social insurance recipients. Finally, and probably most important, AFDC, often considered to be synonymous with welfare, is viewed by many as discouraging work, disrupting families, and encouraging dependency. (Yet research evidence shows that these disincentives are relatively minor; see S. Danziger, Haveman, and Plotnick 1981, and S. Danziger and Gottschalk 1985.)

The AFDC program serves mainly female-headed families with children, and it has grown as divorce rates and out-of-wedlock births have increased. In addition, as a result of expanded rights and entitlements in the late 1960s and

Table 7.2. Average Monthly Benefit Levels in Selected Income Transfer Programs, Nationwide and in Several States, 1969 and 1979 (1979 dollars per month)

Program	1969					1979				
	U.S.	Wis.	Mich.	Minn.	Ill.	U.S.	Wis.	Mich.	Minn.	Ill.
Social security[a]	$197	$203	$217	$192	$209	$294	$303	$316	$285	$312
Unemployment										
Compensation[b]	477	562	392–647[c]	485	358–596[c]	533	641	417–585[c]	645	555–662[c]
SSI[d]										
Cash	234	204	301	283	345	236	301	242	242	249
Food stamps	0	0	0	0	0	39	0	37	37	35
AFDC[e]	420	438	521	572	533	327	458	470	454	333
Medicaid[f]	32	NA	NA	NA	NA	135	132	170	163	142

	Percentage Change in Inflation-Adjusted Benefits, 1969–79[g]				
	U.S.	Wis.	Mich.	Minn.	Ill.
Social security	+49.2	+49.3	+45.6	+48.4	+49.3
Unemployment Compensation					
Individual	+11.7	+14.0	+6.4	+33.0	+55.0
Family	—	—	–9.6	—	+11.1
SSI: Cash plus					
food stamps	+17.5	+47.5	–7.3	–1.4	–17.7
AFDC	–22.1	+4.6	–9.8	–20.6	–37.5
Medicaid	+321.9	NA	NA	NA	NA

Sources: *Statistical Abstract of the United States,* 1971 and 1981; U.S. House of Representatives, Committee on Ways and Means (1985).

Note: NA = not available.

[a]Average per month for retired worker.

[b]Maximum benefit.

[c]Higher amount includes dependent benefit.

[d]Maximum for aged individual living independently; in 1969 Old Age Assistance Benefit.

[e]Maximum benefit for four-person family with three children.

[f]Estimated market value of Medicaid as insurance for four-person family with three children.

[g]Defined as 100 × [(1979 level – 1969 level)/1969 level].

early 1970s, a larger proportion of eligible persons applied for and received AFDC. Concomitantly, food stamp and Medicaid expenditures also rose, since many AFDC recipients are automatically eligible for these programs.

The Supplemental Security Income program (SSI), implemented in 1974, replaced three previous state-run welfare programs—Old Age Assistance, Aid to the Blind, and Aid to the Permanently and Totally Disabled. The federal government establishes and pays for a nationally uniform basic benefit level. States, at their own expense, supplement the federal benefit. Wisconsin is one of the few states to do so. As do AFDC participants, SSI recipients receive Medicaid benefits and, in most states, food stamps. Wisconsin, however, is one of two states which "cash out" food stamps for SSI recipients, by increasing the SSI payment in lieu of food stamps.

There are significant variations in the probability of receiving a benefit and in the amount of benefits across states, programs, and over time. For example, benefit levels in social security and food stamps are federally determined and have been indexed to the Consumer Price Index since the early 1970s; SSI has a federally established and indexed minimum that states may choose to supplement (Wisconsin provides a supplement, but does not index it); and AFDC benefit levels are determined on a state-by-state basis within broad federal guidelines.

The top panel of table 7.2 presents average monthly benefit levels in 1969 and 1979 in constant 1979 dollars for Wisconsin, several surrounding states, and the United States as a whole. The greatest variation across states occurs in AFDC, where individual state policy has the greatest impact on benefit levels, and in SSI, for which Wisconsin provides a much higher than average supplement. It is clear that, compared to the national average, Wisconsin is relatively generous in the level of income transfer payments.

The bottom panel of table 7.2 shows the percentage change in real benefits between 1969 and 1979. The difference between programs with and without indexed benefits is striking. For example, for the United States all benefits in real terms are higher, except for AFDC benefits, which declined by about one-fifth. And the largest gains are in social security, not only because benefits are indexed, but because benefit levels were raised across the board several times in the early 1970s. Program by program, the rate of benefit increases in Wisconsin equals or exceeds that in the nation.

What effect do these benefits have on alleviation of poverty? The next sections of this chapter address that question. We begin by discussing the measurement of poverty and then examine the antipoverty effectiveness of income transfers in Wisconsin.

The Incidence of Poverty and the Antipoverty Impact of Transfers

The official measure of poverty provides a set of income thresholds that vary by household size, the age of the head of the household, the number of children under 18, sex of the household head, and farm-nonfarm residence (after 1981, sex of the head and farm-nonfarm were no longer used as distinctions). Each year the poverty thresholds are adjusted to reflect change in the Consumer Price Index, thereby maintaining a constant level of purchasing power over time and providing an absolute measure of poverty. In 1979 the poverty lines ranged from $3,469 for a single elderly woman, to $7,412 for a nonfarm family of four, and to $12,293 for a family of seven or more.

The official income measure is total money income received by the household in a calendar year. It includes wages and salaries, net income from self-employment, social security and other government cash transfers, property income, and other cash income (e.g., private pensions, alimony). This measure does not include public or private benefits in kind (such as food stamps, Medicare, or employer-provided insurance), nor does it subtract direct taxes paid. Because these benefits and taxes affect a household's consumption, their exclusion will bias upward official estimates of the poverty population (see S. Danziger, Haveman, and Plotnick 1986). Nonetheless, we employ the official measure because it is widely used and is the only measure we can compute with the data that are available for the state of Wisconsin for the 1969–79 decade.

Table 7.3 shows the incidence of poverty among persons in 1969 and 1979 in the United States, Wisconsin, and several surrounding states. *Pretransfer* poverty rates show the percentage of all persons living in households whose money income from private sources (such as earnings, property income, private pensions) fails to raise them over the poverty line.[2] The official or *posttransfer* poverty rate is determined by adding all cash transfer program benefits (such as social security and AFDC) to pretransfer income. The comparison of these rates provides a measure of the antipoverty effectiveness of cash transfer programs.

In 1969 Wisconsin had lower posttransfer poverty rates than the nation as a whole and very similar rates to its surrounding states (column 2). In 1979 Wisconsin had maintained its margin of difference with the national posttransfer poverty rate (3.6 percentage points lower in 1979 compared to 3.7 points in 1969), but it had gained on its neighbors (column 5). Between 1969 and 1979 Wisconsin's rate decreased, Minnesota's remained almost constant, and rates in both Michigan and Illinois increased.

Table 7.3. The Incidence of Poverty, Nationwide and in Selected States, 1969 and 1979

	1969			1979		
	Pretransfer Poor (1)	Posttransfer Poor (2)	Percentage Change in Poverty[a] (3)	Pretransfer Poor (4)	Posttransfer Poor (5)	Percentage Change in Poverty[a] (6)
United States	18.5%	14.4%	−22.2	19.1%	13.1%	−31.4
Wisconsin	14.9	10.7	−28.2	16.4	9.5	−42.1
Michigan	13.5	9.9	−26.7	17.7	11.2	−36.7
Minnesota	15.2	10.8	−28.9	16.0	10.3	−35.6
Illinois	14.5	10.9	−24.8	17.1	12.0	−29.8

Source: Computations from 1970 and 1980 *Census of Population* computer tapes.

[a]Defined as the percentage point difference between posttransfer and pretransfer rates divided by the pretransfer rate and multiplied by 100.

Although a portion of Wisconsin's lower posttransfer rate in 1979 can be attributed to its lower pretransfer poverty rates (column 4), column 6 indicates that the effectiveness of its cash transfer system was a major contributing factor. The largest share of the reduction is attributable to federal benefits, such as social security. However, Wisconsin's relatively generous level of state-determined (or partly determined) benefits certainly adds to its lower posttransfer rates.

Transfers not only have a differential impact across states in any year, but also differ dramatically in effectiveness across family types. Table 7.4 shows the incidence of poverty among persons in 1979 in Wisconsin and the nation, by demographic group. Almost every such group in Wisconsin has lower poverty rates than its national counterpart. In 1979 Wisconsin ranked sixth lowest among the states in terms of poverty rate, even though its median family income was very close to the U.S. average. Some of this difference is due to Wisconsin's lower unemployment rate (4.5% versus 5.8% for the nation). Wisconsin also, however, has an income distribution that is more equal than that of most other states, above-average transfer payments, and a work force that is better educated than average.

In both Wisconsin and the nation, the groups that are at highest risk of pretransfer poverty are families with children headed by women and households headed by the elderly. Poverty rates for persons in these groups are about 50%, but the risk of poverty rises to about 60% if the head of the household belongs to a minority group. The lowest poverty rates are for families headed by nonaged men, although again minorities have much higher rates than whites. Transfers do little to lower the poverty of female-headed households, but have a dramatic impact on rates among the elderly. For example, in Wisconsin pretransfer poverty rates among the aged and female household heads are quite similar—48.6% and 46.0% respectively. But the posttransfer poverty incidence among the elderly falls to about one in ten, while it remains above one in three for households headed by women.

The differential impact of transfers on the various demographic groups is a function of differences in both the proportion of the poor within the group who receive benefits and the average amount of the transfer. Table 7.5 shows that almost all of the pretransfer elderly poor receive a transfer.[3] In addition, their average benefit levels are higher than those of most other demographic groups, even though their average family size is smaller. In fact, the maximum SSI benefit for an aged couple and the maximum AFDC benefit for a family of four are quite similar in Wisconsin. Thus, the transfers of the elderly are more effective in reducing poverty than are those received by the nonaged: 79.6% of Wisconsin's elderly were removed from poverty by transfers (column 7), and 90.1% of their poverty gap—the difference between pretransfer income and the poverty level—was eliminated (column 8).

Table 7.4. The Incidence of Poverty among Persons, by Demographic Group, Nationwide and in Wisconsin, 1979

Characteristics of Household Head	United States		Wisconsin	
	Pretransfer Poor (1)	Posttransfer Poor (2)	Pretransfer Poor (3)	Posttransfer Poor (4)
Age under 65				
White male with children	6.8%	6.0%	5.5%	4.7%
Nonwhite male with children	18.5	16.2	16.3	14.1
Hispanic male with children	20.4	18.3	14.4	13.7
All males with children	9.3	8.2	6.0	5.2
White female with children	38.2	32.0	39.4	28.3
Nonwhite female with children	61.5	54.1	62.3	53.7
Hispanic female with children	64.8	58.2	73.5[a]	64.7[a]
All females with children	50.0	43.3	46.0	35.6
All unrelated individuals and childless households				
Male	10.9	8.7	9.4	7.3
Female	31.2	26.4	29.9	28.5
Age 65 and over				
White	44.6	12.2	48.1	9.1
Nonwhite	62.1	32.4	68.0	39.9
Hispanic	56.2	26.8	56.3[a]	0.0[a]
All aged	46.9	14.9	48.6	9.9
Poverty rate, all persons	19.1	13.1	16.4	9.5

Source: Computations from *1980 Census of Population* computer tapes.

[a]Fewer than 100 persons in this group. As a result, poverty rates have large standard errors.

Families headed by poor nonaged males with children and childless households are the least likely to receive a cash transfer. Across racial groups, 28.8% of pretransfer poor nonaged, male-headed households with children in Wisconsin receive transfers, as compared to 76.8% of all poor female-headed households with children and 97.1% of poor aged households. These participation rates are slightly lower than the national average for men, but are slightly higher for the other groups. But families headed by men have by

Table 7.5. The Receipt and Antipoverty Effect of Cash Transfers, by Demographic Group, Nationwide and in Wisconsin, 1979

Characteristics of Household Head	United States				Wisconsin			
	Percentage of Pretransfer Poor Households Receiving Transfers (1)	Average Annual Transfer per Recipient Household (2)	Percentage of Pretransfer Poor Persons Removed from Poverty by Transfers (3)[a]	Percentage Reduction in Poverty Gap (4)	Percentage of Pretransfer Poor Households Receiving Transfers (5)	Average Annual Transfer per Recipient Household (6)	Percentage of Pretransfer Poor Persons Removed from Poverty by Transfers (7)[a]	Percentage Reduction in Poverty Gap (8)
Age under 65								
White male with children	29.9%	$4,247	11.8%	23.6%	26.8%	$4,228	14.5%	18.7%
Nonwhite male with children	39.0	3,855	12.4	25.3	40.6	4,108	13.5	22.1
Hispanic male with children	29.2	4,255	10.3	21.9	45.5	5,669	4.9	41.3
All males with children	31.8	4,142	11.8	23.8	28.8	4,289	13.3	20.2
White female with children	59.6	3,505	16.2	41.8	74.0	3,859	28.2	59.0
Nonwhite female with children	69.5	3,356	12.0	39.1	81.4	4,305	13.8	54.8
Hispanic female with children	70.0	3,736	10.2	43.4	76.9[b]	3,688[b]	12.0[b]	44.9[b]
All females with children	65.2	3,467	13.4	40.1	76.8	3,996	22.6	56.8

(continued on following page)

Table 7.5. The Receipt and Antipoverty Effect of Cash Transfers, by Demographic Group, Nationwide and in Wisconsin, 1979 (continued)

Characteristics of Household Head	United States				Wisconsin			
	Percentage of Pretransfer Poor Households Receiving Transfers (1)	Average Annual Transfer per Recipient Household (2)	Percentage of Pretransfer Poor Persons Removed from Poverty by Transfers (3)[a]	Percentage Reduction in Poverty Gap (4)	Percentage of Pretransfer Poor Households Receiving Transfers (5)	Average Annual Transfer per Recipient Household (6)	Percentage of Pretransfer Poor Persons Removed from Poverty by Transfers (7)[a]	Percentage Reduction in Poverty Gap (8)
Unrelated individuals and childless households								
Male	29.0	3,757	20.2	27.1	26.1	3,909	22.0	25.6
Female	32.0	2,896	15.3	28.1	28.3	2,944	4.7	27.5
Age 65 and over								
White	95.9	4,367	72.6	87.1	97.1	4,460	81.1	90.5
Nonwhite	94.0	3,853	47.8	76.6	94.2	4,202	41.3	77.5
Hispanic	93.0	4,159	52.3	79.3	100.0[b]	5,227[b]	100.0[b]	100.0[b]
All aged	95.6	4,297	68.2	85.2	97.1	4,456	79.6	90.1
All persons	60.8	4,000	31.4	51.3	64.1	4,231	42.1	58.5

Source: Computations from 1980 Census of Population computer tapes.

[a]Defined as the difference between pre- and posttransfer poverty divided by pretransfer poverty. Computations are based on the poverty rates shown in table 7.4

[b]Fewer than 100 persons in this group. As a result, poverty rates have large standard errors.

far the lowest incidence of posttransfer poverty because of their low pre-transfer rates. Moreover, the average annual transfer per recipient household is somewhat higher in Wisconsin. Compared to the national average, the largest difference is in households headed by women with children—$3,996 in Wisconsin, 15% above the U.S. average of $3,467. Nonetheless, these benefits are lower than those received by nonaged men and the elderly.

In nonaged childless households, men and women are almost equally likely to receive transfers. However, women again have substantially higher post-transfer poverty rates (table 7.4), a reflection of both their higher pretransfer rates and their lower average level of transfers compared to nonaged childless men as well as to other demographic groups (table 7.5). The high rates for some of these women might well reflect the phenomenon of the "displaced homemaker"—the divorced, never married, or widowed woman whose primary responsibility had been as wife and/or mother. They consequently have a spotty, or nonexistent, employment record and present a particular challenge to policymakers because no specific income support programs are in place to assist them. Also, to the extent that women who do work earn less than men, their earnings-related unemployment and social security benefits will be lower.

Although about three-quarters of poor families headed by women with children in Wisconsin receive transfers (compared to about two-thirds in the nation), their posttransfer poverty rates remain extremely high because only a little more than half of their poverty gap is eliminated by transfers (compared to about 40% in the nation). Why don't transfer programs do more for this group? The major reason is that the transfer most often received by these households is AFDC, and as noted in table 7.2, even the maximum allowable benefit ($458) is below the poverty level of $618 a month for a family of four in 1979. In addition, real benefit levels have deteriorated recently. Between 1969 and 1975 the maximum benefit for a family of four in Wisconsin (in constant 1984 dollars) rose from $627 to $778, then fell as inflation outpaced benefit increases, to $636 in 1984. For the same years, the national average inflation-adjusted benefits fell steadily—from $601 in 1970 to $542 in 1975 to $383 in 1984 (U.S. House of Representatives 1985). Thus, even if almost all of these households received transfers, as is the case for the aged, the antipoverty impacts of transfers for them would still be smaller than those for the elderly.

The high rates of poverty for single-mother households, their continued reliance on the transfer system, and their increasing numbers make the situation of these households the most pressing poverty problem in Wisconsin and the United States. For a further discussion of what is being done for this group in Wisconsin, see chapter 9 in this volume.

Recent Increases in Poverty

The data we have presented so far come from the 1980 census, the only data source which can provide the demographic detail such as was shown in tables 7.4 and 7.5. Unfortunately, the census provides a misleading picture of poverty in the early to middle 1980s, because poverty increased in each subsequent year, rising nationwide from 11.4% of all persons in 1978 to 15.2% in 1983 before declining to 14.0% in 1985. As a result, we have taken data from the Census Bureau's annual Current Population Surveys to present, in table 7.6, a picture of the recent increase in poverty in the United States, Wisconsin, and neighboring states.[4] Wisconsin's poverty rate is below that of the United States and the neighboring states in each year. Thus, the patterns of poverty and the antipoverty effects of transfers discussed above are likely to be valid in the mid-1980s, even though the poverty level is much higher than at the time of the decennial census. We now return to further analysis of the census data for Wisconsin.

Female-Headed Families and the Feminization of Poverty

Female-headed families with children not only have the highest poverty rates, but they also compose the greatest share of Wisconsin's poor. In 1979, 13% of all families with children under 18 were headed by women, yet these households accounted for 53% of all such families in poverty. This results from two factors. First, the number of female-headed families increased rapidly between 1969 and 1979: the number of all families with children rose by 6.7%, but the number of those headed by women increased by 75%. Second, even

Table 7.6. The Incidence of Posttransfer Poverty among Persons, Nationwide and in Selected States, 1978 and 1985

	1978	1985	% Change	Percentage Point Change
United States	11.4%	14.0%	22.8%	2.6%
	(0.19)	(0.22)		
Wisconsin	7.5	11.6	54.7	4.1
	(1.07)	(1.72)		
Michigan	8.3	14.5	74.7	6.2
	(0.82)	(1.03)		
Minnesota	8.1	12.6	55.6	4.5
	(1.21)	(1.83)		
Illinois	10.2	15.6	52.9	5.4
	(0.81)	(1.04)		

Source: Computations from March 1979 and March 1986 Current Population Survey computer tapes.

Note: Standard errors of poverty rates appear in parentheses. Because the Current Population Surveys have many fewer observations than the census, these standard errors are relatively large. As a result, the Census Bureau does not publish annual poverty data for states.

though the poverty rates of single-mother families declined somewhat over that period, declines were much larger for other groups, especially the elderly. For example, poverty rates for mothers heading households declined from 37.9% in 1969 to 35.5% in 1979, while the rate among the elderly dropped from 24.3% to 9.9%.

Three major demographic and economic trends have contributed to this increase in the number of families headed by women and their persistently high poverty rates: (1) increased numbers of divorces and out-of-wedlock births; (2) employment barriers; and (3) poor performance of the child support system.

The Route to Single Parenthood

As figure 7.1 indicates, female household headship in Wisconsin is most often a result of marital disruption. Almost 82% of the 84,000 women heading families with children in 1979 were divorced, separated, or widowed. According to a national study (Duncan and Morgan 1983), family income drops sharply after a marital breakup—by 43% for divorced women, 51% for sepa-

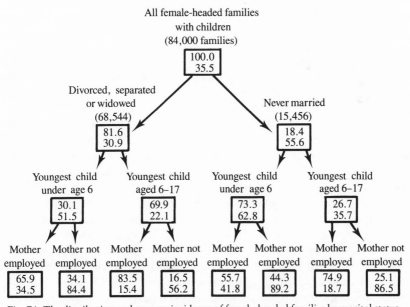

Fig. 7.1. The distribution and poverty incidence of female-headed families by marital status, age of children, and mother's employment, Wisconsin, 1979. Note: The top number in each box is the percentage of the referent family type, and the bottom number is the incidence of poverty for that family type. The number in parentheses is the number of families. (Source: Computations from *1980 Census of Population* computer tapes.)

rated women, and 30% for widows. It has further been estimated that 45% of the poverty beginnings for female-headed households come from marital breakup and almost half of all spells of receiving AFDC commence when a wife becomes a household head (Bane and Ellwood 1983).

The highest rates of poverty among women who head households, however, are for those who never married—their rate of 55.6% is almost double that of the ever-married heads. And among this group, teenaged parents are at greatest risk of poverty. A study of births in Wisconsin shows that in 1980, 44% of all births to unmarried women were to teenagers and 20% were to women 17 years or younger. And while the birthrate for all never-married women increased by 25% (from 17.1 to 21.3 births per 1,000 unmarried women) between 1970 and 1980, the birthrate for unmarried teens increased by almost 64% (from 13.0 to 21.3 births per 1,000 unmarried women ages 15–19) (Wisconsin Department of Health and Social Services 1984).

Teenage parenthood affects not only the current but also the future economic status of the family. Unmarried teenaged mothers are less likely to complete high school and are more likely to receive welfare and have longer periods of welfare receipt. They are likely to escape poverty via the most common route for women (through marriage), but if they do marry, they have a higher probability of divorce or separation.

Poverty, Work, and Welfare

Current societal expectations view employment as the best means for women heading families to escape poverty. Figure 7.1 shows that women with young children (under six) are much more likely to be poor than those with older children, and that, holding age of children constant, mothers who worked at some time during the year were much less likely to be poor than those who did not work at all. However, employment does not always guarantee a way out of poverty. Among all single mothers, three-fourths work at least part time, yet about one-quarter of these remain poor. Poverty remains high because on average women work fewer hours and earn lower wages than men.

Several factors contribute to the male-female earnings differences—discrimination, occupational segregation, and, for many, lack of education, training, and job experience. In addition, the responsibilities of child care make it difficult to work full time, full year. The U.S. Commission on Civil Rights (1981) reviewed data on the relationship between child care and employment and concluded that (1) some women were unable to work, (2) others could work only in part-time jobs, and (3) others were unable to seek the kinds of jobs that provided opportunities for promotions.

Figure 7.2 presents the same type of information as that in figure 7.1, but classifies women by the age of youngest child rather than by marital status and provides further information on welfare recipiency. About 39% of all female

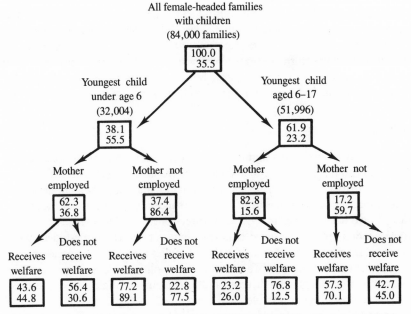

Fig. 7.2. The distribution and poverty incidence of female-headed families by age of children, mother's employment, and welfare recipiency, Wisconsin, 1979. Note: The top number in each box is the percentage of the referent family type, and the bottom number is the incidence of poverty for that family type. The number in parentheses is the number of families. (Source: Computations from *1980 Census of Population* computer tapes.)

household heads received welfare (AFDC) in 1979. Because AFDC is income-tested, when earnings increase, benefits decrease. Thus, welfare recipiency is lower among employed mothers than those not employed. And, controlling for employment, welfare recipiency is greatest among women with children under six.

Over 43% of employed mothers with young children combined work and welfare in 1979, yet almost 45% of them remained below the poverty line. And as a result of changes in AFDC rules introduced by the Reagan administration in 1981, AFDC benefits are now reduced, dollar for dollar, for all earnings after four months of employment, and deductions for work-related expenses are significantly curtailed. These changes mean that fewer women can mix work and welfare in the mid-1980s and that poverty among female household heads is even higher than shown in figure 7.2.

The Child Support System

Child support, or more accurately the lack of it, also contributes to the poverty of families with single mothers. For almost every single mother, there is a father who should be contributing to the support of his children. Yet, more often than not, absent fathers pay no child support. It is clear that lack of child support awards, inadequate amounts of awards, and nonpayment of awards contribute to the impoverishment of women and their children, and their combined effect often shifts the burden of responsibility to the public sector. This issue is discussed in detail in chapter 9.

Policy Recommendations

Income transfer programs significantly reduce poverty and are more effective in Wisconsin than in most other states. The transfer system, particularly the social security component, has succeeded in moving a large percentage of the elderly out of poverty. It has been much less successful with solo-mother families. As we have shown, in 1979 over three-fourths of Wisconsin's poor female-headed families received cash transfers, yet less than one-fourth were removed from poverty. In addition, these families now form the greatest proportion of the state's poor. We conclude that policies to alleviate poverty in Wisconsin must be policies directed at the problems of single-parent families. Several reforms appear feasible.

First, AFDC should include opportunities for recipients to combine work and welfare. Prior to the 1981 federal changes in AFDC, the first $30 plus one-third of subsequent earnings were disregarded in the determination of benefit levels. These "disregards" are now eliminated after four months of employment. Although the 1980 census data presented here have shown that, even when earnings were disregarded, combining work and welfare did not eliminate poverty for these families, a Wisconsin study on the effects of the 1981 changes that were introduced by the Omnibus Budget Reconciliation Act of 1981 (OBRA) concluded: "As a whole, by 1983, the OBRA-affected womens' lives are marked by substantially reduced income and increased poverty levels (compared to their 1981 status), despite continued commitment to working and probable success at work, judging from overall increases in earnings" (S. K. Danziger 1984, 23–24).

Because these changes were federally mandated, the state cannot rectify the situation by changing its policies. The state can, however, reintroduce a Wisconsin earned income tax credit (EITC), to supplement the federal credit. The EITC is an effective way to increase the earnings of all low-wage workers with children, whether or not they receive welfare.

Second, Wisconsin needs to address itself to barriers that are preventing these women from achieving economic self-sufficiency through employment. Although there are policies in place that enable disadvantaged individuals to prepare themselves for jobs that can make them self-supporting—notably the Job Training Partnership Act (JTPA)—there is evidence to suggest that insuf-

Data on JTPA programs from the Wisconsin Governor's Employment and Training Office (GETO) indicate that the enrollment rate of women is much lower than their eligibility rate, that they have a much lower enrollment rate than men, and that when employed through JTPA, they are in jobs paying low average wages (the average wage for women at placement was $4.31 per hour—scarcely enough to raise a family over the poverty line).

Major contributing factors to these inequities are inadequate supportive services, including child care, and stereotyped placement into "female" occupations. If employment is going to be a viable option for reducing the poverty of female-headed families, these factors must be addressed. There is ample evidence to suggest that employment programs for single women with children can be successful (Bassi and Ashenfelter 1986). Major barriers, however, include lack of participation by many employers and inadequate funding.

Third, "workfare" programs for welfare recipients should be endorsed. While some workfare programs seek only to reduce the number of recipients, this need not be the case. The issue should not be whether able-bodied persons must earn their income, but rather how much income they can earn. Under many workfare programs, a recipient can work only until he or she has earned an amount equal to that of the welfare benefit. But if the program allows the recipient to work full time, workfare becomes a work opportunity program, even if the job provides no training. And if unemployment rates remain high, then a workfare job may be the only employment opportunity available to welfare recipients who have little work experience.

Our final antipoverty policy recommendation is one that is currently being demonstrated by the state of Wisconsin. It concerns a child support assurance system, in which all parents who live apart from their children would be obligated to share their income with the child. The sharing rate is proportional to gross income and varies with the number of children to be supported. The obligation is collected through paycheck withholding, as are social security and income taxes. All children with a living absent parent would be entitled to benefits equal either to the child support paid by the absent parent, or an assured benefit, whichever is higher. Should the absent parent pay less than the assured benefit, the difference would be financed out of general revenues, and the custodial parent would be subject to a surtax up to the amount of the public subsidy. Preliminary estimates on the costs and benefits of this program indicate that it has the potential to lower poverty and welfare dependence as well as to reduce welfare costs. Chapter 9 discusses the child support assurance system in detail.

NOTES

1. The Census Bureau publishes annual data on poverty and income transfers for the United States, but the number of households sampled is too small to provide detailed

estimates for individual states. Thus, income data for calendar years 1969 and 1979 from the 1970 and 1980 decennial censuses are used in this chapter.

2. The pretransfer poverty rates tabulated from the decennial censuses differ from those from the annual Current Population Surveys (CPS), the usual sources of poverty data. The census reports Unemployment Compensation and Workers' Compensation in a single category along with private nonemployment income (e.g., private pensions, annuities), rather than in a separate social insurance category. Thus, our measure of pretransfer income does not really exclude all cash income transfers. This produces an underestimate of the extent of pretransfer poverty and of the antipoverty effectiveness of transfers. Census and CPS posttransfer rates also differ, even though each counts the same cash income sources. Census Bureau officials attribute the discrepancy to such things as differing public attitudes about responding to the two surveys, differences in the training of census interviewers, and the varying emphasis on income information in the two surveys.

3. Because the census data do not count noncash benefits, such as food stamps, Medicare, Medicaid, or public housing, the posttransfer poverty rates shown in table 7.4 are overstated and the number of people receiving public transfers and the effectiveness of those transfers, shown in table 7.5, are understated.

4. These data are not published by the Census Bureau because of the small number of observations in some states. As a result, no demographic detail by state can be provided. There are, for example, less than 1,000 Wisconsin households in each CPS.

8

The Status of Youth in Wisconsin:
Lessons for Policy

SANDRA K. DANZIGER, JOHN F. LONGRES,
AND MICHAEL R. SOSIN

Introduction

Public spending for children tends to flow to such specific areas as education, health services, or income support. Policy is also typically formulated on an issue-specific basis. As a result, while rather high-quality work exists on the nature of each area, much less has been accomplished in examining the inter-relationships between areas, for example, between schooling and health or welfare. A broader perspective on children's policy issues is thus not well developed.

When considering this broader level, it is possible to assess whether the typical child's needs or resource requirements that may be prerequisite for a satisfactory adult life are being met. Also to be assessed is whether certain groups of children demonstrate needs in several problem areas. In either case, a needs-based approach might suggest that a number of specific program areas should take into account the more basic issues of childhood, or even that certain basic issues need more attention in new types of programs.

Such a needs-based approach is particularly crucial when conditions are changing so that new needs may be developing. And life in Wisconsin, as in the nation as a whole, has changed significantly over the last two decades. The economy, shifting emphasis from industry to services, has experienced inflation, recession, and debt. Family life has also changed in many ways: in the divorce rates and living arrangements of children and families, in the household division of labor, and in the increased likelihood that mothers will work.

This chapter reports on the changing economic and demographic charac-

151

teristics, household composition, and family life in Wisconsin. It searches for
resulting trends in needs and characteristics of children from such data as well
as from some indicators of the well-being of children. It also examines the
implications of these findings for the general direction of policies toward children and their families.

Frame of Reference

We conceptualize the well-being of children as a function of the material
and social resources available to them in the course of their development. We
do not claim that the well-being of every child is determined by external constraints; we suggest only that general patterns often respond to available
resources.

There are, of course, innumerable aspects of well-being, each of which
might respond to the level of very specific resources. Many specifics are outside the scope of trends reported here. Rather, we examine general patterns.
Evidence for general problems exists, for example, if well-being is improving
or deteriorating overall; if certain types of well-being are altering in similar
ways; or if certain subgroups of children are experiencing consistent declines.

We assume that material resources that originate at the level of the state and
the counties influence the quality of the social institutions that deal with children. The shape of the economy—income and labor market conditions, for
example—determines the public and private income that can be spent on
schools, medical facilities, recreational programs, social services, and the like.

Families serve as a major channel through which community resources
reach children. The family provides the basic material goods for survival,
growth, and development. The ability of parents to provide these goods is, in
turn, affected by demographic factors, ethnic status, occupation, income,
household structure, the nature of the community, and so forth.

Families provide social and affectional resources as well as material support. These resources, which may be more readily dispensed by families that
are not under great economic and social stress, are very important to child
development and to the society's future. Productive citizens who become part
of the community, reshape it, and maintain its vitality result in part from
families that function well.

Children—especially older youth—contribute to their own welfare and
make use of the resources available to them. It is reasonable to expect communities and families to provide opportunities, but children must learn to use
them. To the extent that economic, emotional, and social resources are adequate, children grow to promote their own well-being.

Measuring the Well-Being of Children

Measures of child well-being are particularly difficult to obtain. For example, the data do not enable us to report, with appropriate detail, the attitudes

of young people toward the quality of life. Nor can we completely judge the relationship of present conduct to future development. Rather, only objective measures of certain attributes or behaviors exist from which well-being must be inferred. At its broadest level, well-being means that children will be living in stable and nurturing households, attending and achieving in schools, or, when they choose, being productively involved in the economy. Sometimes, however, well-being can be defined only as an absence of measured problems.

Another issue is that the data for our analyses come primarily from widely available government sources, including the U.S. census and state data. Reliance on official sources of data has its limitations. Although they are the best available because they are based upon the broadest scale samples and allow comparisons over time, the measures used are not always the most precise. For example, instead of criminal behavior rates, only arrest rates are available. In addition, the data are often not available by such important dimensions as income level of families.

In this chapter we attempt to select what appear to be the most relevant measures of community and family resources, such as income, family size, and family composition. When examining specific indicators of well-being we rely on selected measures of "social problems" that reflect our judgments about what is measured most successfully, albeit imperfectly. The measures are also meant to illustrate the range of relevant issues, although we focus on older children and adolescents. The status of younger children is measured by such different indicators that it could not be covered along with the examination of older children.

We focus on four specific areas as indicators of the general status of youth: education, employment, delinquency, and births to adolescents. Education represents an area in which universal trends in the population can be assessed. Youth employment also affects many typical youth, more so than in the recent past, as more young people enter the labor force. Two specific problem areas, delinquency and adolescent births, reflect a lack of normal adjustment or a high probability for a problematic future.

TRENDS. The well-being of children is likely to fluctuate with time. At different historical periods, communities and families can provide more or fewer resources; this leads, in turn, to increased or reduced child well-being. The lack of precise measures of well-being suggests that a relative standard should be adopted. At times, we compare children in Wisconsin to children in the nation. In addition, we often compare relative well-being of children over time. When trends are measured, we frequently compare 1970 to 1980. The choice of these years largely has to do with the availability of the most thorough census data from which to report.

By comparing 1970 to 1980, we underestimate probable recent declines in the material and social resources being provided by communities and families, since a national recession from 1979 through 1983 increased unemployment and related declines in family income among white, black, and Hispanic families (S. Danziger and Gottschalk 1985). To help offset the possibility of overestimating the economic and social resources currently available to children, we do, at times, make comparisons to data later than 1980.

VARIATION. One of the most important issues is whether children with certain characteristics are facing a particularly difficult time. The most obvious expectations are that poor and minority youth or those with one-parent families are in unusual jeopardy. When possible, we explore whether the trends in well-being for such youth differ from trends for youth at large.

In addition, we examine variation across counties. Here, we ask whether in some environments children in general seem to be worse or better off. Do rural children fare better than urban, for example? Even though we use some indicators of general family functioning in the communities in this analysis, we acknowledge that it takes a leap of faith from such measurements to impute that individuals with given backgrounds are better or worse off.

Opportunities and Resources for Families with Children

Population Characteristics: Fewer Households with Children

Children live in 648,000 families, just over half of Wisconsin's households. Even though the number of these families grew (by about 41,000 from 1970 to 1980), their proportion of all households decreased from 56% of all families in 1970 to 53% in 1980. This downward trend held for all racial groups except blacks. Over 70% of black families had children in 1970 and 73% in 1980. Also in 1980, approximately three-quarters of Hispanic and American Indian households had children in them.

Within the category of families with children, the mean number of children under 18 declined for all groups, from almost three to two children per family. This trend of declining family size is also reflected in the overall changing age distribution of the state's population. In 1980, more than one in nine blacks were preschool-aged or younger. For Hispanics, the figure was one in seven, whereas for whites it was more like one small child among every fifteen persons. Though there are now more adults per child in the state, fewer of these adults are living in families with children; instead, they live alone or in adult-only households. Thus, this potential social resource may not be as available to the young.

Household Composition: Fewer Adults Living with Children

Of families with children, greater numbers were headed by single parents in 1980 than in the previous decade, which suggests that more children have

Table 8.1. Percentage of Wisconsin Children Younger than Age 18 Living with Two Parents, by Race, 1970 and 1980

	1970	1980
White	90.0%	86.4%
Black	57.1	37.2
American Indian[a]	NA	59.3
Hispanic[b]	86.7	69.2

Source: U.S census extract, prepared by the Institute for Research on Poverty (1986).

Note: Census definition: The number of children living with two parents includes the number of stepchildren and adopted children as well as sons and daughters born to the couple. This includes "blended" families.

NA = Not available.

[a]Includes Eskimos and Aleutians.

[b]May be of any race.

only one adult in the position to provide direct resources. The overall number of Wisconsin's children and youth (under age 18) living with two parents declined from 89% to 83%. The racial and ethnic differences here are striking. As table 8.1 indicates, black children are the most likely to live in single-parent families; over 60% did so in 1980.

The causes of single parenthood have changed over the decade: divorce and separation rates and illegitimacy have risen while widowhood has declined in families with minor-aged children. The number of divorce decrees and annulments granted in the courts in a year increased from 2 per 1,000 persons in 1970 to 3.7 per 1,000 in 1980.

By 1983 and 1984, the number of divorces and annulments was down from the 1980 and 1981 figures by about 2,000. Whereas 17,589 were granted in 1980 and 18,459 in 1981, only 16,625 occurred in 1984. In contrast, the number of marriages occurring over the 1980s was more stable, 41,000 a year. The number of children affected by the marital disruptions (which do not include separations or desertions) is high—18,410 in 1984, the most recent year for which data were available.

The majority of breakups involve families with children. In families with children under 18, the changes in marital status of the women indicate that children in 1980 were less likely to live with married or widowed women then in 1970, and more likely to live with divorced, separated, or never-married women. In 1980, 87.1% of the women with children were married; in 1970, 92.6% were. Those who were widows declined from 2.4% of women with children to 1.5% from 1970 to 1980. The divorced or separated grew from 4.3% to 8.9%, while the never-married grew from 0.7% to 2.5%.

The increase in families with never-married mothers is reflected in the rise in births to unmarried women. Both the actual numbers of births to unmarried women and their percentage of all births almost doubled from 1970 to

1984. In Wisconsin, births to unmarried mothers rose from 8.6% of all births in 1970 to 13.8% in 1980, and up to 16.6% by 1984 (Wisconsin Bureau of Health Statistics, loose table 16, 1970 and 1980; *Wisconsin Vital Statistics* 1984). The pattern is nationwide and attributed to a number of causes, such as the decline in births among married women and reduced incidence of marriage after premarital conception (O'Connell and Rogers 1984). Thus, the number of children who are born to a single parent has increased; and many studies suggest that children who grow up in families with never-married single mothers have the least promising economic and social futures (e.g., S. K. Danziger and Nichols-Casebolt forthcoming; Hofferth 1985).

Employment in Families with Children: More Working Mothers

Despite an overall growth in the labor force participation of women, general unemployment in the state has risen over the decade, from 4.0% in 1970 to 6.6% in 1980. Interestingly, the unemployment levels of persons who are heads of households are lower than the averages. Fewer individuals who have primary responsibility for others (both children and adults) report spells of being out of work. However, in 1980, family heads who were black, Hispanic, or American Indian experienced a disproportionate share of unemployment—family-head unemployment was approximately twice the rate of whites for blacks and Hispanics and over three times the white rate for American Indians.

The number of working mothers (no matter what their marital status) increased dramatically. For all women with children under six, the proportion in the labor force—working or looking for work—rose from under a third to almost half; for women with school-aged youth, the proportion in the labor force increased from over one-half to over two-thirds. Table 8.2 shows that black and white mothers are almost equally likely to be in the labor force.

Income Levels and Poverty in Families with Children

The increases in maternal employment may have mixed effects for children. While more employment should provide more economic resources for children, we find that overall, median family income in Wisconsin has not increased significantly since 1970. The median stood at $10,068 in the 1970 census and was $20,915 ten years later. This seems a sizable increase, but when the inflation rate is taken into account (using the Consumer Price Index), family income increased by only 1.5%. That amounts to roughly a $300 increase in 1979 dollars. Children in white families and Asian families obtain or exceed this median family income. Other children, however, are likely to share in far lower levels of income. The median family income for black families with children was $11,701 in 1979. Indian and Hispanic families with

Table 8.2. Percentage of Wisconsin Mothers Aged 16 and Over, in the Labor Force, by Age and Race of Children in Family

Age and Race of Children in Family	1970	1980
Children under age 6		
Total	31.3%	48.6%
White	30.6	48.8
Black	49.5	48.4
American Indians[a]	NA	42.9
Hispanics[b]	33.5	39.8
Children aged 6–17		
Total	52.8	67.3
White	52.6	67.3
Black	63.0	70.5
American Indians[a]	NA	61.9
Hispanic[b]	44.2	61.8

Source: U.S census extract, prepared by the Institute for Research on Poverty (1986).
Note: NA = Not available.
[a]Includes Eskimos and Aleutians.
[b]May be of any race.

children fared somewhat better, with median incomes of $13,141 and $16,505, respectively.

Because female labor force participation is increasing while income has been about constant, it may be that more individuals (i.e., women) within families are participating in the work force just to maintain the same level of income that a typical family obtained ten years earlier without the mother going off to work (see also S. Danziger and Gottschalk 1985). This suggests that many parents have less time available for interacting with children, even though they on average have fewer children.

For single-parent families, women's employment definitely reduces time adults allocate to children. It also may not provide sufficient income. A growing proportion of families that fall below the poverty line are headed by both employed and unemployed single mothers with children. Although overall poverty rates have slightly declined since 1970, there are striking differences in incidence by the race and sex of the parent who heads a family with minor-aged children. Chapter 7 in this volume shows that the highest poverty rates are for Hispanic and nonwhite children with single mothers, while the lowest rates are for white children who live in families headed by men (p. 140).

Finally, as elsewhere in the country, the proportion of children in poverty has increased over the decade. In 1970 8.9% of Wisconsin's children under age 18 lived in poverty. The percentage of children who lived in families with incomes below the poverty line (the child poverty rate) increased to 10.4% by 1980 (see table 8.3).

Table 8.3. Trends in Poverty Status of Wisconsin Children Aged 18 or Under, by Race,
         1970 to 1980

	Number of Children in Families with Incomes below the Poverty Line	Percentage of Total Population of Children Aged 18 or Under
1970		
Total, aged 18 or under	139,981	8.9%
Whites	116,569	7.8
Blacks	20,037	33.6
Others	3,375	NA
1980		
Total, aged 18 or under	139,418	10.4
Whites	102,761	8.3
Blacks	29,057	38.9
Others	7,600	NA

Source: U.S. census extract, prepared by the Institute for Research on Poverty (1986).
Note: No other ethnic category was given in these data on poverty status.
NA = Not available.

The number of children in poverty has declined slightly over the decade, from 139,981 in 1970 to 139,418 in 1980, but because the overall population of children has declined even more, the percentage of children in poverty has increased. For minority children, the number as well as the percentage has increased. As table 8.3 shows, the percentage of black children who were poor rose from 33.6% in 1970 to 38.9% in 1980, and this represented an increase of over 9,000 poor children.

Opportunities Available to Youth: Education and Employment

Levels of educational attainment of children may reflect changing family conditions (Preston 1984); for example, nationally, children in poverty-level female-headed families complete fewer years of schooling (McLanahan 1985). In addition, one might expect the economic stagnation to result in pressure for some youth to exit school and search for work.

School Performance

One measure of school performance is competence in the basic skills. For the last decade, Wisconsin students at each of the grade levels tested—fourth, eighth, and eleventh—consistently outperformed the nation in the Comprehensive Tests of Basic Skills (CTBS). These tests are given in the three major subject areas of mathematics, reading, and language arts. Trends in the scores for basic skills are difficult to interpret, particularly because we uncovered no

Table 8.4. Wisconsin High School Students Taking College Entrance Exams, and Mean
   Scores, 1974–75, 1979–80, 1984–85

	1974–75	1979–80	1984–85
ACT takers	13,179	21,707	24,402
% minority	3.0	2.0	5.0
ACT mean composite score	20.4[a]	20.4[a]	20.3[a,b]
SAT takers	6,585	7,419	8,769
% minority	3.6	5.2	7.0
SAT verbal score	492[a]	472[a,b]	477[a,b]
SAT math score	544[a]	533[a,b]	534[a,b]

Sources: Reports from American College Testing (ACT) Research Services (1979–80, 1985)
and the College Board Admissions Testing Program (SAT) (1980, 1985).
   Note: Minority is defined here by self-report of students taking exams.
   [a]Higher than national mean score.
   [b]Higher than Midwest-region mean score.

comparable data before 1976. From the mid-1970s, however, the fourth and
eighth-graders improved in reading and language arts, but not in math,
where they showed declines or stability. The scores of eleventh graders
showed little change from 1976 to 1980.

Another performance measure—college entrance examination scores—
also reflects this picture of overall stability over time. Table 8.4 shows the
number of high school students who take these tests, their minority composition, and mean scores for 1974–75, 1979–80, and 1984–85. It is clear that
more and more of Wisconsin's youth are taking these examinations. Yet the
scores for the American College Testing Examination (ACT) have remained
stable. The Scholastic Aptitude Test (SAT) trends show declines from 1974 to
1980 but stability in the 1980s.

On both groups of tests and in most subscales, trends in Wisconsin mirror
national ones, but at significantly higher levels. For example, the Wisconsin
ACT composite score in the school year 1969–70 was 21.1, compared to the
national average of 19.9. Since regional norms have been available, Wisconsin
students have outperformed their Midwest peers in both types of tests. Also
on the positive side, in 1984–85, 5% of the ACT takers and 7% of the SAT
takers reported that they were members of an ethnic minority. This is lower
than their proportion in the overall school enrollment but has increased over
time. The average ACT and SAT scores of Wisconsin's black, American Indian, and Hispanic students were higher than the national average scores for
these minority groups.

School Completion and School Dropouts

Two different measures of school drop-out rates are consistent with national trends in indicating an increase in the problem from 1970 to 1980.

Table 8.5. Wisconsin Youth Aged 16 and 17 Who Are Not Enrolled in School, by Race and Sex, 1970 and 1980

Youth Aged 16–17	Percentage Not in School	
	1970	1980
Total population aged 16–17	6.0%	7.9%
White males	5.8	7.6
White females	5.6	7.2
Black males	12.3	11.6
Black females	15.1	15.2
American Indian, Eskimo, Aleutian males	NA	25.4
American Indian, Eskimo, Aleutian females	NA	21.0
Hispanic[a] males	10.0	20.8
Hispanic[a] females	17.0	19.9

Source: U.S. census extract, prepared by the Institute for Research on Poverty (1986).
Note: NA = Not available.
[a]May be of any race.

According to census reports (table 8.5), almost 8% of youth aged 16 and 17 were out of school in 1980, compared to 6% in 1970. According to school enrollment estimates, almost 20% failed to graduate in 1980 because they dropped out in one of the four years. The proportion is up by 3.8%, compared to 1970. The census figures show that only among black males did the percentage in school continue to increase from 1970 to 1980. However, according to the Wisconsin Department of Public Instruction (DPI), the general picture of declining enrollments may have reversed by 1985, when drop-out rates were estimated at 15.5% (that is, the proportion of enrolled ninth graders who failed to graduate from twelfth grade four years later).[1]

Differential rates from year to year and discrepancies in DPI and census figures can reflect measurement problems. If we look at overall high school graduation rates among Wisconsin's youth, we find that a significant proportion of Wisconsin's population fails to graduate from high school. In 1980 about 20%— one in five youth—aged 18 to 24 had not obtained high school degrees. The proportion of minority youth who had failed to graduate is double this—about two in five. There was indeed improvement over the 1970–80 decade (in 1970 less than 75% graduated), but given its probable economic consequences, the extent of inadequate education among our youth is important.

Postsecondary Education

Table 8.6 shows the proportion of youth aged 18–19 who were enrolled in academic schooling. This is the best available measure of college attendance,

Table 8.6. Youth Aged 18 and 19 Enrolled in College or High School, by Race and Sex, 1970 and 1980

Youth Aged 18–19	Percentage Enrolled in School	
	1970	1980
Total population aged 18–19	61.6%	53.6%
Whites	62.3	54.2
Blacks	40.0	45.6
American Indian, Eskimo, Aleutians	NA	34.1
Hispanics[a]	53.0	45.8
Males	66.8	54.2
Females	56.6	53.1

Source: U.S. census extract, prepared by the Institute for Research on Poverty (1986).

Note: "In school" as defined in the census data includes students enrolled in high school or college that leads to a diploma or degree. It excludes specialized vocational, technical, or business schools, on-the-job training, and correspondence courses.

NA = Not available.

[a]May be of any race.

although it overestimates actual college enrollments, because some youth are in high school at ages 18 and 19. Nevertheless, according to the data, the proportion in school, most likely in college, declined quite markedly between 1970 and 1980 for all groups except blacks.

Although these data exclude most vocational and technical training, the trends are striking. Whereas two-thirds of young men and over half of young women were academically enrolled in 1970, the figures dropped to close to half, or about 54%, by 1980. It is also important that just over a third of American Indians and less than half of Hispanics and blacks were obtaining schooling at this age in 1980.

Youth Employment

Declines in schooling may be related to changes in patterns of work. Labor force participation rates of youth include those looking for work and those who have part-time and full-time jobs. Youth in the job market typically work in entry-level service-related positions (Marini 1985; Greenberger 1986). In Wisconsin, job opportunities for youth are mostly in retail (restaurants, fast-food chains, and stores), in food processing, in nursing homes and other health care facilities, and in the public sector in schools, libraries, and parks (*Wisconsin Youth, Work and the Economy*, 1981).

The statistics on youth employment and labor force participation present conflicting trends. Table 8.7 reports that a greater proportion of youth were in the labor force—working or looking for work—in 1980 than in 1970. On

Table 8.7. Labor Force Participation of Wisconsin Youth Aged 16–19, by Minority Status and
Educational Status, 1970 and 1980

Youth Aged 16–19	1970	1980
Total in the labor force (civilian)	47.1%	56.4%
Nonwhites in the labor force	33.0	36.6
Employed who work part time	62.4	65.9
Employed nonwhites who work part time	51.5	58.7
In-school youth who are in the labor force	39.5	48.0
Nonwhites in school in the labor force	24.0	28.9

Source: U.S. census extract, prepared by the Institute for Research on Poverty (1986).

the other hand, the unemployment rates also increased. From 1970 to 1980, the official unemployment rates for youth aged 16–19 who were looking for work increased from 9.4 to 12.1% (not in table). Among employed youth, the proportion who worked full time (over 35 hours per week) decreased from 35.1% to 31.8%. Finally, the proportion of youth who worked part time increased, as did the proportion of youth attending school who worked.

The labor force measures reported in table 8.7 also reveal that nonwhite youths have lower participation rates than the general population. Approximately one-third of all nonwhite youth and only one-quarter of those nonwhites who are enrolled in school are in the labor force. Of those nonwhites who are employed, a high percentage work full time rather than half time, compared to whites. Those nonwhite youth who are in the labor force work more hours and also have higher unemployment rates than whites. Trends among nonwhites, however, are similar to the population as a whole, in that, since 1970, labor force participation, part-time work, and employment while attending school have increased.

Indications of Problems: Juvenile Arrests and Births to Teens

Adolescents try out a variety of social roles as they strive toward adulthood (Adams 1980). Through trial and error, young people formulate values and beliefs, build self-esteem and identity, and determine their goals and expectations as adults. The adolescent years are often fraught with self-doubt and questioning including concerns over morality and sexuality. As a result, it is not unusual for youth to engage in behaviors that can get them into trouble.

The troubles that we examine here are juvenile arrests and teen births, but there is no way of knowing the exact number of youth who commit delinquent behaviors and participate in sexual intercourse. It has been estimated that one-third of all children in the nation are arrested by the police before the age of 19 (Wolfgang, Figlio, and Sellin 1972). The overwhelming majority of these, especially for the more serious crimes, are males. Estimates from national self-reports indicate that one in three females aged 15–17 and seven out of ten at age 19 have engaged in premarital sexual activity (Alan Guttmacher Institute 1981). The rates for young men are even higher, but sexual activity carries a higher penalty for young women because in the event of pregnancy, they are the ones who "get caught." One in ten sexually active girls becomes pregnant, and of these, approximately half give birth (Alan Guttmacher Institute 1981).

While neither the arrest rates nor the birthrates measure the true incidence of delinquent or sexual behavior, both may reflect broader trends in the welfare of youth. We rely on them, here, as admittedly imperfect measures of conduct that is potentially troublesome for children, their families, and the community.

Arrest Rates

Trends in juvenile arrest rates may reflect not only changing police practices but also changing definitions of problem behavior among youth. Some offenses that in 1970 were treated in the juvenile justice system, such as "status offenses" (e.g., truancy, running away), are now handled in the state by county social services. In addition, the same behavior that leads to an arrest in one community may in another be treated by the mental health service system. We thus restrict our examination to trends in serious offenses, the Part I offenses according to the FBI definition. These include murder, robbery, aggravated assault, and forcible rape, classified as violent crimes; and arson, burglary, larceny-theft, and motor vehicle theft, the so-called property crimes.

In 1980, about 25% of the recorded juvenile arrests were for these Part I offenses. Of these, only 20% were for crimes of violence, whereas the overwhelming majority were property crimes. About 80% of arrests for all Part I offenses were of males. Table 8.8 presents trends in juvenile arrests from 1970 to 1984. Youth are far more likely to be arrested for property crimes than for violent crimes. However, the rate of arrests over time is decreasing for property offenses and increasing for crimes of violence.

Table 8.9 presents the minority distribution of these arrests, indicating that black youth are far more likely to be arrested than are members of other groups. Their arrest rates for violent crimes are particularly high compared to the rates for white and American Indian youth. The rates for all crimes and for all groups have increased over time, except for the property crime arrests of black youth, which decreased over the 1970–80 period.

CHRONIC AND VIOLENT DELINQUENTS. This increase in arrests for violent offenses certainly deserves attention. The Youth Policy and Law Center investigated chronic and violent offenders using 1980 arrest data and court records in Milwaukee County, the county with by far the largest number of arrests for violent offenses (Youth Policy and Law Center 1983). "One-time

Table 8.8. Wisconsin Juvenile Arrests, 1970 to 1984

	Part I Offenses	
	Violent Crimes	Property Crimes
1970		
Number of all arrests	597	19,337
% of total arrests		
that were to juveniles	26.2	67.5
Rate per 1,000 youth	0.7	21.7
1980		
Number of all arrests	1,196	25,873
% of total arrests		
that were to juveniles	27.1	55.2
Rate per 1,000 youth	0.9	19.5
1984		
Number of all arrests	1,436	25,009
% of total arrests		
that were to juveniles	26.5	51.2
Rate per 1,000 youth	1.1	18.4

Source: Wisconsin Statistical Analysis Center (1970, 1980, 1984).

Table 8.9. Wisconsin Juvenile Arrests by Race, 1970 and 1980

	Violent Crimes		Property Crimes	
	Percentage of All Juvenile Arrests	Rate per 1,000 Youth (each race)	Percentage of All Juvenile Arrests	Rate per 1,000 Youth (each race)
1970				
White	51.3	0.2	84.1	10.8
Black	46.6	5.1	14.6	51.5
American Indian	1.3	0.9	1.1	23.1
1980				
White	61.4	0.6	85.3	18.0
Black	35.0	5.9	12.9	44.7
American Indian	2.4	2.5	1.5	31.1

Source: Wisconsin Statistical Analysis Center (1970, 1980).
Note: Category for Asian is left out.

offenders" were distinguished from "recidivists" (with two to four arrests) and "chronic offenders" (with five or more arrests).

The results led the investigators to conclude that the violent crimes committed by youth may usually be on the less serious side of the range of criminal acts they examined. Thus, most (79%) of the juveniles arrested for a violent crime were apprehended on robbery and aggravated assault, while murder and rape were not common. In addition, most juveniles (67%) were not likely to possess or use a weapon during the commission of a violent crime. Indeed, having committed one violent offense does not mean that a child will enter into a career of violent crime. Even counting all the arrests of children who had been arrested at least once on a violent offense, 75% of all arrests in the sample were for nonviolent crimes.

The study suggests that 3% of the sample were chronic offenders, who had been arrested five or more times and were responsible for 84% of all arrests, violent and nonviolent, in the sample. And these chronic offenders started young. Ninety-two percent of those arrested prior to age 12 ended up as chronic offenders and were more likely than others in the sample to be arrested more than once for a violent crime. According to this report, arrests for violent crime went together with a number of social and demographic characteristics:

1. Males were responsible for 87% of all arrests for violent offenses.
2. Juveniles between the ages of 15 and 17 were responsible for 59% of all arrests for violent offenses.
3. Race was not related to frequency of arrest but was related to the nature of the arrest. Black males were more likely to be arrested for violent offenses than white males. Yet, black females were no more likely to be arrested for violent offenses than white females.
4. Socioeconomic status, measured by census tract income distributions, was found to be related to arrest for violent behavior, though not in a direct linear fashion. While youth from less-well-off census tracts were likely to have higher arrest rates, youth from census tracts with the lowest income levels also had the lowest average arrest rates.
5. Although the presence of two parents was related to lower average arrest rates, it was not related to the number of arrests for serious and violent crimes (Youth Policy and Law Center 1983).

Birthrates

The number of teenagers who carry a pregnancy to birth has received much national, statewide, and even local attention in recent years. Yet, in the United States from 1970 to 1980, for both black and white teen women aged 15–19, the actual birthrates—the numbers of live births per 1,000 girls—declined (Ventura 1984). This is also true in Wisconsin, according to recent state reports (McIntosh 1986; *Population Estimates and Vital Rates* 1983 and 1984). In 1970, there were 45.1 births per 1,000 girls aged 15–19. By 1980, this had declined to a rate of 39.1. By 1983 this rate dipped to 38.6. The U.S. rates for these three years were 68.3, 53.0, and 51.7 (National Center for Health Statistics, 1986, 17). The state thus has proportionately fewer births to teenagers than the nation as a whole.

UNMARRIED AND MINORITY TEENAGED MOTHERS. An unfavorable trend in adolescent parenthood is the rising proportion of births to unmarried teenagers and the overall increases in single teen motherhood. Birthrates of unmarried white teenagers increased from 9.1 per 1,000 white women aged 15–19 in 1970 to 15.5 by 1980. The rates for nonwhites are much higher, although they have declined. The nonwhite single teen birthrate fell over this period from 108.4 per 1,000 nonwhite women aged 15–19 to 95.1 (McIntosh 1986, 10).

Table 8.10 summarizes Wisconsin's trends in numbers of births to teenagers by marital and minority status over the 1970–84 period. We highlight the percentage of babies with low birth weight born to teens, as this is one of the major risks of adolescent childbearing. Although the numbers of births to teens are declining, the proportion of births to unmarried women and to minority women who are nonwhite (this excludes most Hispanics) is increasing. While the overall rate of low birth weights has declined over the period, it is markedly higher among nonwhites. For nonwhite teens, the proportion of low-birth-weight babies actually increased over the 1970s, with a high of 14.2% in 1980. By 1984, this fell below the 1970 percentage, probably reflecting better prenatal care for young nonwhite pregnant girls.

Table 8.10. Number of Live Births to Wisconsin Adolescents Aged 19 and Under, by Marital and Nonwhite Status, 1970, 1980, 1984

	1970	1980	1984
Total number of births	9,697	9,213	7,376
Percentage unmarried	32.9	50.5	62.5
Percentage with low birth weight[a]	9.4	8.0	7.9
Percentage nonwhite[b]	15.5	17.7	23.8
Number of nonwhite births[b]	1,507	1,629[c]	1,757[d]
Percentage unmarried	69.6	87.3	88.6
Percentage with low birth weight[a]	13.0	14.2	12.1

Sources: Wisconsin Bureau of Health Statistics (n.d.), and *Wisconsin Vital Statistics* (1984), 28, table 1.6.

[a]"Low birth weight" is defined as under 2,500 grams in 1984 and as 2,500 grams or less in 1970 and 1980.

[b]Nonwhite is race reported as other than white on birth certificate and does not include Hispanics.

[c]In 1980, 1,402 of these were blacks and 168 were American Indians.

[d]In 1984, 1,502 of these were blacks and 159 were American Indians.

PROBLEMS OF TEENAGED PARENTS. In addition to being at higher risk for infants with low birth weights than are older pregnant women, adolescent mothers experience many health, social, and economic problems. Teens, relative to women in their twenties, face higher rates of maternal and infant mortality, pregnancy complications (including toxemia), labor complications, lower Apgar scores, more congenital abnormalities, and birth defects. These girls are less likely to get prenatal care and nutritional guidance early in the pregnancy.

A recent Wisconsin report (McIntosh 1986) cites the positive trend that fewer teens who give birth receive little or no prenatal care during the pregnancy. But despite improvement since the late 1960s, by 1984, one in three teen mothers and their babies were not obtaining adequate health services (McIntosh 1986, 18). Younger teens and minority teens are even more likely not to get care. Infant mortality rates have generally declined over the last decade and a half; however, these trends for teen mothers in particular are not available. In 1984, fetal and infant deaths were more likely to occur to mothers in their teens than to mothers in their twenties and early thirties (McIntosh 1986, 22).

For the young teen who gives birth and becomes a single mother, the prospects for her and the child's long-term economic and social well-being are bleak. Some of the most likely long-run socioeconomic consequences of teenagers becoming mothers rather than delaying parenthood are the following: lower chances of completing high school or going beyond in their education; higher probability of future single motherhood and marital dissolution; higher subsequent fertility; and higher rates of poverty and welfare dependence (S. K. Danziger 1986).

Impact of Family Resources on Youth: County-level Comparisons

The trends in well-being we have examined show some similarities and some differences over the 1970–80 period. Resources available to families have fallen slightly or remained constant. Among youth, education test scores have remained about constant, while graduation rates and college attendance have fallen. Labor force participation and part-time work showed increases, as did arrest rates for serious crimes and out-of-wedlock birthrates. In this section, we look at cross-sectional data to explore whether conditions of family life bear some direct relation to the extent to which youth pursue opportunities and/or develop problems. We utilize a series of aggregate-level multivariate regression analyses to examine the effect of a community's level of family social and economic conditions for the status of its youth.

The model of conditions for family life selects a few indicators of social and economic conditions that might affect children. It includes the following five variables measured at the county level from 1980 census data: (1) percentage of the population residing in urban areas; (2) percentage of children in families headed by single parents; (3) civilian adult unemployment rate; (4) percentage of families with children who have income at or below the poverty line; and (5) percentage of adults who have four or more years of college.

The model is run for four dependent indicators of the status of youth, each of which is measured at the county level and based upon teen population figures: (1) drop-out rate—percentage of all youth 16–17 years old not enrolled in school in 1980; (2) work rate—percentage of youth 16–19 years old who were employed in 1980; (3) arrest rate—number of juvenile arrests for Part I offenses per 1,000 youth aged 0–17, 1984; and (4) birthrate—annual number of births per 1,000 females 15–19 years old, averaged over the three years of 1980, 1981, and 1982.

Results

Table 8.11 shows the results of the regressions. We present the (standardized) beta coefficients, which estimate the extent to which variation in one particular county characteristic on average is associated with a change in the particular indicator of youth status when all other county characteristics included in

Table 8.11. Regression Model of Community Conditions on County Indices of Teen Well-Being ($N = 72$)

	(Standardized) Beta Coefficients			
Community Resources	Percentage of Youth 16-17 Years Old Not Enrolled in School, 1980	Percentage of Youth 16-19 Years Old Who Work, 1980	Juvenile Arrest Rates for Part I Offenses, 1984	Average Annual Birthrate to Females 15-19 Years Old, 1980-1982
Percentage of population residing in urban areas, 1980	-.336*	.236	.350*	-.225*
Percentage of children in single-parent families, 1980	.719*	-.077	.744*	.660*
Civilian adult unemployment rate, 1980	.038	-.285*	.059	-.104
Percentage of families with children in poverty, 1979	-.087	-.431*	-.260*	.050
Percentage of adults with 3 or more years of college, 1980	-.152	-.067	-.186*	-.459*
Adjusted R^2	.585	.616	.649	.758

Source: U.S. census extract, prepared by the Institute for Research on Poverty (1986).
*Reaches statistical significance at .05 level (for Betas).

the model are held constant. The standardized coefficient corrects for differences in measurement scale across the five resource conditions, so that the predictive value of each can be compared with the others.

For school continuance among youth 16–17 years old, two county characteristics remain significantly associated with drop-out rates when the other measures are held constant. More youth drop out in areas with more children living with single parents and in less populous areas. If county phenomena indicate something about individuals, perhaps the results imply that rural youth and those with limited parental resources are less motivated to continue schooling.

On the other hand, youth employment levels are lowest in areas with two other characteristics: higher rates of family poverty and higher general unemployment. These suggest that the existence of limited economic opportunities in a county makes for lower work rates for youth.

Arrest rates for Part I offenses are directly influenced by four of the indicators in the model. More youth are arrested where more children live in single-parent families, where the county is more urban, where educational attainment is lower, but also where family poverty rates are lower. Perhaps here the poverty rate is a proxy for lower community expenditures on public institutions such as the police force. The urban results are in keeping with the frequently found correlation between urbanization and crime, which may indicate that opportunities for these offenses are greater where there is more anonymity. Results involving single-parent family rates and the level of education may suggest a relationship between arrests and limited social and family resources.

Finally, when we analyze the role of a county's level of family resources for its teen birthrate, we find very strong relationships. Three county measures emerge statistically significant. Higher proportions of single-parent families, lower levels of educational attainment, and a less urban population are related to higher rates of teen childbearing. It may be that the teen birthrate is higher when role models are inappropriate, or when knowledge of and access to contraception are limited. The lack of significance of the economic indicators of unemployment and poverty rates in a county suggest that the material resources in the community do not exert independent direct influence on this outcome measure of adolescent well-being.

Given our aggregate level of analysis comparing the counties, the interpretation of the associations between various measures of the status of children and demographic attributes of the communities in which they live must be viewed with caution. Nevertheless, it is notable that the proportion of one-parent families tends to be positively associated with the problems of school dropout, juvenile delinquency, and teen birth. Degree of urbanization is associated with these same problems, but in a mixed way, and it tends to have less of an effect. The problems we measure are not confined to the more urban or the more rural areas. Measures of economic resources in a community—for example, poverty and unemployment—also bear some relation to the status of youth, such as to the level of their employment. Finally, lower educational level of adults affects the rate of teen births and juvenile arrests in a county.

These results may imply that in one-parent families—those with the fewest resources—adolescents may be vulnerable to many problems. Lack of resources in the form of education and income may also contribute to problems, but to a reduced degree. On the other hand, some variables that we were unable to measure may account for such relationships. Indeed, the complicated pattern of relations between the proportion of one-parent families and the concentration of family poverty in urban areas and among minority groups may be implicated in ways that we cannot isolate here. (The uneven representation of minority youth across counties precluded the use of minority status in these equations, for example. And the high correlations between levels of unemployment, poverty, family income, and urban density complicate the isolation of possibly different effects of these factors on the status of youth.)

Summary and Policy Implications

Failing to complete one's education, having a baby in one's teen years, and getting arrested are all behaviors that jeopardize an individual's future as a productive adult. Each, however, might also reflect the general changes in social conditions in Wisconsin. Given their similarities in the above analyses, we conclude that these problems call for a broad, needs-based policy approach targeted to some youth. We find that family resources that reach children have stabilized or fallen since 1970. Moreover, poverty among children, rates of single-parent families, and rates of mothers working have increased. While these trends affect all of Wisconsin children, minority youth bear a disproportionate share of the burden.

The most striking such trend is the growth in single-parent families in Wisconsin, as in the rest of the nation. The rates are especially high for racial minorities. Nevertheless, white single-parent families are also increasing. Single-parent families come about increasingly as a result of out-of-wedlock births, divorce, and separation. Few result from widowhood.

Despite the general stagnation of resources, we do not find a great deal of evidence from educational achievement or employment that the typical child is affected by this decline. Perhaps the largest problems we uncovered are that early sexuality can result in pregnancy and disaffection from normal adolescent development and that a few measures of test scores indicate moderate deterioration. The most striking findings in the measures of well-being are that specific subgroups seem to be facing severe problems. The analysis suggests, for example, that counties with high percentages of children in single-parent families have the highest rates of school dropout, juvenile arrests for serious crimes (both violent and property offenses), and births to women 15–19 years old. Individual-level data suggest great hazards for minority youth as well as one-parent families—less school continuation, more full-time employment for those who have jobs, more teen parenthood, more arrests for violent crime.

We thus find no particular mandate for altering or targeting general policies to the typical child—except when policies affect the adolescent birthrate. However, if improvement in overall well-being is desired, a broad-based focus on policies to increase general levels of schooling, employment, and so forth, would be warranted.

Although stability is the general rule, deterioration in well-being apparently occurs in counties and to children with the fewest economic and social resources. This seems to demand a policy response. In education, for example, reduced class size, special types of community involvement, or supportive services might be needed where the drop-out problems are greatest. Various general family supports might be useful to prevent some children from having the types of social problems we have reported. Social policy also might do well to encourage the two-parent family, while at the same time promoting services to address the stresses of existing one-parent families. Finally, these findings support the need for targeting programs to minority families and youth.

Family and racial issues highlighted here might in themselves reflect broad economic realities. For example, family life may have worsened for single parents and minorities as a result of changing economic conditions. Or, high rates of youth unemployment may reflect a general shortage of jobs. Similarly, a growing proportion of nonwhite families face economic difficulties, and nonwhite children and families, perhaps as a result, often demonstrate high rates of troubles. Thus, the general health of the economy, particularly as it affects minority groups and the poor, is likely to be one of the most important factors to consider when formulating youth policy.

NOTES

This chapter reports on a project funded by the Wisconsin Office for Children, Youth, and Families, Bureau of Human Resources. We thank the many people in state agencies and on the University of Wisconsin–Madison campus who provided us with information, sources of data, reports, and so forth. We are especially grateful to Charles Nagatoshi, Liz Uhr, Cathy Cameron, Kay Hendon, and Kathe Thorpe. Any errors, omissions, or opinions are those of the authors.

1. School graduation and drop-out estimates were provided by Donald Russell of the Wisconsin Department of Public Instruction.

9

Reforming Wisconsin's Child Support System

ANN NICHOLS-CASEBOLT, IRWIN GARFINKEL,
AND PATRICK WONG

Introduction

One of every five children in Wisconsin is now potentially eligible for child support.[1] That is, they have a living parent not residing with them who could be contributing to their financial support. Demographers project that nearly one-half of all children born today will become potentially eligible for child support before they reach adulthood (Bumpass 1984). Therefore, the quality of Wisconsin's child support institutions is of great importance.

Unfortunately, though Wisconsin's child support system is one of the best in the nation, it is still plagued by serious problems. It condones and therefore fosters parental irresponsibility. It is inequitable. And it leaves thousands of children and their mothers impoverished and dependent on welfare.

In response to these problems the state has embarked upon a major reform effort to create a new child support assurance system. If successful, Wisconsin's system will likely become the model for the nation.

In the first two sections of this chapter, we describe Wisconsin's current child support system and document its shortcomings. The third section outlines the contents of and presents the rationale for a new child support assurance system. The fourth section provides estimates of some of the benefits and costs of the proposed new system. In the last section, we discuss the status of the reform effort and prospects for the future.

The Current System

The child support system consists of two major parts: the family court system and the welfare system. The former establishes and enforces noncustodial parents' obligations to provide financial support for their children. This part

172

of the system may be thought of as engaging in the public enforcement of private child support obligations. In contrast, the second part, the welfare system, provides publicly financed economic support for poor children and their custodial parents.

Family law is traditionally a province of the states. Wisconsin, like most states, has statutes that establish the obligation of noncustodial parents to contribute financial support to their children. The amount to be paid, however, is determined on a case-by-case basis, and historically the guidelines given the court have been very broad. Prior to 1983, Wisconsin statutes instructed courts to apply the following criteria in determining the amount of child support: (1) the financial resources of the child; (2) the financial resources of both parents; (3) the standard of living the child would have enjoyed had the marriage not ended in annulment, divorce, or legal separation; (4) the desirability that the custodian remain in the home as a full-time parent; (5) the cost of day care if the custodian works outside the home, or the value of custodial services performed by the custodian if the custodian remains in the home; (6) the physical and emotional health needs of the child; (7) the child's educational needs; (8) the tax consequences to each party; and (9) any other factors that the court deems relevant. These guidelines are so vague that Wisconsin courts have had tremendous discretion in setting child support awards.

Until recently, nearly all states allowed wide judicial discretion.[2] In some jurisdictions, however, judges use a child support obligation schedule, which is similar to a tax table. Most counties in Michigan, for example, use only two facts to determine child support: the noncustodial parent's income and the number of children owed support. Though such schedules remain the exception rather than the rule, an increasing number of states have begun to adopt simple standards. As we describe below, recent federal legislation requires all states to establish at least nonbinding standards as of October 1987. Wisconsin legislation in 1985, described below, takes the state well beyond the federal requirements.

Wisconsin law in the area of enforcement of the parental child support obligations is also among the strongest in the nation. It provides that all child support be paid through a government body—the county clerk of courts. Only six other states have a similar requirement (Melli 1984, 36). Moreover, since 1978, Wisconsin law has also provided that when a court order for child support is entered, a contingent income assignment must be issued. This means that if payments are a month late (changed to ten days in 1983), the county clerk of courts is authorized to send notice to the delinquent noncustodial parent. Unless the parent can show cause within ten days, the child support payments will be withheld from the delinquent parent's paycheck. Although these statutory provisions appear comprehensive, the logistics involved in contingent income assignments are too cumbersome for successful implementation. As we will see below, Wisconsin is now moving beyond withholding in response to delinquency to a universal, immediate withholding law, while the federal government is requiring all states to adopt at least a law mandating withholding in response to delinquency.

Although income withholding is the most effective collection tool, the ultimate sanction for those who do not pay is jail. In Michigan, thousands of noncustodial fathers are jailed each year for failure to comply with child support orders.[3] In Wisconsin and most other states, however, jail is used infrequently.

The second part of the child support system is welfare, of which the Aid to Families with Dependent Children (AFDC) program is the most important component. AFDC provides cash assistance to low-income families with dependent children. Most families eligible for AFDC are also eligible for food stamps and for Medicaid, a medical assistance program for the poor.

The AFDC program was enacted in 1935 as part of the original Social Security Act. Initially the principal beneficiaries were the children of widows. Once the Survivors Insurance Program was enacted in 1938, AFDC was expected to shrink in importance. Instead, owing to dramatic increases in divorce, separation, and out-of-wedlock births, AFDC caseloads grew. Today, widows and their children constitute less than 2% of the caseload.

As AFDC costs mounted, congressional interest in private child support payments grew. Between 1950 and 1984, Congress enacted a series of bills to strengthen public enforcement of private child support. Although the initial motivation was to reduce public child support costs, by the 1980s strengthening private child support had become an end in itself.

In 1950, Congress enacted the first federal child support legislation. This required state welfare agencies to notify law enforcement officials when a child receiving AFDC benefits had been adandoned. Other legislation, enacted in 1965 and 1967, required states to enforce child support and establish paternity, and allowed them to request the addresses of absent parents from the Internal Revenue Service (IRS) and the Social Security Administration within the Department of Health, Education and Welfare.

The most significant legislation was enacted in 1975, when Congress added Part D to Title IV of the Social Security Act, thereby establishing the Child Support Enforcement (or IV-D) program. The states are responsible for running this program. They are reimbursed by the federal government for about 70% of the cost of establishing paternity, locating noncustodial parents, and collecting child support. Use of the IRS to collect child support owed to AFDC beneficiaries was authorized by the 1975 law. In 1980, this use was extended to non-AFDC families, and new legislation in 1981 required the IRS to withhold tax refunds in cases when states certified that the individual had an overdue child support obligation.

In the summer of 1984, Congress voted unanimously to enact the strongest federal child support legislation to date. It requires all states to (1) initiate a process to withhold child support from the wages of noncustodial parents who are delinquent in their child support payments for one month, and (2) appoint blue-ribbon commissions to devise statewide standards for child support. In addition, for the first time, the law gives the states financial incentives to collect child support for non-AFDC and out-of-state cases.

As of 1985, about 147,000 Wisconsin families had about 250,000 children potentially eligible for child support. Table 9.1 indicates that about 103,000 or nearly 70% of these families were headed by single mothers. Most of the remaining children lived with their married mothers. Less than 13% of the children lived with their fathers. Thus, although we use the term "noncustodial parents" throughout most of this chapter, the reader should bear in mind that in the overwhelming majority of cases the noncustodial parent is the father.

Forty-six percent of families with children potentially eligible for child support were on welfare. About six of every ten such female-headed families received AFDC in 1985, but only about three in ten of the families with remarried mothers did.

Public transfers in Wisconsin to poor families with children eligible for child support substantially exceed private child support transfers to all

Table 9.1. Number of Wisconsin Families and Children Potentially Eligible for Child Support in 1985 by AFDC Status

Headship Status of Custodial Parent	Total	Non-AFDC Recipient	AFDC Recipient
		Number of Families	
Female head	102,708	41,910	60,798
Remarried female	20,681	14,138	6,543
Male head (single)	14,065	13,765	300
Remarried male	9,575	9,575	0
Total	147,029	79,388	67,641
		Number of Children	
Female head	183,050	67,605	115,445
Remarried female	35,509	23,938	11,571
Male head (single)	20,322	19,793	529
Remarried male	11,371	11,371	0
Total	250,252	122,207	127,545

Sources: Non-AFDC recipient data from Wisconsin Survey of Children, Income, and Program Participation 1985. AFDC recipient data from Wisconsin Computer Reporting Network 1985.

Wisconsin children. Whereas about $163 million in private child support was paid in 1985, AFDC expenditures on families eligible for child support were equal in that year to about $356 million. If the costs for Medicaid and food stamps are added in, public transfers were equal to nearly $597 million, or more than three times private child support transfers.[4]

Problems with the Current System

Although Wisconsin's child support system is better than most, it faces the same problems that obtain in the rest of the nation: parental irresponsibility, inequity, impoverishment of children, and fostering dependence on welfare.

Nationwide, slightly less than 60% of mothers with children eligible for child support even have a child support award. The proportion with an award varies dramatically with the marital status of the mother. Whereas about eight out of ten divorced and remarried mothers have child support orders, less than 40% of separated mothers and less than two in ten never-married mothers have such orders. Of those with orders, only about half receive the full amount due them, and about one-quarter receive nothing (U.S. Bureau of the Census 1985). In all, over half the families eligible for support receive nothing.

There are two ways in which the child support system is inequitable. First, it treats equals unequally. Second, it is regressive because it establishes child support obligations that are a greater proportion of the incomes of low-income men than of those who are well-off. The first inequity of the system stems directly from its toleration of irresponsibility—a problem compounded by capricious enforcement of the law. The majority of noncustodial parents pay no child support. Most who do not pay suffer no consequences. Yet others, albeit a very small percentage, are sent to jail. The amount of support an absent parent pays depends not just on the ability to pay, but on the varying attitudes of local judges, district attorneys, and welfare officials; the beliefs, attitudes, and relative power of both parents; and the skill of their lawyers. Nearly every absent parent knows someone earning more who pays less. And nearly every custodial parent knows someone who is receiving more though the child's father earns less.

Data for Wisconsin indicate that child support awards range from zero to over 100% of the noncustodial father's income.[5] The data in table 9.2 from twenty-one Wisconsin counties indicate that in 20% of the cases, child support awards for one child are less than 10% of the noncustodial father's income; in 50% of these cases, awards are between 11% and 20%. Similar data in table 9.3 indicate that average award levels as a percentage of the noncustodial parent's income vary substantially across counties. The average for

Table 9.2. Child Support Order as a Percentage of Gross Income by Number of Children

Order as % of Noncustodial Parent's Income	Percentage of Cases		
	1 Child (N = 1,087)	2 Children (N = 829)	3 Children (N = 277)
0–10%	20%	10%	6%
11–20	50	36	27
21–30	21	30	33
31–40	5	15	20
41–50	3	5	9
More than 50	2	5	6

Source: Family court record data file from Wisconsin Child Support Reform Demonstration Project, 1985, Institute for Research on Poverty, University of Wisconsin–Madison.

Note: This table covers custodial families with a child support award and with three or fewer children. Cases with 4 or more children (N = 102) are not tabulated because the sample size is too small for reliable estimates. Of the 3,806 cases meeting the sample requirements, income information is missing in 1,536 cases. In addition, 77 cases have zero reported income and are also excluded. This results in a final N of 2,193.

one child varies from 12% to 24%. For two and three children respectively, the ranges are 18% to 36% and 13% to 37%.

Child support awards are also regressive. Table 9.4 indicates that orders decline as a percentage of income as the noncustodial father's income increases. For one child they range from a high of 32% for those with incomes less than $5,000 to a low of 12% for those with incomes between $30,000 and $40,000.

Finally, our welfare system, in relieving poverty, encourages dependency. Most of the poor in female-headed households receive welfare, and the overwhelming majority of mothers on welfare do not work during the months they receive benefits.[6] Given the confiscatory tax rates on earnings in the AFDC program, this is not surprising. Because AFDC, like any welfare program, is designed to aid only the poor, benefits are reduced when earnings increase. After four months on a job, a woman on AFDC faces a benefit reduction of a dollar for every dollar of net earnings. This is equivalent to a 100% tax on earnings. What we give with one hand, we take with the other. Yet, because they have little education and experience, and would have childcare expenses if they did work, most women on AFDC could not earn enough to lift their families from poverty even if they worked full time. Isabel Sawhill finds that even if fully employed, one-half of welfare recipients could earn no more than their welfare grant, while another quarter could earn only up to $3,200 more in 1985 dollars (Sawhill 1976).[7] If they also received child support from the children's noncustodial father, some but not all of these families would attain an income above the poverty level. Clearly, the only way to alleviate this kind of poverty without creating dependency is to supplement rather than replace the earnings of these custodial mothers.

Table 9.3. Percentage of Wisconsin Child Support Eligible Cases with Child Support Orders, and Relationship between Awards and Noncustodial Parent's Income by Number of Children and by County

| County | % Cases with Child Support Orders | Child Support Award as % of Gross Income | | |
		1 Child	2 Children	3 Children
Calumet	90 (N = 154)	20	26	25
Clark	83 (N = 151)	18	21	16
Dane	85 (N = 397)	18	22	25
Dodge	81 (N = 148)	19	30	29
Dunn	78 (N = 151)	12	20	13
Green	91 (N = 149)	24	24	26
Jefferson	83 (N = 147)	18	25	29
Juneau	81 (N = 141)	19	28	34
Kewaunee	83 (N = 138)	18	22	30
La Crosse	83 (N = 198)	21	23	28
Marathon	84 (N = 199)	17	22	31
Milwaukee	85 (N = 648)	18	22	24
Monroe	87 (N = 153)	20	18	18
Oneida	90 (N = 152)	15	22	23
Ozaukee	90 (N = 188)	16	23	37
Price	81 (N = 144)	12	23	27
Racine	91 (N = 201)	23	36	35
Richland	91 (N = 143)	15	19	24
St. Croix	87 (N = 154)	13	18	15
Sheboygan	90 (N = 221)	16	22	24
Waukesha	85 (N = 399)	16	21	24
Winnebago	86 (N = 223)	18	22	27
Weighted average	86 (N = 4,599)	18	24	27

Source: Family court record data file from Wisconsin Child Support Reform Demonstration Project, 1985, Institute for Research on Poverty, University of Wisconsin–Madison.

Note: There is an upward bias in the estimates for child support as percentage of gross income. Because of coding error, net income is used for about 280 cases for which gross income is not available.

Child Support Assurance: The Proposal and Its Goals

In the summer of 1980, a research team from the Institute for Research on Poverty (IRP) at the University of Wisconsin contracted with the Wisconsin Department of Health and Social Services (DHSS) to examine the state's child support system and find ways to improve it. The IRP report concluded that a child support assurance system gave promise of reinforcing parental responsibility, increasing equity, and reducing poverty and welfare dependence.

Under a child support assurance system, all parents living apart from their children would be obligated to share income with their children. The sharing rate would be specified in the law and would depend only upon the number of

Table 9.4. Relationship between Noncustodial Parent's Income at the Time of the Child
Support Order and Level of Child Support Awards by Number of Children and
Gross Income Category, Selected Wisconsin Counties

Income Category of Noncustodial Parent	N	Percentage of Income		
		1 Child (N = 1,087)	2 Children (N = 829)	3 Children (N = 277)
Less than $5,000	151	32%	41%	33%
$5,000–$10,000	538	20	27	28
$10,000–15,000	506	18	25	31
$15,000–20,000	443	15	22	30
$20,000–30,000	450	13	21	24
$30,000–40,000	107	12	20	32
$40,000 or over	100	16	19	14
Weighted average	2,295	18	24	27

Source: Family court record data file from Wisconsin Child Support Reform Demonstration
Project, 1985, Institute for Research on Poverty, University of Wisconsin–Madison.
Note: See note to table 9.3.

children owed support. The obligation would be collected through payroll
withholding, as social security and income taxes are. Children with a living
noncustodial parent would be entitled to benefits equal to either the child
support paid by the noncustodial parent or a socially assured minimum benefit, whichever was higher. Should the noncustodial parent pay less than the
minimum, the custodial parent would be subject to a small surtax up to the
amount of the subsidy. Any remaining difference would be financed out of
general revenues.

The report examined the pros and cons of the rationales for dozens of
features of the proposed new system. Here we describe briefly the rationales
for only the four major features of the program: (1) standardized income
sharing rate, (2) automatic income withholding, (3) assured support, and
(4) custodial parent surtax. The report argued that a legislated formula for
child support would eliminate many of the worst problems of the current
system. First, it would be "horizontally" equitable, since absent parents with
the same income and the same number of children would pay the same
amount. Second, the current regressiveness in the child support obligation
would be corrected by using a proportional formula. Third, the formula
would reduce one of the principal conflicts between former spouses by eliminating the possibility of disputes over the size of the child support payments.
A final justification for the transfer of jurisdiction from the judiciary to the
legislative branch is simple: Child support belongs under the control of taxpayers, who already provide for the large number of children whose absent
parents do not pay sufficient support.

Withholding for income and payroll taxes attests to the effectiveness of withholding in general. Wisconsin's preliminary experience with selective, court-ordered wage withholding attests to the effectiveness of withholding for child support collections. We already have one of the best collection records in the country (Oellerich 1982), but withholding in response to delinquency is neither equivalent to nor likely to be as effective as universal withholding. Does anyone imagine that social security payroll tax collections would be as great if we withheld only from those who were delinquent? The principal reason for advocating universal automatic wage withholding for child support, therefore, is that it has been proved in practice.

The assured support of the system consists of two components. The first component assures a minimum amount of child support to each custodial family as a function of the number of eligible children. If the collection from the noncustodial parent is less than the assured level, the difference is subsidized by the government. The second component provides an hourly work-expense offset to low-income custodial parents who work and who do not receive welfare. The offset covers child-care expenses and is meant to improve the appeal of the reform system relative to the guaranteed benefit of AFDC, which is quite generous in Wisconsin.

The argument for a socially assured benefit is twofold. First, it would reduce the risk to children whose noncustodial parents became unemployed or unable to work. In such cases, child support payments would fall only to the socially assured benefit level, not to zero. Second, the assured benefit, when combined with earnings, would lift many single-parent households out of poverty and remove them from welfare. Custodial parents going to work would not face a dollar-for-dollar reduction in their child support payments, as they do under AFDC. On the contrary, the availability of the work-expense offset encourages low-income custodial parents to both work and leave AFDC. Any reduction in their child support receipts would be small and would occur only if the absent parent was paying less than the assured benefit. Thus, custodial parents would have the usual incentive for acquiring jobs—the knowledge that by so doing they would be enhancing the well-being of their families. Also, benefits would no longer be seen as welfare for the poor alone, but as social insurance for which all children eligible for child support were entitled. Therefore, the child support assurance system would not demean the recipients. AFDC, with its built-in negative incentives and stigma, should dwindle into a program of last resort for a destitute few.

Finally, there are two related arguments for the custodial-parent surtax in the event that the noncustodial parent pays less than the assured benefit. First, in the absence of a custodial parent surtax, in a few cases, well-to-do custodial parents will receive a public subsidy. Second, a custodial-parent tax will reduce the cost of the program.

Benefits and Costs of Child Support Assurance

Both the benefits and costs of a child support assurance program will depend upon the level of the assured benefit, the tax rates on noncustodial and custodial parents, and the effectiveness of the new system.

The impact of the reform also depends on the behavioral response of the custodial parents. The reform makes available a set of economic incentives very different from the existing welfare system. Relative to the latter, the assurance system has a lower tax rate and in fact subsidizes work through the work-expense offset. Some of the custodial parents currently on welfare are therefore expected to opt for more work and to leave welfare. At the same time, many of those not on welfare will experience an increase in unearned income through either increased private child support payment or the assured benefit. They may reduce their work effort.

In table 9.5, estimates of net savings or costs and of reductions in poverty and AFDC caseloads are presented for child support assurance programs

Table 9.5. Costs and Benefits of Alternative Child Support Assurance Plans in 1985

Award and Collection Rate		Benefits for the 1st child[a]		
		$2,000	$3,000	$3,500
100%	Net savings[b]	68	59	50
	% poverty gap reduction	34	38	44
	% AFDC load reduction	18	24	35
Mid-range[c]	Net savings[b]	11	-1	-9
improvement	% poverty gap reduction	26	29	33
	% AFDC load reduction	11	15	22
Current[c]	Net savings[b]	-28	-38	-45
state	% poverty gap reduction	17	19	21
average	% AFDC load reduction	6	9	14

Sources: Non-AFDC recipient data from Wisconsin Survey of Children, Income, and Program Participation 1985. AFDC recipient data from Wisconsin Computer Reporting Network 1985.

[a]Assured benefits for additional children are gauged to the benefit for the first child and set at the same proportion of increments in the state's AFDC scale. The noncustodial parent is taxed at 17%, 25%, 29%, 31% and 34%, for one child up to five children, respectively. The custodial tax rate is the same as the noncustodial rate.

[b]Net savings are reported in millions of 1985 dollars, and are relative to net public AFDC expenditure on families eligible for child support in Wisconsin in that year.

[c]The award and collection rates are both estimated from our 1985 Wisconsin data sets as functions of demographic characteristics of the custodial parent. We estimated the relationship of income to percentage paid to be 39% plus 1.4% for each additional $1,000 of income. This is the relationship used in our estimates. For the mid-range improvement we shift the intercept to 60% and retain the same slope. The likelihood of award as estimated implies an increase of 50% in award probability among those never-married and separated, and an increase of 27.5% among divorcees.

with three different assured benefit levels. The labor supply response of the custodial parents is incorporated in the simulation. (A description of the methodology used for obtaining these estimates is available from the authors.) The benefit levels for the first child—$2,000, $3,000, and $3,500— are all less than the welfare benefit for one child and the child's custodial parent ($5,539 in 1985 in Wisconsin). This is in keeping with the purpose of the program, which is to supplement—rather than substitute for—earnings. Moreover, unlike welfare, the child support benefit is for the children only. The assured benefit levels for subsequent children in the family are set in proportion to the corresponding family size increments in the Wisconsin AFDC scale. The work-expense offset is set at $1.00 or $1.75 per hour, depending on whether one or more than one child is eligible in the family. This subsidy to work is provided up to $8,000 in income. Beyond this level it is gradually phased out in the manner of the earned income tax credit. The offset disappears at $16,000 of income. The tax rates for noncustodial and custodial parents alike are equal to 17% for one child, and 25%, 29%, 31%, and 34% respectively for two, three, four, and five or more children.

The estimates in the top panel of table 9.5 assume that 100% of eligible families obtain awards, and that all of the noncustodial parents' child support obligations are collected. Under these circumstances, all three proposed plans result in net savings to the state and federal government, ranging from $68 million for the least generous plan to $50 million for the most generous plan. All of the plans reduce the poverty gap—the difference between a family's income and the poverty line—by one-third or more. AFDC caseload reductions range from 18% to 35%.

The bottom panel presents estimates of the effects of instituting the same child support assurance plans, assuming, however, that award and collection effectiveness were no better than the system's performance in Wisconsin in 1985. In this case, in all three of the plans, there are added costs instead of savings—ranging from $28 million to $45 million. The costs are due primarily to the much lower private child support collection. At the same time, the poverty-gap reduction is cut in half and welfare reduction by even more because, under current performance of the system, 40% of the population do not have awards and would not be covered by the reform.

Wisconsin already does better than the national average in enforcing awards. Moreover, there is every reason to believe that universal immediate income withholding will lead to further substantial improvement in collection effectiveness. The existence of the assured benefit will also encourage more custodial families to obtain awards. On the other hand, it is unrealistic to expect that awards and collections will ever be perfectly efficient. For this reason, the middle panel presents estimates based on the assumption that collection enforcement is about midway between perfect and the current state average. We believe that this panel provides the most realistic estimate of collection effectiveness when immediate withholding is universally applied among all cases with awards. In this case, the least generous plan saves $11 million, while the most generous would cost an additional $9 million. The plan with a $3,000 assured benefit approximately breaks even relative to the current welfare system, but it will reduce poverty and welfare dependency by 29% and 15% respectively.

The Status of the Wisconsin Child Support Reform Initiative

Wisconsin is now in the process of moving toward a child support assurance system. For two reasons, the state has implemented the collection phase of the system before the benefit phase. First, improving collections before instituting a new benefit is fiscally prudent. Second, the assured benefit and custodial-parent tax are more complicated administratively and fiscally.

At the request of then Governor Anthony Earl and Assembly Speaker Thomas Loftus in July 1983, the Wisconsin legislature enacted a budget bill that directed the DHSS to (1) contract with ten counties to withhold child support payments from the wages of all new obligors, and (2) publish a child support standard based on a percentage of the noncustodial parent's income that judges and family court commissioners could use in lieu of the nine guidelines discussed at the beginning of this chapter. The bill also contained a provision which requires all Wisconsin counties to adopt universal income withholding in new cases as of 1 July 1987.

The standard was published by the DHSS and sent to all judges and family court commissioners in December 1983. It provides for a child support obligation equal to 17% for one child, and 25%, 29%, 31%, and 34% respectively for two, three, four, and five or more children. (For the source of these rates, see Appendix A.)

By May 1984 ten counties had contracted with the DHSS to pilot the use of immediate income assignments. The counties were selected on the basis of the willingness of the judges and family court commissioners to implement immediate income assignments, the interests of related agencies in participating in the pilots, and the willingness of a majority of the county board to contract with the DHSS to participate in the pilot. In addition, factors such as diversity in geographic location were considered. The ten pilot counties are Clark, Dane, Dunn, Kewaunee, Monroe, Oneida, Ozaukee, Richland, Sheboygan, and Winnebago.

Meanwhile, state officials also successfully sought federal legislation that allows Wisconsin to use federal funds to help finance the state's assured child support benefit. Because the assured benefit will reduce AFDC costs, of which the federal government pays about half, the federal government agreed to allow Wisconsin to use the resulting savings to help finance the assured benefit if a request is submitted by the governor. The agreement, contained in the 1984 landmark federal child support legislation, extends for seven years—from the last quarter of 1986 through 1993.

The July 1985 budget bill for the 1986–87 biennium contains new child support legislation that permits additional counties to begin immediate withholding prior to 1 January 1987, and makes the DHSS percentage-of-income standard the presumptive child support award as of July 1987. This means that awards can depart from the standard only if the judge makes a written finding that justifies such a departure. Finally, the new bill gives the DHSS authority to implement the assured benefit on a demonstration basis in several counties.

Soon after the 1985 legislation was enacted, nearly twenty additional counties began implementing universal immediate income assignments. By July 1987 nearly fifty counties, including Milwaukee, were using immediate withholding. It appears that this part of the proposed new system is no longer politically controversial in Wisconsin.

The standard is more controversial. During the 1985 legislative session, there was vociferous debate among interested parties about the grounds that judges could use to depart from the standard. The DHSS favored language that would have allowed a departure from the standard only if it was "in the best interests of the child." A Child Support Advisory Committee appointed by the DHSS had recommended a much broader escape clause, which would have allowed a departure if the judge found that it was "in the best interests of justice." The DHSS thought this escape clause was too broad, while the judiciary and bar mobilized against the narrow escape clause. The final legislation contained both a general escape clause and some specific criteria.

Though the standard is now used in most cases to establish the initial child support order, as yet it is only infrequently used as a way of automatically adjusting the order as the noncustodial parent's income changes. County clerks of courts currently have no way of monitoring income changes. This problem should disappear when immediate income withholding is implemented in all cases, employers are required to report earnings along with withheld child support, and the computer capabilities of the child support system are updated.

The 1987 budget bill provides for administrative funds to pilot the assured benefit in two counties. Governor Tommy Thompson has submitted a proposal to the federal government which will enable the state to receive federal funds to help finance the assured benefit. Implementation is scheduled for mid-1988. How controversial the assured benefit turns out to be is certain to depend upon the results of the demonstration.

At this point the contrast between the dismal reality of the current system and the bright promise of a child support assurance system warrants a thorough test of child support assurance. Whether the new system proves to be as promising in reality, of course, remains to be seen. If so, the rest of the nation will almost certainly follow Wisconsin's example, and child support assurance will join Workers' Compensation, income taxation, and Unemployment Compensation as successful social policy innovations that bear the stamp "Made in Wisconsin."

Appendix A. Determining What Proportion of Their Incomes Absent Parents Should Pay

The income sharing rates levied on noncustodial parents are based upon research conducted by the Institute for Research on Poverty and the recommendations of a joint IRP-DHSS task force. The first principle upon which the Child Support Assurance System is based is that when individuals parent children, they incur an obligation to share their income with the children. In determining what proportion of their income absent parents should share with their children, a good starting point is the proportion that they would have devoted to their children had they lived with the children.

Estimating how much income married parents share with their children is very difficult because so many expenditure items, like housing, are jointly consumed. As a consequence of this difficulty, estimates of the costs of children vary. As part of the child support project, Jacques van der Gaag conducted a review of the literature on the costs of children (Garfinkel and Melli 1982, 1–44) and found the following:

1. The cost of a first child is between 20 and 30% of gross income.
2. The cost remains roughly proportional up to very high income.
3. The second child costs about half as much as the first, the third as much as the second, and subsequent children about half as much as the second and third.

For several reasons, the proportion of their incomes that absent parents share with their children should be lower than the proportion they would have shared had they been living with the children. First, some of the costs of raising the child will be borne by the custodial parent. Second, a parent derives less benefit from a child when he or she lives apart from rather than together with the child. Third, the noncustodial parent will incur some costs for the children in the course of normal visitation. Finally, extremely high child support tax rates on noncustodial parents should be avoided because they will encourage evasion.

None of these reasons for expecting absent parents to share less of their income with their children than if they lived with them suggests an exact amount. Ultimately, decisions about how much the noncustodial parent should pay depend also upon judgments about how to balance the conflicting objectives of providing well for the children, minimizing public costs, and retaining incentives and a decent standard of living for the noncustodial parent.

Combining the midpoint of the estimated range of what percentage of income parents who live with their children share with their first child—25%—with the first three reasons for expecting absent parents to contribute a smaller percentage of their income to the children led the joint task force to recommend a child support rate of 17% for the first child. Based upon estimates of the cost of a child, the additional rate for the second and subsequent children should be about half the rate for the previous child. The committee also suggested that the highest rate for children in one family be 34%. Hence the recommended rates of 17%, 25%, 29%, 31%, and 34% for one, two, three, four, and five or more children.

NOTES

1. From computer runs of the Wisconsin Basic Needs data set.

2. For a general description of child support laws, see Krause (1981), Melli (1984), and Chambers (1979).

3. For an evaluation of the effectiveness of jail as an enforcement tool, see Chambers (1979).

4. Estimates of private child support are taken from the Wisconsin Survey of Children, Incomes, and Program Participation for non-AFDC recipients and from the Wisconsin Computer Reporting Network (CRN) for AFDC recipients. Estimates of public child support transfers were derived from CRN for AFDC, and the *Statistical Abstract of the United States: 1987,* 107th edition, 1986, tables 610 and 184, for Medicaid and food stamps. The expenditures for Medicaid and food stamps in *Statistical Abstract* were multiplied respectively by 0.18 and 0.48, estimates of the portion of total expenditures in these programs on female-headed households (see Garfinkel and McLanahan 1986, chap. 4.) Most female-headed households are eligible for child support. The small percentage which are not (those headed by widows) should be more than offset by the families headed by men who are eligible for child support and receive welfare.

5. These figures and the data for tables 9.2, 9.3, and 9.4 are derived from court records in twenty-one Wisconsin counties. The court records are being used to evaluate the effects of the child support reform. In making calculations of orders as a percentage of noncustodial parent income, the sample was limited to cases in which orders existed, the income of the noncustodial parent was known, and the noncustodial parent was a male.

6. On the other hand, nearly half of those who receive welfare during the course of the year also work at some point during the year.

7. The figure $3,200 is our inflation adjustment to 1985 dollars. In the original article the number is $1,000 in 1968 dollars.

10

Improving the Economic Well-Being
of Indians in Wisconsin

GARY D. SANDEFUR AND ARTHUR SAKAMOTO

In 1980 there were 29,320 American Indians in the state of Wisconsin (U.S. Bureau of the Census, *1980 Census of Population*, PC80-1-B51, 1982). American Indians accounted for approximately 0.6% of the population of the state, and for approximately 0.6% the population of the United States. Most of the Indians in Wisconsin are members of one of six groups: Chippewa, Menominee, Oneida, Potawatomi, Stockbridge Munsee, and Winnebago. The Chippewa are divided into "bands" who have traditionally lived on six major reservations in the northern part of the state: Red Cliff, Bad River, Lac Courte Oreilles, Lac du Flambeau, St. Croix, and Mole Lake. By 1980, however, approximately one-third of the Indians in Wisconsin lived on reservations, one-third lived in central cities of urban areas, and one-third lived elsewhere in the state (Christenson 1984).

Published statistics indicate that Indians in Wisconsin were economically disadvantaged relative to white residents in 1980.[1] Twenty-two percent of the American Indian families in Wisconsin had incomes that placed them below the poverty line, compared to 5% of the white families. The median family income for Indian families was $13,520, whereas the median family income for white families was $21,164. Thus, median family income for Indians was only 64% of white median family income. Among persons 16 and older, the unemployment rate for Indians was 16.1%, whereas the unemployment rate for white Wisconsinites was 6.3% (U.S. Bureau of the Census, *1980 Census of Population*, PC80-1-C51, 1983).

Among Indians, those who lived in central cities and on reservations fared substantially worse than those who lived elsewhere. In central cities, 29% of American Indian families had incomes that placed them below the poverty line, compared to 23% of reservation residents and 17% of Indians who lived elsewhere in the state (Christenson 1984). Economic conditions varied across the different reservations. For example, on the Lac Courte Oreilles reservation, the poverty rate among persons was 29.2%, whereas on the Menominee reservation the poverty rate among persons was 16.9% (U.S. Bureau of the Census, *1980 Census of Population,* PC80-1-C51, 1983).

In this chapter we explore in more detail the picture portrayed by the summary statistics published by the Census Bureau. First, we briefly review the history of Indians and of Indian policy in Wisconsin. Second, we examine the household structure of the American Indian population, the prevalence of poverty among different types of households, and the impact of transfers on the reduction of poverty. Finally, we suggest ways to improve efforts to reduce the poverty and economic disadvantages faced by Indians.

The American Indian Population of Wisconsin

Although there is no way to know for sure how many Indians lived in what are now the contiguous forty-eight states of the United States, anthropologists and historical demographers have estimated that between 1 million and 15 million indigenous people resided here in 1492. Most scholars accept a figure of around 5 million (Thornton forthcoming). By 1900, the indigenous population of this country had declined to 237,000, or less than 5% of its size at the time of Columbus, if we accept the 5 million estimate. This drastic population decline was largely due to the introduction of European diseases such as smallpox and measles into a population which had not previously been exposed and therefore had no resistance. War, genocide, and forced migration also helped reduce the size of the indigenous population. All these forces were active in Wisconsin, so it is reasonable to assume that the size of the indigenous population in Wisconsin suffered a similar drastic decline.

At the beginning of this century, the American Indian population of Wisconsin was approximately 8,372 (Stanley and Thomas 1978). Its size has grown considerably in the past few decades. By 1960 it had grown to 14,297, in 1970 it was 18,924, and in 1980 it was 29,497 (Passel and Berman 1985). Thus, the Indian population grew by 32% between 1960 and 1970, and 56% between 1970 and 1980. This population growth was due to higher fertility than that of the general Wisconsin population, to improvements in efforts to enumerate Indians, and to "recruitment" into the Indian population through changes in self-identification (i.e., some people who did not classify themselves as Indians in the 1960 or 1970 censuses changed their self-identification in a later census). Although it is impossible to know how many people in Wisconsin changed their designation, evidence indicates that recruitment was not a significant factor in Wisconsin and other traditional Indian areas, compared to states in which Indians have not traditionally lived.[2]

Among the major Indian groups residing in Wisconsin, some (the Menominee, Chippewa, Winnebago, and Potawatomi) were living here prior to the arrival of Europeans, whereas others (the Stockbridge Munsee and Oneida) were forced to move here from the eastern United States (Lurie, 1980). Other Indian groups resided in parts of Wisconsin prior to the arrival of Europeans but were forced to move west of the Mississippi in order to open up Wisconsin for white settlement. These groups include the Santee Sioux, Sauk, Fox, Kickapoo, Iowa, Illinois, Ottawa, and Miami Indians (Thornton forthcoming). Not all of these groups were involved in formal bargaining and cession of lands to the U.S. government, however. Some simply abandoned their lands in Wisconsin. The U.S. government did force the Chippewa, Sioux, Menominee, Winnebago, Sauk, Fox, Ottawa, and Potawatomi to cede land through formal agreements. Between 1804 and 1842, these groups of Indians were forced to give up most of what later became the state of Wisconsin (Lurie 1980). The original plan was for most of the Indians in Wisconsin to be relocated in Oklahoma, Minnesota, and other areas west of the Mississippi, but because of various factors, not all Indians moved, and the groups that currently live in Wisconsin were eventually granted reservations in the state. Although only one-third of Wisconsin's Indians currently live on these reservations, most nonreservation Indians are former reservation residents or descendants of Indians who lived on these reservations.

The Role of the Federal, State, and Tribal Governments in Indian Affairs

Just as it is impossible to understand the current situation of American Indians in Wisconsin without at least some knowledge of the history of the Indian population of the state, it is also neccessary to understand the complex roles of the federal, state, and tribal governments. These roles have evolved over time through treaties between the United States and different Indian tribes, Supreme Court decisions, and legislation passed by Congress. The early policy of the British colonial governments and the U.S. government toward American Indians was based on the doctrine of discovery. This doctrine recognized the "use rights" of Indian groups and their ability to transfer title of the land to the colonial government and to the U.S. government. Neither individuals nor states were given the right to acquire land from Indians, and the U.S. government assumed the responsibility for "protecting" Indians from non-Indians. The predominant role of the federal as opposed to state governments in dealing with Indian affairs was codified in Article I, section 8 of the U.S. Constitution. Treaties were the primary mechanisms for reaching agreement between the U.S. government and Indian tribes until 1871, when the federal government ceased dealing with tribes through treaties and began to deal with them through statutes.

The most important Supreme Court decision regarding American Indians was written by Chief Justice John Marshall in 1831. Marshall referred to Indian tribes as "domestic dependent nations," which did not relinquish sovereignty over their lands when they put themselves under the control of a "stronger nation" by treaty. In addition, Marshall likened the role of the federal government to that of a guardian protecting the property of a ward. This was interpreted by many federal officials over the years as giving them the right to control the lives and decisions of individual Indians. However, it also excluded the states from exerting such control and provided the legal basis for tribes to perform many of the functions that state and local governments perform, including police protection, civil and criminal matters, and taxation. This decision and subsequent decisions have been used to justify current Indian practices as diverse as bingo (e.g., the Oneida bingo operation near Milwaukee), Chippewa hunting and fishing rights, and the license plates for cars issued by the Menominee tribe. In addition, Indian land held in trust by the federal government is not subject to taxation by the states. Not all Indian groups have used all of their rights, so the state and local governments perform roles on some reservations that are performed by tribal governments on other reservations.

Although the reservation system, institutionalized by treaties and upheld by the Supreme Court, was seen as the final solution to the Indian problem, it was not long before white Americans and the American government became dissatisfied with this arrangement.[3] Near the end of the nineteenth century, the federal government proposed and began to implement allotment policy through two major pieces of legislation—the Dawes Act and the Curtis Act. The purpose of allotment policy was to integrate Indians into American society through breaking reservations into individually owned parcels of land and opening up "surplus" reservation land to white settlement. Once Indians owned individual parcels of land, they were expected to become farmers—the prevailing occupational role model of the time. Also, alloted land would be subject to taxation, and Indians living on alloted land would become citizens of the United States and of the state in which they lived. Unfortunately, the land on which many Indians lived was not suitable for farming. Also, the 160-acre tracts which most Indians received quickly became divided among many people through inheritance. The major consequence of allotment policy was to deprive Indians of land. Nationally, Indians lost about three-quarters of the land they controlled prior to allotment; in Wisconsin, Indians lost approximately one half of their land (Lurie 1980).

Allotment policy was not uniformly administered across Wisconsin. The Menominee were most successful in retaining their land, but there is non-

Indian owned land within the boundaries of the Menominee reservation just as there is within all of the other reservations in Wisconsin. After the allotment legislation and the turn of the century, World War I captured the attention of the nation, and there was little legislative activity involving Indians. The 1920s, however, produced two significant pieces of legislation. The Snyder Act of 1921 provided authorization for appropriations by Congress to provide a number of services and types of aid to Indians including general support, "civilization," education, health services, economic assistance with development, agricultural development, buildings, Indian police, and general expenses associated with the administration of Indian affairs. All Indians, regardless of whether they lived on allotments or on trust land, were made citizens of the United States through the Citizenship Act of 1924. It is ironic that the original inhabitants of the United States were not granted citizenship in this country until well into the twentieth century.

The 1930s also produced a number of significant pieces of Indian legislation. The Johnson O'Malley Act of 1934 authorized the federal government to contract with other organizations, including state agencies, to provide services (including medical services and education) to Indians. Through the Johnson O'Malley Act, states began to play an important role in health care and education. Many Indian students began to attend public schools, especially in states such as Wisconsin and Oklahoma, where allotments had led to the geographic intermixture of Indians and non-Indians. Public schools were given, and continue to be given, per capita payments for each Indian student who is in attendance.

Gradually, policymakers came to the conclusion that allotment policy was disastrous for most Indians, and the United States reversed its position on the assimilation of Indians to one promoting the distinctiveness of Indian life. The Indian Reorganization Act of 1934 restored some reservation land and provided mechanisms through which tribes could organize governments and exert limited control over their own affairs. Many tribes reorganized their system of government under the provisions of this act. However, after World War II, the federal government again reversed itself and moved to the position that complete integration was the final solution, and in the 1950s began a policy of terminating the special legal status of Indian tribes. Another feature of termination policy was relocation of Indians from traditional rural areas to urban areas, where they were expected to adopt the prevailing occupational role of that era—the urban industrial worker. Existing evidence indicates that termination would have been disastrous for most Indians, but that relocation, later renamed employment assistance and made completely voluntary, was beneficial to some, but not all, Indians (Sorkin 1971). One of the first tribes to be terminated was the Menominee, who, after years of fighting, finally had their special legal status restored.

Most Indians were opposed to termination, and in the 1970s the federal government again reversed itself with passage of the Indian Self-Determination Act of 1975, which transferred responsibility to the tribes for many functions that had previously been handled by the federal government, including the provision of health services. This brought about the current phase of U.S.-Indian relations that is commonly referred to as Indian self-determination. Since 1975 most tribes have assumed more and more responsibilities for themselves.

The various policies of the U.S. government toward American Indians since the American Revolution have had two major sets of consequences for the poverty and well-being of Wisconsin Indians. First, removal, allotment, termination, and self-determination produced the current geographical distribution of American Indians in Wisconsin which is reflected in the map, figure 10.1. This map also shows the amount of land guaranteed to the different Indian groups through treaties with the U.S. government, and the amount of land they controlled around 1980. As we pointed out above, prior to the early 1800s all of Wisconsin belonged to these and other Indian groups. The location, as well as the amount of land controlled by Indians, is important, since most reservations in Wisconsin are, by design, far away from the major centers of population and commerce in the state. Second, the accumulated impact of federal policy reversals, Supreme Court decisions, federal legislation, and varying amounts of tribal governmental activism across tribes has led to a very complex system of intergovernmental relations. For example, in Wisconsin many tribes operate their own health clinics; for other tribes, health care is provided directly by the Indian Health Service, which is a federal agency. In order to receive free health care (promised in most treaties), nonreservation Indians must return to a reservation or Indian Health Service clinic. At the same time, the state of Wisconsin works with Indian tribes to administer AFDC programs for Indians living on trust land and provides public assistance through the Relief to Needy Indian People program (RNIP). In some other states, state governments refuse to provide public assistance to Indians living on trust land, and the Bureau of Indian Affairs provides such assistance. Indians who leave reservations in Wisconsin for urban areas, and need assistance, find that they face bureaucracies which operate much differently from the one to which they are accustomed on their reservations.

American Indian Household Structure and Poverty

Given the reduction in land base that Indians have experienced, the inconsistencies and reversals in federal Indian policy, and the complex set of current governmental arrangements and relationships, it is perhaps not surprising that poverty continues to be a significant problem for Indians in Wisconsin.

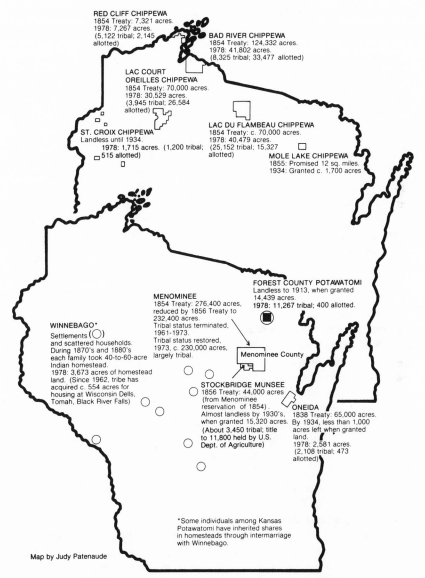

RED CLIFF CHIPPEWA
1854 Treaty: 7,321 acres.
1978: 7,267 acres.
(5,122 tribal; 2,145
allotted)

BAD RIVER CHIPPEWA
1854 Treaty: 124,332 acres.
1978: 41,802 acres.
(8,325 tribal; 33,477 allotted)

LAC COURT
OREILLES CHIPPEWA
1854 Treaty: 70,000 acres.
1978: 30,529 acres.
(3,945 tribal; 26,584
allotted)

ST. CROIX CHIPPEWA
Landless until 1934.
1978: 1,715 acres. (1,200 tribal;
515 allotted)

LAC DU FLAMBEAU CHIPPEWA
1854 Treaty: c. 70,000 acres.
1978: 40,479 acres.
(25,152 tribal; 15,327
allotted)

MOLE LAKE CHIPPEWA
1855: Promised 12 sq. miles.
1934: Granted c. 1,700 acres

FOREST COUNTY POTAWATOMI
Landless to 1913, when granted
14,439 acres.
1978: 11,267 tribal; 400 allotted.

MENOMINEE
1854 Treaty: 276,400 acres,
reduced by 1856 Treaty to
232,400 acres.
Tribal status terminated,
1961-1973.
Tribal status restored,
1973, c. 230,000 acres,
largely tribal.

Menominee County

WINNEBAGO*
Settlements (○)
and scattered households.
During 1870's and 1880's
each family took 40-to-60-acre
Indian homestead.
1978: 3,673 acres of homestead
land. (Since 1962, tribe has
acquired c. 554 acres for
housing at Wisconsin Dells,
Tomah, Black River Falls)

STOCKBRIDGE MUNSEE
1856 Treaty: 44,000 acres
(from Menominee
reservation of 1854).
Almost landless by 1930's,
when granted 15,320 acres.
(About 3,450 tribal; title
to 11,800 held by U.S.
Dept. of Agriculture)

ONEIDA
1838 Treaty: 65,000 acres.
By 1934, less than 1,000
acres left when granted
land.
1978: 2,581 acres.
(2,108 tribal; 473
allotted)

*Some individuals among Kansas
Potawatomi have inherited shares
in homesteads through intermarriage
with Winnebago.

Map by Judy Patenaude

Fig. 10.1. Distribution of American Indians in Wisconsin. (Source: Reprinted by permission of the State Historical Society of Wisconsin from Nancy Oestreich Lurie, *Wisconsin Indians*, 1980.)

193

In order to understand better the nature of Indian poverty, we examine it in the context of an analysis of household structure. Although an individual's economic well-being is obviously related to the state of the surrounding economy, the family constitutes an important mediating agency. In fact, family and household structure is one of the most important factors in understanding poverty and developing programs to eliminate or ameliorate it. Further, anthropological research suggests that the family is an even more important feature of Indian life than of the lives of other groups (Wax 1971).

We therefore consider poverty among Wisconsin's native Americans in terms of their family living arrangements. First, we simply describe the prevalence of different types of family living arrangements among American Indians in Wisconsin. We then compare their distribution of household types to that of American Indians elsewhere, as well as to the household distributions for other ethnic groups in Wisconsin. Next we consider, for each of the ethnic groups, the extent of poverty among different household types. We then examine the impact of transfer payments on the alleviation of poverty by house-hold type in Wisconsin.

Patterns of Household Structure among Indians and Other Groups

We borrow a scheme of household types utilized by Sweet (1984). This classification includes eight different types and distinguishes between family and nonfamily households. Family households are represented by (1) married couples without children, (2) married couples with children, (3) mother-child families, (4) father-child families, and (5) other families; the nonfamily household types include (6) men living alone, (7) women living alone, and (8) multiperson nonfamily households.

We define an Indian household as one in which the household head is Indian.[4] A Hispanic household is one in which the household head is Hispanic but not Indian.[5] For white households the household head is white but not Hispanic, and for black households the household head is black but not Hispanic.

Our analysis of American Indians outside Wisconsin is restricted to those residing in what have been called the traditional "Indian states." Historically, these nineteen states have had relatively large concentrations of native Americans. In addition, demographic analysis by Passel and Berman (1985) suggests that Indian self-identification has generally remained consistent in these areas. That is, in these Indian states (IS) less growth in the Indian population has occurred by way of changes in self-identification or recruitment. Since these new "recruits" to the Indian population may differ substantially from Indians who maintain more consistent racial identification, in this analysis we have chosen to focus on the Indian states in lieu of the national aggregate as a whole. The nineteen Indian states include Alaska, Arizona, Idaho, Michigan,

Minnesota, Montana, Nebraska, Nevada, New Mexico, New York, North Carolina, North Dakota, Oklahoma, Oregon, South Dakota, Utah, Washington, Wisconsin, and Wyoming.

With these definitions in mind, we can now consider table 10.1, which shows for each group the distribution of household types in 1980. The table indicates that 77% of native Americans in Wisconsin live in family households. Married couples with children represent the single most prevalent household type (37%). Mother-child families (where there is no husband present) are the next most prevalent (17%), followed by married couples without children (14%). The other household types each constitute less than 10% of the distribution, while the smallest group is represented by the father-child household type (where there is no wife present).

This distribution of household types for Indians in Wisconsin may be compared to that for Indians in the Indian states in 1980. As shown in table 10.1, in Indian states 79% of Indian households are family households. Thus, family households are 2% more prevalent (i.e., nonfamily households are 2% less prevalent) among IS Indians than among Wisconsin Indians. As for the particular household categories, one difference is that the Wisconsin distribution has a slightly greater percentage of mother-child families than is the case in the Indian states (17% versus 14%). Further, Indian married couples without

Table 10.1. Distribution of Households by Type, Race, and Residence, 1980

Household Type	Wisconsin				IS Indian
	White	Hispanic	Black	Indian	
Family households	71%	79%	73%	77%	79%
Married couple, no children	28	15	11	14	17
Married couple, with children	32	47	25	37	38
Mother-child	3	13	28	17	14
Father-child	2	1	1	1	2
Other family	5	4	7	8	8
Nonfamily households	29	21	27	23	21
Men living alone	11	8	11	9	9
Women living alone	15	8	12	9	9
Multiperson	4	5	4	5	3
N	390	414	397	396	12,844

Source: Computations from the 1980 public use microdata samples, U.S. Bureau of the Census.

Notes: Indian household: Householder is Indian. Hispanic household: Householder is Hispanic but not Indian. Black household: Householder is black but not Hispanic. White household: Householder is white but not Hispanic. IS refers to the Indian states, which include Alaska, Arizona, Idaho, Michigan, Minnesota, Montana, Nebraska, New Mexico, New York, Nevada, North Carolina, North Dakota, Oklahoma, Oregon, South Dakota, Utah, Washington, Wisconsin, and Wyoming.

children are less prevalent in Wisconsin than in the Indian states (14% versus 17%). The other household categories, however, do not show significant differences between the two groups.

We can also compare the Wisconsin distribution of Indian household types to the distributions for other groups in Wisconsin, particularly whites, blacks, and Hispanics. These figures are also shown in Table 10.1. From the table it is evident that though the percentage of Wisconsin Indians in family households is two points less than the IS percentage, Wisconsin Indians nonetheless have proportionately more family households than either whites or blacks (6% more than whites and 4% more than blacks). However, Hispanics are the group that is most highly represented by family households (79%).

The percentage of households that are mother-child families varies dramatically by race. The highest level is found among blacks (28%) while the lowest level, for whites, is much smaller (3%).[6] Indians and Hispanics are intermediate between these two extremes, though mother-child families are more prevalent among Indians than among Hispanics (17% versus 13%).

There are also substantial racial differences in the proportion of households that are married couples without children. Again, the extremes are evident among whites and blacks (28% versus 11%), whereas Indians and Hispanics are intermediate (14% and 15% respectively). Some racial variation pertains as well to married couples with children. For this category, blacks have the lowest percentage (25%) while Hispanics have the highest (47%). Whites, Wisconsin Indians, and IS Indians are intermediate (32%, 37%, and 38% respectively). The percentages for the other household categories do not exhibit great racial variation—in part perhaps because they are smaller to begin with—but it is probably worth noting that individuals living alone (i.e., men living alone and women living alone) are most prevalent among whites and blacks.

Poverty Rates and Household Structure

Given that some of these household categories represent only a small proportion of households, we utilize a simpler classification that may be more immediately relevant to our discussion of poverty rates. So in the following, four household types are recognized: (1) families with children and nonaged male heads; (2) families with children and nonaged female heads (with no husband present); (3) all childless households with nonaged heads; and (4) all households with aged heads (65 or more years of age).

In accordance with Danziger and Nichols-Casebolt's definitions (see chapter 7), two types of poverty are examined here. The first is pretransfer poverty. Households are said to be pretransfer poor when their total household money income from private sources falls below the poverty line that is applicable to a household of their type (where the thresholds are differenti-ated by age, sex, number of children, and farm/nonfarm residence). Pre-transfer poverty does not count transfer payments (i.e., social security and public assistance incomes) in determining whether the household falls below the poverty line. Posttransfer poverty, on the other hand, refers to a household which falls below its poverty line after including transfers.

Pretransfer and posttransfer poverty rates by household type are shown in table 10.2 for each of the two Indian groups. Across all households in 1979 the pretransfer poverty rate was 35% among Wisconsin Indians and the post-transfer rate was 23%. In the Indian states both the pretransfer and the post-transfer poverty rates were higher: 38% and 30%.

Except for nonaged female-headed households with children, the pre-transfer poverty rate for each of the household types is lower in Wisconsin than in the Indian states. In the case of nonaged female-headed households with children the rates are about equal (i.e., about 65%) between the two areas. Across Wisconsin and the Indian states, there are also some similarities in the rank ordering of the pretransfer poverty levels by household types. In both groups, aged households and nonaged female-headed households with

Table 10.2. Poverty Rates among American Indian Households by Household Type and Resi-dence, 1979

Household Type	Indian States		Wisconsin	
	Pretransfer	Posttransfer	Pretransfer	Posttransfer
Nonaged male-headed with children	25%	22%	21%	17%
Nonaged female-headed with children	64	56	65[a]	49[a]
Other nonaged households	31	25	25	17
Aged households	71	40	60[a]	17[a]
All households	38	30	35	23

Source: Computations from the 1980 public use microdata samples, U.S. Bureau of the Census.

Notes: Pretransfer poverty is the percentage of households that are below the poverty line before counting the social security and public assistance income of the household head. Post-transfer poverty is the percentage of households that are below the poverty line after counting social security and public assistance of the household head. Indian states include Alaska, Ari-zona, Idaho, Michigan, Minnesota, Montana, Nebraska, New Mexico, New York, Nevada, North Carolina, North Dakota, Oklahoma, Oregon, South Dakota, Utah, Washington, Wisconsin, and Wyoming. Transfer income was computed as the sum of the social security and public assistance incomes of the household head. Transfers to other members of the household were counted as pretransfer income.

[a]These poverty rates are based on samples of fewer than 100 people and thus have large standard errors.

children are the poorest household types. Other nonaged households are the next poorest in rank-order terms, although in terms of rates their poverty levels are less than half of those for nonaged female-headed households with children. Nonaged male-headed households with children have the least pre-transfer poverty.

After transfers, poverty by household type is in each case lower in Wisconsin. Posttransfer poverty is 49% among nonaged female-headed households with children in Wisconsin and 56% in the Indian states. While this group clearly has the highest posttransfer poverty in both groups, the pattern for the other household types differs greatly between the groups. For each of the remaining household types, posttransfer poverty is only 17% in the case of Wisconsin Indians. In the Indian states, posttransfer poverty is 22% for nonaged male-headed households with children, 25% for other nonaged households, and 40% for aged households.

We now compare Indian poverty to that of other ethnic groups in Wisconsin as reported by Danziger and Nichols-Casebolt (see table 7.4 in this volume). Because our results are for households while theirs are for individuals, the two sets of poverty rates are not strictly comparable. In general, however, it seems that Wisconsin Indians have rates of pretransfer and posttransfer poverty that are greater than those for whites but roughly similar to those for other minorities. In the case of nonaged male-headed households with children, pretransfer poverty among Wisconsin Indians somewhat exceeds that for nonwhites and Hispanics. For nonaged female-headed households with children, the pretransfer poverty rate for Indians is slightly higher than that for nonwhites but slightly lower than that for Hispanics. For aged households as well, Indian pretransfer poverty is intermediate between that of nonwhites and Hispanics. (Danziger and Nichols-Casebolt do not report results by ethnic group for nonaged childless households.) Posttransfer poverty rates for Wisconsin Indians in nonaged male-headed households appear to be slightly higher than those for other minorities, but nonaged female-headed Indian households have lower rates than other minorities.

We should note, however, that our computation of transfer income in Wisconsin was restricted to the social security and public assistance incomes of the household head. Not included in our figures are the transfers received by other household members, such as spouses and surviving children. In the case of the Indian states, we computed total family transfer income, but for Wisconsin, our figures tend to understate the real extent of pretransfer poverty, because transfers to other household members are counted as the pretransfer income of the household. We can only point out here that the Wisconsin pretransfer figures should be best viewed as lower-bound estimates.

Poverty on Major Indian Reservations in Wisconsin

Poverty rates are generally believed to be greater among Indians residing in reservation areas than among Indians elsewhere. Since our data sources do not allow us to clearly distinguish between reservation and nonreservation Indians, we cannot fully address this issue here. We briefly consider poverty among reservation Indians, however, by referring to published census figures for the four largest reservations in Wisconsin: Oneida, Menominee, Lac du Flambeau, and Lac Courte Oreilles.

The reservation poverty figures are shown in table 10.3. First of all, for any particular reservation, poverty rates by household and by persons are virtually identical. (This suggests that our comparison above with the Danziger and Nichols-Casebolt figures is not very misleading.) The highest household posttransfer poverty rate is 30% (for Lac Courte Oreilles), which is twice the smallest rate (15% for Menominee).

These figures suggest that poverty rates can vary significantly by tribe. The 17% posttransfer rate for Indians on the Menominee reservation is not so much greater than that across all persons in the United States (cf. table 7.4). On the other hand, the 29% figure for Indians on the Lac Courte Oreilles reservation is about as severe as the relatively high posttransfer poverty among all Indian households in the Indian states (cf. table 10.2). In short, we can conclude that for Wisconsin reservations, simple generalizations about poverty levels are not easily made.

Table 10.3. Poverty Rates among American Indians on Selected Reservations in Wisconsin, 1979

	Lac du Flambeau	Lac Courte Oreilles	Oneida	Menominee
% Persons in posttransfer poverty	25	29	19	17
% Families in posttransfer poverty	24	30	19	15
% Posttransfer poor families that are female-headed	55	49	49	57

Source: U.S. Bureau of the Census, *1980 Census of Population,* PC80-1-C51, table 193, issued 1983.

Note: Here "female-headed families" refers to all families headed by a woman without a husband present; she may be with or without children.

The Impact of Transfers on Poverty among American Indians

Table 10.4 allows us to analyze the impact of transfers on the alleviation of poverty for American Indians in Wisconsin and the Indian states. Column 3 of table 10.4 shows the percentage of pretransfer poor households that are removed from poverty by the receipt of transfer payments. It is computed from the figures in table 10.2 and equals the difference between pre- and posttransfer poverty divided by pretransfer poverty. Another measure of welfare efficacy, the poverty gap, is given in column 4. It is defined as the total number of dollars required to raise all households out of poverty. Column 4 shows the percentage reduction in this poverty gap after transfer payments are included in household incomes. Note that table 10.4 corresponds to table 7.5.

For Wisconsin Indians in nonaged female-headed households with children, table 10.4 indicates that 25% were removed from poverty by the receipt of transfers. These transfers, however, brought about a 56% reduction in the poverty gap for this group. In other words, some of these nonaged female-headed families with children benefited from transfers but not to the point where they were completely removed from poverty. This occurred despite the fact that during 1979 the average of their transfer payments was among the highest (i.e., $3,453 in column 2) for any Wisconsin Indian group, and 82% of them received some transfers (see column 1). In short, Wisconsin Indians in nonaged female-headed households with children are so deeply in poverty that present welfare efforts still leave 49% poor (table 10.2).

Among Wisconsin Indians, nonaged male-headed households with children have the lowest receipt of transfers (32% in column 1), the lowest percentage reduction in poverty (19% in column 3) and the lowest percentage reduction in the poverty gap (33% in column 4). In short, transfers are clearly the least effective in ameliorating the poverty of this group. As for Wisconsin Indians who are in other nonaged households which are pretransfer poor, 56% receive some transfers, though the average amount is the lowest across the Wisconsin Indian household types ($2,855). For them transfer payments reduce poverty by 32% and the poverty gap by 50%.

The welfare system is most effective in ameliorating the poverty of Wisconsin Indians in aged households. The poverty gap is reduced dramatically, by 88%, and fully 72% of households are removed from poverty by transfers. Accordingly, transfer payments are almost universal (94%) as well as being the highest among any Wisconsin Indian household type ($3,542).

Before proceeding further, we need to point out that as in table 10.2, transfer income in Wisconsin in table 10.4 was computed as the sum of the social security and public assistance incomes of only the household head. The reader should keep in mind that our Wisconsin figures slightly understate the

Table 10.4. The Receipt and Antipoverty Effect of Cash Transfers among American Indian Households by Residence and Household Type, 1979

Household Type	Percentage of Pretransfer Poor Receiving Transfers (1)	Average Annual Amount of Transfers (2)	Percentage of Pretransfer Poor Removed from Poverty by Transfers (3)	Percentage Reduction in Poverty Gap (4)
	Wisconsin			
Nonaged male-headed with children	32%	$3,142	19%	33%
Nonaged female-headed with children[a]	82	3,453	25	56
Other nonaged households	56	2,855	32	50
Aged households[a]	94	3,542	72	88
All households	68	3,314	34	56
	Indian States			
Nonaged male-headed with children	35%	$3,053	12%	22%
Nonaged female-headed with children	62	3,370	13	37
Other nonaged households	49	2,918	19	35
Aged households	92	3,809	44	70
All households	59	3,354	21	40

Source: Computations from the 1980 public use microdata samples, U.S. Bureau of the Census.

Notes: Column 2 refers to all recipient households. Column 3 is computed from table 10.2 and equals the difference between pre- and posttransfer poverty divided by pretransfer poverty. Column 4 equals the difference between the pre- and posttransfer poverty gaps divided by the pretransfer poverty gap. Transfer income in Wisconsin was computed as the sum of the social security and public assistance incomes of the household head. Transfers to other members of the household were counted as pretransfer income.

[a] These statistics are based on fewer than 100 people and have large standard errors.

percentage of the poor receiving transfers, the average amount of transfers received, and perhaps the percentage reductions in poverty and the poverty gap.

Nonetheless, we will attempt to make some general comparisons of the situation of Indians in Wisconsin to those in the Indian states as reported in the bottom panel of table 10.4. Although the Wisconsin figures for the percentage reduction in poverty may be slightly understated, columns 3 and 4 seem to indicate that for each household type the proportionate reduction in poverty and in the poverty gap is larger in Wisconsin than in the Indian states.

Across all Indian households in Wisconsin in 1979 the percentage reduction in poverty is 34%, while in the Indian states it is 21%. The percentage reduction in the poverty gap is 56% in Wisconsin and 40% in the Indian states. But differences in the average amount of transfers do not appear to account for this difference in efficacy (unless the understatement of average transfers is very large in Wisconsin). For nonaged households with children the average amount of transfers is only slightly higher in Wisconsin, and for childless households and aged households the average amounts of transfers are higher in the Indian states. In fact, over all Indian households, the average transfer amount in Wisconsin is actually $40 lower than in the Indian states ($3,314 versus $3,354).

A better explanation might be that transfers are somewhat more widespread in Wisconsin (even though this figure is understated). That is, households receiving some transfers are 9% more numerous in Wisconsin than in the Indian states (i.e., 68% versus 59%). Also, our earlier results in table 10.2 showed that pretransfer poverty is slightly lower in Wisconsin to begin with (35% across all households in Wisconsin but 38% across all households in the Indian states). An additional factor that might be involved here is that more Indian transfer payments in Wisconsin may go to the Indian poor. That is, column 2 of table 10.4 refers not to the pretransfer poor per se but rather to all Indian households who receive any transfers. Perhaps the transfer system in the Indian states is not highly targeted to poor (rather than nonpoor) Indians. All of these factors may be instrumental in explaining the greater transfer efficacy in Wisconsin.

Danziger and Nichols-Casebolt report that in Wisconsin 42% of pretransfer poor persons were removed from poverty by transfers in 1979 (see table 7.5). Our results in table 10.4 indicate that the corresponding figure for Wisconsin Indian households is 34%. Thus, it seems that the effectiveness of transfer payments in eliminating poverty is greater for the Wisconsin general population than for Wisconsin Indian households. To a lesser extent, this same conclusion seems to apply to the efficacy of transfers in reducing the poverty gap. For Indians in Wisconsin, our results show a 56% reduction across all households, whereas in table 7.5 the corresponding figure for the Wisconsin population is about 59%.

Certainly one reason for this difference is the higher average transfer income for the Wisconsin general population; they receive $4,231 on average while for Wisconsin Indians the average transfer income is only $3,314 (although note here again that this latter figure is slightly understated). Probably more important, however, is the initial difference in the pretransfer poverty rates. Since most of the Wisconsin population is white, the pretransfer poverty rate is much higher for Wisconsin Indians than for the general population of Wisconsin.

In terms of the particular household types and ethnic groups, no obvious patterns are apparent. For example, although in our discussion of table 10.2 it did seem that whites have lower rates of pretransfer poverty, it does not appear to be the case that transfer payments are generally more efficacious in ameliorating their poverty. So for nonaged male-headed households with children, the percentage reduction in poverty is about 15% for whites but 14% for nonwhites and 19% for Indians. The percentage reduction in the poverty gap for this household type is 19% for whites, 22% for nonwhites, 33% for Indians, and 41% for Hispanics. For nonaged female-headed households with children, the percentage reduction in poverty is 28% for whites, 14% for nonwhites, 12% for Hispanics, and 25% for Indians. The percentage reduction in the poverty gap for this group is about 59% for whites, 55% for nonwhites, 45% for Hispanics, and 55% for Indians.

Policy Recommendations

Our analyses indicate that households headed by single mothers constitute a substantial proportion of the poor Indian households in the state. Consequently, the recommendations for improving the economic status of these families in the general population would also benefit Indians. (See chapter 7, pp. 148–50.)

However, poverty rates are also high among other types of Indian households. To make these households self-sufficient, additional efforts are needed in four areas: (1) education; (2) job training; (3) health care; and (4) job opportunities. Efforts in the first three areas would lead to improvements in the productivity of individual Indians, and efforts in the last area would provide Indians the opportunity to be productive.

Statistics from the 1980 census illustrate the ways in which the educational attainment of Indians in Wisconsin lags behind that of white residents. In 1980, 70% of the white people aged 25 and older in Wisconsin had finished high school, whereas only 55% of Indian people aged 25 and older had finished high school (U.S. Bureau of the Census, *1980 Census of Population,* PC80-1-D51, 1983). Ninety-three percent of whites aged 16 and 17 were attending school in 1980, whereas only 77% of Indians in the same age group were attending school. For those aged 18 and 19, 54% of whites were attending school, compared to only 34% of Indians; for those aged 20 and 21, 33% of whites were attending school, compared to a mere 15% of Indians (U.S. Bureau of the Census, *1980 Census of Population,* PC80-1-D51, 1983). These figures suggest that the educational gap between Indians and whites is unlikely to disappear for some time. They also suggest that we have not yet solved the problem of retaining Indian students in the educational system, especially in those crucial years at the end of high school and the beginning of college.

The major programs that provide aid for the education of Indian students are the Johnson O'Malley program, the Title IV program, and higher education assistance. The Johnson O'Malley and Title IV programs provide financial aid, counseling, and other services to primary and secondary school students, while higher education assistance makes it possible for American Indian students to attend colleges and universities. Each of these programs has been cut substantially in recent years, and the Johnson O'Malley program has been targeted for elimination in the near future. Instead of cutting Indian educational aids, more attention should be directed toward evaluating existing programs and to funding the kinds of initiatives that have proved successful in retaining Indian students and ensuring that they graduate.

Another way to prepare American Indians for success in the labor market is through job training. Because of the isolation of many American Indians on reservations and in rural areas, they are less likely to have access to job training opportunities than are most other people in Wisconsin. Improved job training opportunities for isolated Indians are important in two ways: (1) in producing a skilled labor force that would help attract businesses to build and invest in reservation areas; and (2) in providing Indians with marketable skills should they decide to move to urban areas, where they would be competing with individuals who have had many more opportunities.

Improving the health status of Indians in Wisconsin would also enhance their ability to compete in the labor market. A recent assessment of Indian health concluded that the overall health status of American Indians has improved substantially in recent years, but that the health of Indians is still not comparable to that of the general U.S. population (U.S. Congress, Office of Technology Assessment 1986). Statistics produced by the Bemidji, Minnesota, office of the Indian Health Service (the office whose responsibilities include Wisconsin) showed that the age-adjusted death rate for American Indians in its service area was 943.5 per 100,000 compared to 568.2 per 100,000 for all races in the United States. Unfortunately, the Indian Health

Service is under pressure to cut back. Given that progress has been made, but there is still obvious need, thought should be given to increasing rather than reducing expenditures on Indian health. Such expenditures would to a large extent pay for themselves through enhancing the productivity of Indian workers.

An educated, trained, and healthy labor force is of little utility unless there are opportunities to work. Some Indians have dealt with the lack of opportunities on reservations by moving to urban areas. At one time, as we pointed out above, this strategy was promoted and supported by the federal government. In more recent times, many reservations in Wisconsin have attempted to create job opportunities on reservations. This is quite difficult given the location of the Indian reservations in the state. Most efforts at economic development have concentrated on tourism and recreation. There has been little careful research on the effectiveness and impact of these efforts, but what little evidence exists indicates that they have been successful. Bingo parlors, hotels, and motels provide not only a source of revenue but also a source of employment for tribal members. One of the most successful efforts has been the Oneida hotel and bingo complex. A good deal of this success is because this complex is located in the Green Bay area, near the major airport serving Green Bay. This gives the Oneida operation an advantage over other similar operations such as that of the Lac du Flambeau band, whose reservation is not near a major population center.

More cooperation between the state government, tribal governments, and the private sector is needed. However, unemployed and poor Indians cannot wait for jobs, so expenditures to create public jobs on reservations should be increased. A public jobs program would promote individual economic self-sufficiency while providing needed work in depressed areas. In addition, the jobs would give work experience and a work history to Indians who eventually seek jobs off the reservation.

Improving the effectiveness of the transfer system for families headed by single mothers and promoting the economic self-sufficiency of all Indians requires more extensive cooperation among the tribal, federal, and state governments. Wisconsin has done a better job than most states in responding to needs in the Indian community. The federal government, on the other hand, seems uninterested in cooperative ventures when the state government is involved but is willing to participate in cooperative ventures with tribal governments, such as tribal-operated health clinics, when these ventures are mandated by law. The future would seem to demand a more flexible approach on the part of federal agencies.

Any policies adopted by the state of Wisconsin or the federal government to assist Indians in the state should recognize and be rooted in the fundamental right of Indian self-determination. Although the federal government has reversed itself from time to time, there is a firm basis for Indian self-determination in the U.S. Constitution and the 1831 Supreme Court decision affirming the limited sovereignty of Indian nations. The basic principle of self-determination is that Indian tribes should take the responsibility for establishing and administering policies and programs designed to improve the economic well-being of Indian people. With self-determination in mind, the recent struggle over hunting and fishing rights in Wisconsin takes on a larger significance that has perhaps been ignored by both Indians and non-Indians in the state. Although the original intention of the treaties was to guarantee the use of hunting and fishing as a means of subsistence, it is not clear how important these rights are to Indian well-being at this point. Most Indians are primarily dependent on jobs and other sources of income just as are most other Americans. What is clear is the symbolic significance of hunting and fishing. Indians have found over the years that a failure to exercise their rights has led to a steady erosion in their ability to control their own destiny. Exercising hunting and fishing rights is a symbolic way of emphasizing the distinctiveness of the Indian situation and affirming the importance of self-determination.

NOTES

This research was supported by a grant from the Wisconsin State Department of Health and Social Services. Jiwon Jeon provided computational assistance.

1. The most recent information we have on Indians in Wisconsin comes from the 1980 census. More recently collected data, such as the Current Population Surveys, do not have enough Indians in the sample to permit state-level analyses.

2. There is a great deal of controversy over how to enumerate Indians and how many Indians actually live in the United States. For example, the U.S. Bureau of the Census counted 2,377 Indians on the Menominee Reservation of Wisconsin in 1980, whereas the Bureau of Indian Affairs listed its service population as 3,384, and the Menominee had 6,182 on their tribal roll (U.S. Congress, Office of Technology Assessment 1986). Although some of the enrolled Menominees live off the reservation, the Menominee felt that the census was a serious undercount of their resident population and requested a special census which was scheduled for this year. Another aspect of the problem is that different organizations use different definitions of who is an Indian. Although the Bureau of the Census allows self-identification, the Bureau of Indian Affairs requires 1/4 blood quantum (e.g., an individual with one full-blood [1/4 blood quantum] Chippewa grandparent and three white grandparents is 1/4 Chippewa; one of his parents is 1/2 Chippewa), and the Menominee tribe requires proof of descent from a previously enrolled Menominee.

3. The reservation system was used as a model by the South African government to establish homelands for its indigenous population. One major difference between the U.S. and South African situations was that the size of the indigenous population in South Africa was, and continues to be, much larger than the size of the white popula-

tion, whereas in the United States, the indigenous population is only 0.6% of the total population. It is interesting to speculate on what would have happened in the United States if the indigenous population were larger than the white population, or if the indigenous population had not declined so precipitously.

4. Unfortunately, this procedure ignores Indian women who reside in households with non-Indian heads. Including these households would increase the proportion of Indian households with couples and slightly decrease the proportion of Indian households below the poverty line. However, doing this would not alter the principal findings in the analysis.

5. Hispanics are generally considered to constitute an ethnic rather than a racial group. By our definitions, a Hispanic may be either white or black but not Indian in racial identification.

6. A comparison of these percentages with those in Census Bureau publications suggests that our estimate of the percentage of white families headed by single mothers may be slightly lower than is actually the case, whereas our estimate of the percentage of white families headed by single fathers may be slightly higher than is actually the case. However, no direct comparison is possible since the Census Bureau does not use the Sweet (1984) typology. As far as can be determined, the other statistics in table 10.1 reflect those in published census data.

11

Hospital Rate Setting: National Evidence and Issues for Wisconsin

JOHN GODDEERIS, BARBARA WOLFE,
DAVID R. RIEMER, AND NANCY CROSS DUNHAM

Introduction

In Wisconsin as elsewhere in the United States, continuing growth of hospital expenditures at rates far in excess of general inflation has focused considerable effort on the development of mechanisms for controlling hospital costs. From 1970 through 1984, hospital expenses per capita grew nationally at an average annual rate that was about 5% faster than the Consumer Price Index. They more than doubled in real terms over the period.[1] Wisconsin's rate of increase was slightly below the national rate until 1980, but then exceeded the national rate as well as those of its neighboring states. These high and increasing rates were reflected in increasing health insurance premiums for Wisconsin's corporations, and for the state, which paid for coverage of state employes (the State Employe Health Plan [SEHP]) and those on medical assistance. These increases led to pressure for change that culminated in a series of actions by the Wisconsin State Legislature in 1983 to attempt to reduce the rate of increase in hospital costs as well as other components of medical care. The Wisconsin legislature embraced a dual strategy of competition and regulation. Among the regulatory provisions in the 1983–85 budget bill was the establishment of a hospital rate-setting commission. The rate-setting commission was charged with setting up a procedure to control hospital rates that would reduce the rate of increase in hospital costs. It operated until 1987 when it was disbanded under a state sunset provision.

Prospective rate setting as an approach to deal with rising hospital costs first attracted widespread attention in the early 1970s (Dowling 1974). The incentives implicit in prospective reimbursement are allegedly superior to

208

those in the retrospective reimbursement of costs, which had been the predominant method by which hospitals were paid. Proponents argue that the necessity to provide services at costs not exceeding predetermined levels (and the possibility of earning a profit if successful) creates incentives for efficient operations almost totally absent under cost reimbursement.

Theoretical arguments about improved incentives were sufficient to motivate a number of states to experiment with rate setting in the 1970s. Continued interest in this approach in the early 1980s derived from some evidence suggesting that prospective rate setting has worked to restrain hospital costs, at least to a degree, while most other regulatory measures have failed.

This chapter provides a review of the empirical evidence that has now accumulated on the effects of rate setting, some analysis of rate-setting options, and a description of the rate-setting program in effect in Wisconsin in 1986. It aims to provide a realistic assessment of what is known while highlighting important gaps in our empirical knowledge.

The term "rate setting" does not refer to a single well-defined process. The designers of a rate-setting system have a number of key choices to make as to its structure, and existing systems vary widely. We attempt to provide insight into these alternative choices. We focus first on the available evidence on the success of rate setting prior to 1983.[2] We then turn to rate-setting options. Next we focus on Wisconsin's program to point up some of the specific issues that must be dealt with if prospective rate setting is to be efficient and equitable, and finally we present a brief discussion of the 1987 sunset of Wisconsin's Rate-Setting Commission.

Rate Setting and Hospital Costs: A Summary of the Evidence

Beginning in the mid-1970s, the adoption of rate setting by a number of states created a kind of natural laboratory in which to study its effects. Those states that did not adopt it, or had not yet as of a particular time, served as a control group against which to compare the experience of those that did. The most persuasive evidence on the effects of rate setting comes from statistical studies that make such comparisons.[3] The general approach of these studies is to use a statistical model (usually multiple regression analysis) to explain differences in hospital expenditures (measured in a variety of ways) across states. Among the explanatory variables included is whether or not the state had adopted rate setting, or in some cases a measure of the strength of the rate-setting program. If the rate-setting variable adds explanatory power to the model, this is taken as evidence of an influence on hospital expenditures.

But a natural experiment of this type falls short of a true controlled experiment in some important ways. Those states that chose to adopt rate setting did so voluntarily. There are therefore problems in separating the effects of rate setting itself from other factors that may have set this group of states apart. It is also the case that the form of the program varies widely from state to state. Grouping all rate-setting states together obscures the effects of individual approaches, but the alternative of considering each state's program (or in some cases, each revision of it) as a distinct entity also has drawbacks. A much smaller number of observations are available for any particular program than for the whole group, limiting the power of statistical tests. And the influences of other characteristics of a state, or of other developments concurrent with rate setting there, are to some extent inevitably confounded with those of the program.

In spite of these difficulties, the accumulated evidence from a number of studies makes it difficult to escape the conclusion that, since 1976, mandatory rate setting has been successful in reducing the rate of increase in hospital expenditures in at least some places. Studies of the post-1976 period that group mandatory programs together consistently find that rate setting is associated with reduced expenditures in a statistically significant way. The best of these studies is perhaps that of Sloan (1983). He estimates that a rate-setting program, after it has been in effect two years, reduces hospital expenses per patient admitted by about 2% per year, with additional reductions gradually tapering off until a long-run total reduction of about 13% is reached. This is not to say that hospital expenses actually fall, but rather that they grow less rapidly than they otherwise would. An important feature of Sloan's model is that this effect is estimated relative to what the particular state's own experience would have been without rate setting, *not* relative to an average non-rate-setting state. This is of interest because states adopting rate setting tend to have had relatively high expenses before instituting the new procedure. It is therefore entirely possible that rate setting can have an effect while expenses remain above those of non-rate-setting states.

Studies by Coelen and Sullivan (1981) and Morrisey, Sloan, and Mitchell (1983) attempt to estimate the effects of individual state programs separately. Coelen and Sullivan find statistically significant negative effects on percentage changes in expenditure per patient treated and per patient day for a number of states (Connecticut, Maryland, Massachusetts, New Jersey, New York, and Rhode Island [per patient only]) and in expenditure per capita in four (Massachusetts, New York, Rhode Island, and Washington). Morrisey, Sloan, and Mitchell use data from Standard Metropolitan Statistical Areas and as a result are limited to studying a smaller number of programs. They find statistically significant effects on expenses per patient day for New Jersey and Washington, and per patient treated and per capita for New Jersey and New York. Their point estimates suggest expenditure-reducing effects for the other programs they considered as well (in Maryland and Massachusetts), but these are not statistically significant. The estimated effects in both of these studies are of roughly the same order of magnitude as those cited for Sloan, above, and sometimes a bit larger.

The evidence on the success of rate setting as a hospital cost-control mechanism in the late 1970s and early 1980s is thus encouraging if not overwhelming, and as noted earlier it stands in rather sharp contrast to the evidence on other regulatory approaches. The effects of controls on capital expenditures (certificate of need laws) have been examined in a number of statistical studies, including those by Sloan and Coelen and Sullivan discussed above (see also Salkever and Bice 1976; Hellinger 1976; Sloan and Steinwald 1980; Joskow 1981; and Ashby 1984). Almost no evidence that these are an effective constraint on the growth of hospital costs has been found. Findings by Sloan and Coelen and Sullivan on the federal Professional Standards Review Organization program, a form of utilization review in which medical providers (peers) look over medical records to see if the care provided was appropriate, are also quite negative (although Ashby finds contrary results). It should be noted, however, that rate setting is frequently applied in conjunction with capital controls and utilization review. It is possible that these latter programs are crucial to its success, but this hypothesis is difficult to test.

Beyond the strong suggestion that rate setting can constrain hospital costs, the statistical studies unfortunately tell us little more about its effects. There has been attention paid to whether savings in per unit costs are eaten up by increases in volume of care, a subject to which we return below. We have some indications of which state programs have had the strongest impact on costs, but little statistical basis for concluding which program features are most important. As to effects on the costs of health care outside the hospital, on the distribution of costs across payers, on access to care, and on quality, even less is known. Given the limitations of available empirical evidence, it is particularly important to attempt to apply economic theory to make predictions about the consequences of various types of rate-setting systems. We turn to this task in the next section.

Unit of Payment and Volume Adjustments

One of the most basic decisions confronting an agency setting hospital rates prospectively is, for what unit of service should rates be set? There are a large number of conceptual possibilities, and in fact experimentation by the states and federal government has already covered a broad range of choices of unit of payment. Possibilities include charges for particular services, per diem (per patient day) rates, per admission rates, diagnosis-specific per case rates, and total hospital budgets. A closely related issue is how to adjust for changes in the volume of services unanticipated at the time rates were set. Special provisions for volume adjustments make it possible to combine different units of payment. For example, a hospital's total budget may be set prospectively, but some adjustment made if the volume of patient days varies from that projected.

The reason the unit-of-payment decision is particularly important—and difficult—is that the final outputs that hospitals produce, those things that consumers truly value, have eluded precise quantitative measurement. Hospitals treat patients, but each patient is in some ways unique, and the quality of treatment can vary widely. The unit of payment chosen is thus inevitably an imperfect proxy for an ideal output measure. Choosing a unit distorts incentives toward manipulating the cost and quantity of that which is rewarded in ways that may not be socially desirable.

Charges for Services

One natural interpretation of the term "rates" is that it refers to the charges hospitals make for specific services. As the total number of different charges at an individual hospital may be many hundreds, a detailed analysis of each one by the rate-setting agency is administratively infeasible. This approach is therefore typically accompanied by some kind of overall budget review, leaving the hospital some flexibility in setting specific charges, perhaps with some special provisions for unforeseen volume changes.

Review of total hospital budgets by the rate-setting agency would require the hospital to submit a set of charges for services and projected service volumes that would, if realized, generate the total budgeted revenue. Effectively, these charges for services then constitute the unit of payment.

In theory, charges are not a particularly attractive choice of unit of payment. While hospital outputs are very difficult to measure, specific services are probably best thought of as inputs into the production of treatments. Paying fixed rates for services creates no incentive to combine these inputs in a way that minimizes the cost of providing treatment of a given quality. The system is not very different from cost reimbursement in that more payments are received if more services are provided. For those services for which the approved charge exceeds the incremental cost, an incentive to expand volume will exist. Thus, a fee schedule (charges) does not have a very attractive set of incentives.

Per Diem and Per Admission Rates

Paying hospitals a fixed rate per patient day is an administratively simple approach to rate setting that has been used in a number of state programs, including those of New York, New Jersey, and Massachusetts. It is obvious that there are substantial differences in the costs associated with different types of patient days. In short, this system creates incentives to increase the volume of days for which the marginal or incremental cost is less than the per diem rate, and to decrease the volume of days for which the opposite is true. Which types of days fall into which class—and probably the strength of the incentive as well—will depend on where the level of the per diem rate is set.

It is generally agreed that extending lengths of stay—keeping patients a day or two after they would have been sent home[4]—is a simple way of generating net revenue in a per diem system, since these additional days are likely to involve relatively little cost to the hospital. Particularly when occupancy is low, such a strategy involves little conflict with other hospital objectives. A hospital might also be expected to try to select patients who can be treated inexpensively on a per day basis, and steer clear of those who are very expensive. Such strategies would, however, require substantial cooperation from the medical staff, and attempts to stay away from certain types of patients are a potential source of conflict between physicians and hospital administrators.

An unadjusted per admission rate creates the opposite incentive with respect to length of stay, as revenue per case is fixed and any reduction in cost increases profit. An incentive exists, similar to that of per diem rates, to seek out cases that can be treated at less than the per admission and to discourage others. There is also an incentive for the hospital to want to discharge and readmit patients who might otherwise be treated in one continuous stay, as revenue is thereby doubled.

Some systems paying per diem or per admission rates are designed so that changes in volume from a base year affect revenues less than proportionately. For example, the Carter administration's hospital cost containment bill proposed that (beyond a "zone of no adjustment") additional admissions should increase (or reduced admissions decrease) revenues by 50% of the standard per admission rate. A figure in the 50% range is a common choice in such volume adjustment formulas, and apparently derives in part from a body of econometric literature that estimates the ratio of short-run marginal cost to average cost per patient day or admission as somewhere in that neighborhood (Lipscomb, Raskin, and Eichenholz 1978).

The use of econometric estimates of this type is most sensible if the rationale is to avoid rewarding (or penalizing) a hospital for unexpected volume changes that occur as random events beyond the hospital's control. Two points are worth emphasizing here. First, work by Friedman and Pauly (1983) suggests that the marginal cost of volume changes that can be anticipated even a quarter in advance is very close to average cost. They argue that the failure to adjust revenue proportionately with volume may weaken incentives for reducing costs in declining hospitals (since these hospitals would lose only 50% of the excess they received from the rate-setting system). On the other hand, expanding hospitals would obtain insufficient revenue to maintain standards of quality. The second point is that these kinds of volume adjustments by themselves probably do little to discourage deliberate manipulation of volume and case-mix. The marginal cost of extending the stay of a patient requiring very little care is probably quite low, for example, even relative to the marginal cost of a more "typical" patient day. And these adjustments do not weaken the incentive under a per admission rate to seek out a less costly case-mix, holding total admissions constant.

Diagnosis-Specific Per Case Rates

The obvious shortcomings of the patient days and number of admissions as hospital output measures have stimulated interest in the possibility of paying hospitals prospective rates per case varying by diagnosis. One set of diagnostic categories, the Diagnosis-Related Groups (DRGs) (Fetter et al. 1980), forms the basis for the current Medicare hospital reimbursement system, which was implemented starting in October 1983, and which is in effect in Wisconsin for Medicare patients.

The theoretic appeal of diagnosis-specific rates—compared with a single payment for admission—is that since diagnoses that are less costly to treat generate smaller reimbursements, incentives to seek out simple cases are reduced. Furthermore, although case-mix differences among hospitals make the notion of paying all hospitals the same per diem or per admission rate unattractive, the possibility of paying different hospitals the same rates by diagnosis is much more appealing. Indeed, the Medicare prospective payment system is gradually moving in this direction.

Diagnosis-specific rates, while removing or weakening certain of the perverse incentives of per diem and per admission approaches, also have difficulties as a way of reimbursing hospitals. They are administratively costly, since a great deal of information is required for the computation of reimbursements. This may cause serious short-run implementation problems, but in itself is probably not a significant drawback in an era of rapidly increasing data-processing capability and falling data-processing costs. More substantively, like per admission rates, diagnosis-specific rates create a profit incentive to reduce the quantity and complexity of ancillary services provided and length of stay, even if quality is sacrificed.

Furthermore, because the differences among individual cases are far more subtle than any classification system can fully capture, it is inevitable that the treatment of some individuals will generate significantly more—and others significantly less—in costs than in revenues, so that incentives to avoid some cases and seek out others will remain.

Another potential and serious difficulty is that a decision to assign different relative rates to different types of cases involves an implicit judgment that a good deal is known about *appropriate* relative costs. The DRG system used historical cost data (now regularly recalibrated using annual hospital data on Medicare patients), but many believe that the historical patterns reflect inefficiencies and therefore do not represent desirable cost levels. This is an important and more general point. Any aspect of a system—whether it has to do with unit of payment, grouping of hospitals, or something else—that takes for granted that historical cost differences are appropriate certainly limits the potential for eliminating existing inefficiencies.

Finally, diagnosis-specific rates create at least one problem not present in simpler systems. The classification of patients might be manipulated to maximize reimbursement, without any real changes in patient care (Simborg 1981). A variation on this theme is that if the performance of certain procedures is required to justify a classification, incentives to perform procedures will be distorted.

Total Hospital Budget

At the opposite extreme from charges on a fee schedule is the use of an annual prospective hospital budget as the basis of rate setting. Conceptually, the appeal of this approach is that a hospital has an incentive always to be efficient—it is not rewarded for more services, more days, or more cases treated. It should have no incentive to extend the stay of a patient beyond the duration medically needed, or to provide services not justified on grounds of expected health benefits. However, since its budget is set for the year, the hospital would maximize short-run profits by providing only limited days of care and few services (too little care) and by avoiding severely ill patients.

In fact, the process by which annual hospital budgets are set can avoid some of these negative incentives. The hospital's budget in year $t + 1$ can be based on activities (costs, etc.) in year t. Then, if a hospital provides fewer services (days of care), its budget will be lower for the following year. If it provides more care, its budget will be higher, thus reducing efficiency incentives. Alternatively, the budget can be set assuming occupancy at a specified level; if that level is not achieved, the budget can be automatically adjusted (downward for lower occupancy, upward for higher occupancy). Finally, the budget can be set by categorizing hospitals to reflect the number of services offered and the difficulty of treating the patient-mix (severity). This grouping approach may be combined with a projected occupancy rate (along with the associated rewards and penalties for higher or lower rates) to minimize the potential negative incentives. Unfortunately, when grouping has been tried, hospitals, recognizing that their revenues depend heavily on the group in which they are placed, have argued about the appropriate group for their institution. This has led to numerous legal battles and high administration costs.

The Evidence on Volume Responses

Despite frequently expressed concerns about the potential for perverse quantity-of-care responses to rate setting, and despite the admission by at least one commission that an inability to control volume has been a problem (Atkinson and Cook 1981), relatively little hard evidence of rate-setting effects on volume has been found. There is a bit of evidence (Sloan 1983; Worthington and Piro 1982) that rate setting has had some effect on increasing lengths of stay, which would not be surprising given that most of the studied programs set individual charges or per diem rates. But on the whole, those studies that look at effects of rate setting on hospital expenses per capita, a measure that incorporates effects on volume within it, find effects that appear to be comparable to those on expense per patient day and per admission.[5]

Early experience with the Medicare DRG-based prospective payment system is also relevant here. Most analysts predicted that hospitals would respond to fixed-per-case payments by shortening stays and increasing the number of admissions. Length of stay did fall as expected, but admissions (both Medicare and non-Medicare) also fell sharply—reversing the historical trend—just after implementation began (U.S. Congress, Office of Technology Assessment 1985).

There are a number of possible explanations for this failure to find important volume-increasing effects of rate setting. One is the possibility that hospitals cannot, or choose not to, respond as strongly to financial incentives that impinge on medical practice as economists suspect. Another possibility is that utilization reviews, in some combination with volume adjustments and other special provisions built into rate-setting formulas, are successful in preventing perverse effects. A third (not relevant in the Medicare case) is that in the dynamic process by which rates have typically been set—wherein next year's approved rates are determined at least in part as a markup over this year's expenses—short-run incentives to manipulate volume may be blunted. For example, taking additional "easy days" may add to profits this year, but reduce the approved per diem rate in the next. Incentives to expand volume would be stronger in a per diem system that broke the tie between the hospital's own current expenses and its future rates.

Two other points should not be neglected. The first is that the influence of volume-related incentives might be strongly related to the degree of financial pressure that hospitals feel,[6] and perhaps most rate-setting programs to date have not put them under significant stress. To expand on this briefly, research by Wennberg, McPherson, and Caper (1984) and others has shown that very substantial variation exists in rates of hospitalization for specific diagnoses, even across geographic areas in the same state. This suggests that there is much room for altering rates of hospitalization, at least by physicians, while staying within the bounds of "acceptable medical practice."

The second point is that more subtle kinds of responses to incentives created by the unit of payment—for example, manipulation of case-mix—have apparently not yet been studied. These responses would presumably show up in part as changes in the distribution of patients across types of hospitals, as some are in a better position than others to select patients on the basis of profitability.

Interhospital Differences in Rates and Case-Mix

No one would deny that differences in the mix of patients treated can be a legitimate reason for differences in hospital operating costs. There is no reason to expect, or to desire, that the per diem costs of a small rural hospital treating relatively routine cases will be identical to those of an urban teaching hospital providing tertiary care. At least for some choices of unit of payment—per diem and per admission, for example—differences in rates across hospitals are to be expected. The more interesting question is whether case-mix differences alone can justify differences in rates. Is the ideal system one in which payments are made on a diagnosis-specific per case basis with all hospitals subject to the same rates, or should other factors, such as a hospital's size and location, be somehow taken into account?

The location at which a service is provided is likely to be an important element of its value to the recipient. For an individual living one mile from hospital A, for example, the fact that hospital B, forty miles away, can provide care in the case of a heart attack at lower cost and equivalent quality is not likely to be an overwhelming consideration. The extra time required to get to B in an emergency makes B's care an imperfect substitute for care at hospital A for this individual. As long as travel time matters for the outcome of treatment (or even for the convenience of the patient), the argument in favor of paying the same price for treatment of a particular case type to all hospitals is not immediately persuasive.

Related to the location issue, the average cost of treating a certain case type efficiently might depend on how frequently such cases are encountered—particularly if there is expensive specialized equipment involved. A hospital that deals with such cases more often can spread the fixed costs of the equipment over a greater number of patients. If location of service did not matter, it would be desirable to treat particular case types only at hospitals for which volume is sufficient to minimize average cost of treatment. But if it is deemed essential to have a service available at a particular location—even if infrequently utilized—it may be necessary to accept relatively high costs as a consequence.

Even in an ideal system, then, there can be sound economic reasons for paying hospitals different prices for treating similar patients. But justifications for such differences are limited. After adjusting for case-mix, for example, hospital size should not be considered as an independent factor in setting rates per patient. Hospitals of different sizes serving the same patient population ought to be expected to meet the same cost standards. If this is not possible owing to the existence of economies or diseconomies of scale, then it is desirable that the rate-setting system make life difficult for the nonoptimally sized hospitals. In addition, if a particular case type can only be treated at high cost in some location (perhaps a rural area where demand is low), the question should be asked whether treatment for it ought to be available there. If the answer is no—if local residents needing such treatment can be referred to more distant hospitals without serious harm or unacceptable inconvenience—then from an economic perspective the higher rates necessary to cover the costs of providing such treatment locally should not be granted.

Attempts to cover by means of hospital rates other costs not directly related to the care of paying patients (such as costs of medical education, research, and charity care) may also lead to differences in rates across hospitals. These issues are touched on below in the section on rate setting and competition.

Updating of Rates and Changes in Intensity of Care

The distinguishing feature of prospective rates is that they are set in advance of the period in which costs are incurred. How rapidly rates are permitted to increase from year to year therefore becomes a crucial issue. The evidence to date (Anderson and Lave 1984) suggests that it is in limiting across-the-board increases, rather than by increasing the efficiency of particularly poorly run hospitals, that rate setting influences hospital expenses over time. If allowable increases are "too large," the system is unlikely to significantly influence hospital behavior relative to cost reimbursement. If "too small," hospitals will be unable to provide increases in quality of care that the public is willing to pay for, and may even have difficulty in maintaining existing quality standards. The problem, however, is that no simple rules of thumb exist for creating incentives for limiting expenditure growth and promoting high-quality hospital care. Given this lack of knowledge, our discussion will be brief despite the importance of the issue.

Typically, the stated policy of a prospective payment system is to permit annual percentage increases in rates equal to the projected increase in an index of hospital input prices, plus some small additional amount, say 1%. If the hospital product remained constant over time, such an add-on factor would be difficult to justify. Merely adjusting rates in accordance with input price changes would be sufficient to allow a hospital to continue to produce the same services it had been producing, assuming previous rates were adequate. Indeed, with any improvement in productivity, rate increases could be held below those of input prices without any damage to the quality of output. The willingness to accommodate increases in rates in excess of those in input prices reflects an acceptance of the fact that the nature of the hospital product constantly changes, partly in response to the development of new, more costly but presumably quality-improving, technologies, and partly in response to rising public expectations about the level of amenities to be provided.

Over the past two decades, hospital expenses have increased several percentage points faster than would be justified by input price increases alone, suggesting that requests for increases beyond the 1% add-on are likely to be common. There are no easy answers as to how to respond to such requests. Nearly any increase in hospital expenses not accounted for by input price inflation can be claimed to result from increases in "intensity" (such as increases in the number and kind of ancillary and nursing services provided). Standards of intensity established by the medical profession are never precise and have tended to drift upward over time. One point worth emphasizing, however, is that if increases in "intensity" of care are always treated as legitimate reasons for increases in rates, then the potential for a rate-setting agency to have an impact on the growth of hospital expenses will be severely constrained.

To point this out is not to claim that all increases in service intensity are bad and should be resisted. As always, costs should ideally be weighed against benefits. But standards of care "established by the medical profession" have involved little consideration of economic costs, and acquiescence to changes in these standards will likely limit a rate-setting agency's role.

Rate Setting in a More Competitive Environment

The initial interest in rate setting stems from a period in which nearly all buyers of hospital care reimbursed the hospital for the cost of service or paid whatever charges the hospital made, exercising little oversight. Patients covered by government programs or private insurance had free choice among hospitals and no reason to pay attention to costs in making that choice. It is now commonplace to observe that incentives for efficient hospital operations were lacking in that system. State rate setting had a strong conceptual appeal when viewed against that background.

But times have changed. The Medicare program is now operating its own prospective reimbursement system. Medicaid programs have explored various cost control measures and are frequently unwilling to participate in state rate-setting systems. Private purchasers of care have also taken matters into their own hands and have begun to rely more heavily on "managed care" approaches to health insurance, including Health Maintenance Organizations (HMOs) and Preferred Provider Organizations (PPOs).[7] In general, the market for hospital care has become much more competitive than it was in the 1970s.

Increasing competition in health care raises some important questions about rate setting. An obvious one is whether relying on competition is a preferred alternative, with rate setting only likely to get in the way. Empirical evidence relating to that question is currently very limited, but the superiority of competition as a cost control measure is still being debated. (See McLaughlin, 1987; Mitchell, Morrisey, and Sloan, 1987, for two different perspectives.) If rate setting is to coexist with increasingly activist payers, questions about the terms of that coexistence emerge. Are the approved rates to be paid by *all* private payers (assuming public programs do not participate), or should they be maxima, with the individual payer free to negotiate discounted rates?

The question of whether granting discounts must result in higher costs for other payers is clearly an important one, but is also more subtle than it first appears. To answer it, one needs to specify the relevant alternative to granting the discount. If the alternative is that the payer in question continues to utilize the hospital as it would have, but pays the full rates, then granting the discount creates a loss of revenue that must be made up (assuming it is not absorbed as a change in profit, which it could be in a for-profit hospital). This is true regardless of the relationship of rates to the costs of providing services to those covered by the payer in question. If, however, the alternative to the discount is that the payer takes much or all of its business elsewhere, then granting it has no detrimental effect on the revenue that must be raised from other payers, as long as the discounted rates cover at least the incremental costs of providing services to that particular payer.

The second alternative seems the more realistic one. What incentive has a hospital, after all, to offer a discount unless it perceives a threat of loss of patient volume if it fails to do so? It also seems clear that a hospital has little or no incentive to agree to a discount so large as to leave the rates of payment below the incremental costs of providing services to a covered group. Here the fact comes into play that most rate-setting systems attempt to cover through rates *more* than the current costs of providing services to those covered by participating payers. If this were not true, then permitting hospitals to negotiate discounts would presumably lead to some differences in rates among payers, reflecting differences in the costs of treating particular groups. And it would be difficult to argue that such differences constituted inequitable cost-shifting, as each payer would still be paying the costs associated with its covered group. If discounts are allowed, payers who have the option of using several different hospitals (such as HMOs in urban areas) may, by threatening to steer their covered patients away from uncooperative hospitals, successfully negotiate rates that may exclude additional costs to a hospital (such as the costs of bad debts, charity care, medical education programs, etc.). The result would be to create a higher burden of such costs for those payers who are unable to evade them.

Perhaps more disturbing is that an analogous process could go on even if discounts are not allowed. Instead of negotiating discounts, "mobile" payers would then simply begin directing patients to those hospitals for which these added-on costs are smallest (and therefore rates lowest, other things equal). As some paying patients leave, rates to those remaining must go up further, and the incentives increase for others to leave. Hospitals that serve relatively large indigent populations must over time find it more and more difficult to attract paying patients and ultimately to survive. The general point here is that as more competition enters the system from the buyer's side (through HMOs, PPOs, and so forth) the ability of a rate-setting agency to simply establish by fiat differences across hospitals in rates for equivalent services becomes more and more limited. Shifting significant portions of the costs of treating indigent patients into the rates paid by others may well prove to be impossible in the long run, so that some other method of financing their care will need to be devised.

The controversy over discounts and cost-shifting is based in large measure on fundamentally different philosophies about the proper allocation of hospital costs among payers. One way of thinking—which hospital rate-setting agencies have traditionally embraced—is that the costs of running a hospital, including not only "normal" operational costs but capital, charity care, bad debt, and medical education and research costs, should be proportionately borne by all payers. However, there is little that a rate-setting agency can do if Medicare and Medicaid refuse to bear proportionate shares of hospital costs for charity care, bad debt, and medical education and research; federal law dictates what costs Medicare will or will not pick up.

Thus, in practice, rate-setting agencies that have adopted a philosophy of proportionality have had to settle for the principle that the operational costs of serving the hospital's nongovernmental patients, plus much of the hospital's capital, charity care, bad debt, and medical education, should be borne by nongovernmental payers. Given this constraint, it is not unreasonable for a rate-setting agency to conclude that further cost-shifting (i.e., causing costs to fall disproportionately on *particular* nongovernmental payers) is wrong and that, to the extent that cost-shifting results from a negotiated discounted price for a particular payer, the discount that caused the cost-shifting should be prohibited.

An alternative philosophy is that there is nothing wrong with the ability of a hospital to distribute in any manner it wishes—proportionately or disproportionately—its operating costs among its various payers. According to this philosophy, not only should government allow Medicare and Medicaid payments to be restricted, but it should also allow similar discounting arrangements for other payers.

The proponents of this viewpoint recognize that, in the short run, the legitimization of cost-shifting will result in the more powerful or clever payers paying less than their proportionate share while other payers pay more than their share, and that there may initially be no net reduction in the costs borne by all payers. However, these proponents maintain that, in the long run, competitive forces will compel hospitals to reduce their total costs in order to avoid losing the victims of their cost-shifting to other hospitals. In sum, the long-range impact of a philosophy that tolerates cost-shifting may be the triggering of market forces which will permanently hold down costs for all payers. According to this philosophy, however regrettable may be the short-term pain to certain payers, it would be justified by an expected long-range gain for all payers.

Competition is an important feature of Wisconsin's system to control hospital costs, and intensifies the problem of discounts for payers negotiating for large groups. These issues are discussed below.

Establishing a Rate-Setting Program in Wisconsin Hospitals

In 1983, the Wisconsin legislature incorporated in the 1983–85 Biennial Budget Act (1983 Senate Bill 83, enacted as 1983 Wisconsin Act 27) a series of new programs designed to hold down health care costs. The major changes were (1) the establishment of a Wisconsin Hospital Rate-Setting Commission; (2) a comprehensive revision of the state's Certificate of Need (CON) law—a law which requires prior approval for large new investments in health care institutions and which established statewide bed limits for hospitals and nursing homes; (3) the legalization of Health Maintenance Organizations (HMOs—prepaid insurance programs) and Preferred Provider Organizations (PPOs—a fee-for-service discount system under which consumers using specified providers pay less than if they use other providers who are not part of the PPO and the physician members accept fees according to a specific fee schedule); and (4) the introduction of new competitive methods of purchasing health care for Medicaid recipients and state employes. These last established an HMO initiative for Medicaid AFDC recipients in counties with more than one HMO, and a State Employe Health Plan (SEHP) which changed the state contribution for employe health insurance from 90% of a comprehensive fee-for-service plan to the lower of the 90% figure or 107% (later 105%) of the lowest bid of any qualified HMO. These led to the formation of many new HMOs in an attempt to retain patients.

The principle guiding the legislature was that the incentives encouraging health care cost inflation were so pervasive and so ingrained in the health care delivery system that it was necessary and desirable to adopt almost any measure which held out the hope of cost restraint. Thus, unlike most other states, Wisconsin chose not to rely on only one type of solution (i.e., a hospital rate-setting commission only, or CON law revision only, or competitive methods of purchasing health care only). Instead, the legislature decided to inaugurate—as a single package—a broad range of cost-control measures.

Three major questions are highlighted here with respect to Wisconsin's Rate-Setting Commission's policies:

1. What unit of payment did they select to prospectively establish rates?
2. How did they deal with varying missions of hospitals?
3. How did the rate-setting system adjust to the new competition in which discounts were offered to purchasers of large volumes of service?

Setting Hospital Rates

The legislation establishing the commission gave it broad, but by no means complete, discretion with respect to the unit of payment to use in setting hospital rates. However, the legislative language did require the commission to "establish maximum hospital rates on a prospective basis" (sec. 2, §54.05). Thus, whatever unit of payment was used, it had to be one which could be applied prospectively.

Under the rate-setting legislation, a hospital's rates were tied to its approved budget. The commission established a total budget for each hospital consisting of two revenue totals: total gross patient revenue and net patient revenue (net of bad debt and discounts, in other words, the amount the hospital expected to receive) which the hospital could generate during the budget year under review. In addition, the commission established a list of one hundred service charge elements, the rates for which were to be submitted by each hospital for approval. With its submission of proposed rates, the hospital had to document its actual volume for each of the charge elements for the year preceding the budget year under review.

Peer group rates were used to evaluate the proposed total budget. This placed a great deal of importance on the peer group for each hospital. These peer groups of hospitals were based on special services offered (31.6%), hospital volume (27.4%), intensity (16.8%), whether they had certain education programs (12.7%), and outpatient volume (11.6%). Between five and fifteen hospitals were in each peer group cluster (Wisconsin Hospital Rate-Setting Commission 1985). This system, then, was primarily based on total hospital budget (using peer groups) with some attention paid to charges for specific services.

Wisconsin's decision to use approved budget levels that were not rigidly enforced, along with a rate per charge element, offered hospitals substantial incentives to generate increased revenue by increasing the volume of services provided to patients. Under a system of rates per charge element, the more patients admitted, the longer they stayed, the more tests, services, and drugs they got, the more the hospital would make. A hospital could continue generating expenditures with the certainty that, at least in the case of adequately insured individuals, it would be reimbursed.

Interhospital Differences: Teaching and Rural Hospitals

Most of Wisconsin's hospitals fall in the category of community hospitals; however, there are several facilities in the state which clearly do not fit into the community hospital category (e.g., the Milwaukee Regional Medical Complex and the University of Wisconsin Hospital in Madison). Rural hospitals have a special mission to serve individuals scattered across a wide geographic area. In an emergency, they may be the only practical source of hospital care. They also attract both primary and secondary-care physicians to rural areas. Teaching hospitals not only provide care to patients but also serve as clinical classrooms for future doctors and sponsor medical research which may advance the frontiers of medical knowledge. It is hardly surprising that these differences were taken into account when hospital rates were established.

Wisconsin's policy with respect to interhospital differences was a mixture of normal and special considerations, exemptions, and expedited review. The legislation took account of special hospitals in several ways. First, hospital budgets to be considered by the commission were defined to include certain costs which were incurred disproportionately by teaching hospitals with large indigent populations (i.e., direct and indirect costs of medical education and research programs as well as bad debts and charity care).

Small rural hospitals could also receive special consideration. Under the legislation, the commission could adopt rules under which small hospitals meeting specific criteria could receive expedited review of rate requests and even, in some cases, automatic approval.

The Issue of Discounting

Perhaps the most controversial issue which the commission faced, and which any new commission would face, was the issue of discounts: dealing with the discounted (i.e., below the maximum allowable level) unit prices that hospitals wish to grant to HMOs and other payers, typically in return for some sort of guaranteed volume of patients.

The commission's discount policy prohibited cost-shifting on the grounds that it violated the principle of proportionality by causing costs to be picked up disproportionately by particular nongovernmental payers while sparing other nongovernmental payers costs they would normally incur.

The commission attempted to distinguish those situations in which discounts resulted in cost-shifting from those in which no cost-shifting occurred, and to treat the two situations differently. On the one hand, the policy prevented hospitals from raising the maximum charges that the majority of their payers were expected to pay in order to compensate for the discounts that certain of their payers had succeeded in obtaining. On the other hand, the commission's policy allowed discounts which did not produce cost-shifting. In other words, a discount was permitted if the hospital, rather than raising its maximum charges to compensate for a discount, instead reduced its expenses through "savings" of one sort or another which equaled or exceeded the discount it granted to a payer.

Ironically, one of the side effects of the way in which the commission's policy was translated into administrative rule was that, when the savings associated with a discount actually exceeded the discount itself, these "excess" savings could not be used to benefit payers who did not generate the savings. According to such an interpretation, just as cost-shifting to payers other than those granted discounts was prohibited, *savings-shifting* to other payers would also be prohibited.

The Wisconsin Rate-Setting Commission's position can be both defended and criticized. The strongest argument in favor of the policy is that it prevented price discrimination against payers who, for one reason or another, did not have the power to protect themselves in the marketplace. One of the traditional functions of regulatory agencies has been precisely to prevent the seller of a service from using its monopoly or dominant position in the marketplace to force most purchasers to pay much higher prices than a small number of comparatively powerful purchasers.

It is arguable, however, that the commission had the legal authority to prohibit hospitals from engaging in cost-shifting in conjunction with discounting. There was nothing in the legislation to indicate that costs shifted to certain payers because of discounts granted to other payers were, per se, unreasonable.

To the extent that cost-shifting occurred, the economic harm may ultimately have been far outweighed by the economic good. Cost-shifting often makes patients and payers become more aware of less expensive alternatives; it makes them *do* something about the costs they are paying. From this perspective, cost-shifting is a good thing, because it compels victims to develop innovative arrangements to secure comparatively lower health care costs.

Other Issues

One of the issues raised in the earlier part of this chapter is the updating and modification of rates to reflect changes in intensity of care. The Wisconsin Rate-Setting Commission automatically allowed for inflation. It did so by allowing an adjustment of revenue based on actual inflation as measured by the nationwide hospital market index. For increases in wages, actual increases were permitted, but not if the hospital had "excessive wage increases" based on a comparison with other hospitals in the same community. This use of a nationwide rate and some limitation to wage increases inhibited the complete pass-through of increases in inputs, yet was likely to permit a large enough increase to prevent hospitals from being unable to provide "the quality of care the public is willing to pay for." Issues of intensity of care were not separately addressed.

A current important concern in Wisconsin (as elsewhere in the nation) is providing care for the uninsured. To hospitals this question is one of how to finance care provided to this population—uncompensated care. To encourage the provision of uncompensated care, the Wisconsin Rate-Setting Commission required, beginning in 1987, that hospitals report the actual amount of charity care they provided. This was to be part of the rate-review process, with some influence on the approved budget.

Summary

The Wisconsin Rate-Setting Commission was established by the 1983 Wisconsin legislature following a 36.8% increase in hospital costs (hospital revenue) from 1981 through 1982. It was one part of a multifaceted approach to reduce the rate of increase in overall health insurance expenditures in the state. The commission made a number of choices that were controversial— using an annual budget but allowing some deviation from the budget, permitting price differentials only if they were based on real underlying cost differences, and treating certain hospitals with special consideration. Even with these controversial decisions, hospital revenue increases were down dramatically—to less than 2% after the two-year period from 1 February 1984 to 1 March 1986 (Oestricher 1986). While the role of rate setting versus the other forces influencing hospital and health care in Wisconsin has not been sorted out, this reduction in expenditure increases suggests that rate regulation, along with competition, has been a successful approach to holding down hospital expenditure increases.

After four years of attacking health care costs with both regulatory and competitive tools, however, Wisconsin has decided to abandon regulation and proceed solely with a competitive approach. The legislature concluded that adequate savings in hospital costs could be gained through competition. The costs of the rate-setting process (including lawyers' and experts' fees, administration, etc.) were assumed to make regulation impractical. And the nationwide introduction of DRGs (the Medicare version of prospective rate setting; see Schramm et al. 1986) appears to have diminished the pattern of hospital savings per capita in regulated states. In other words, the introduction of rate setting nationwide for one group of patients has diminished the gains from programs to cover additional groups. Yet, evidence in Wisconsin suggests that rate setting may be important in the future. To date, Wisconsin corporations and local governments have had only limited success in using managed care such as HMOs to control health care costs (premiums). Only the SEHP—a model not replicated by the private sector—has translated potential competitive pressures into substantial savings over a four-year period.[8] And, immediately after the demise of the rate-setting commission, a large number of hospitals announced increases in their rates (or plans for increases).

The issues discussed in this chapter may for the present seem moot in Wisconsin. The chapter should, however, serve as useful background to understanding the Medicare rate-setting program (DRGs) in effect in Wisconsin and the nation. Other states are turning to additional rate setting—eight states introduced rate-setting bills in their legislatures in 1984 and 1985. Should hospital rate setting reemerge as a strategy in the future for Wisconsin, the state's experience and issues raised by the state's program and by the DRG program will provide valuable lessons in how to proceed.

NOTES

1. The figure is for "nonfederal short term general and other special hospitals," from American Hospital Association, *Hospital Statistics* (various years).

2. Early studies of the effects of individual programs were limited by lack of data and frequently by methodological problems. They have been reviewed elsewhere. We confine attention also to studies which make use of data extending at least through 1978. Studies based on earlier data found little evidence of important effects of rate setting, but methodologically similar studies with more recent data reach different conclusions.

3. A number of these studies are critically reviewed in Goddeeris and Noren (1984). Another useful review is Eby and Cohodes (1985).

4. Extending patient stays is frequently criticized as a particularly serious form of resource misallocation on the grounds that hospital care, costing hundreds of dollars a day, is wasted on individuals who could be sent home. In truth the situation is much more complicated. The incremental cost to the hospital may be for less than the hundreds of dollars it is reimbursed. From the point of view of efficiency of resource allocation, it is this incremental cost that should be compared with any costs (monetary or otherwise) imposed on the patient and the patient's family as a result of earlier discharge.

5. An even more important issue is the effect of rate setting on total health care costs, including those incurred outside the hospital, but there is virtually no evidence on this point.

6. Some evidence to this effect for the Maryland program is contained in Salkever, Steinwachs, and Rupp (1986).

7. PPOs contract selectively with preferred providers at negotiated rates, and also emphasize controls on utilization of services.

8. A key difference in the use of HMOs or competition more generally between the state and these other employers is that the state pays a fixed-dollar amount per employe while most others pay a *percentage* of the premium. In the fixed-dollar approach, the employe pays 100% of any additional premium of a more expensive plan, while in the percentage approach the employe only pays a share of the additional premium.

PART THREE

AGRICULTURAL AND NATURAL RESOURCE POLICY

12

Agricultural Policy

EDWARD V. JESSE

Introduction

The state of agriculture in Wisconsin is probably more uncertain now than at any time in recent history. The "farm financial crisis" of the mid-1980s affected Wisconsin less seriously than other midwestern states because of Wisconsin's heavy emphasis on dairying, which was more protected by federal programs from price drops than other farm commodities. But Wisconsin's dairy farmers now face the prospect of large cuts in dairy price supports and the reality of strong competition from rapidly expanding milk production in the southwestern United States. There is ominous evidence that financial stress in Wisconsin agriculture may intensify.

It is with this backdrop that this chapter examines the agricultural sector of the state and the policies affecting it. The focus is long-run—on likely trends over the next twenty years or so, and on state and federal policies to accommodate these trends. But the current depressed status of agriculture has long-run implications; evidence of the chronic tendency of U.S. agriculture toward overcapacity.

This chapter begins with a brief discussion of the nature of Wisconsin agriculture, followed by a review of government policies that have helped shape the industry. Next, current and emerging issues that will influence the future viability of agriculture are identified, and, finally, policy options are noted and recommendations offered.

The discussion and recommendations were influenced by and draw from three recent organized efforts to identify means by which Wisconsin can assist its agricultural sector: (1) January 1984 conference titled "Wisconsin's Agricultural Economy: An Urban-Rural Perspective" (Wingspread Conference), which was held "to seek economic policies for enhancing Wisconsin agriculture in the context of statewide urban and rural economic development"; (2) a 1984–85 task force on agriculture sponsored by the Wisconsin Strategic Development Commission (1985b), which was charged with the responsibility to develop long-range public- and private-sector strategies to improve agriculture's future in Wisconsin; and (3) a spring 1985 Wisconsin Governor's Commission on Agriculture, which made numerous recommendations to assist agriculture in the areas of state agricultural policies, taxation, state rural development policies, and federal policy initiatives.

Profile of Wisconsin Agriculture

Farm Products and Income

Agriculture, farming plus allied farm service and food manufacturing industries, makes a significant contribution to Wisconsin's economy. From 1980 to 1983, gross farm income averaged $5.75 billion, and Wisconsin farmers spent $4.6 billion per year for production items and farm services. Agriculture is estimated to have accounted for 13% of total Wisconsin industry value added in 1979, split about evenly between farming and agriculture-related industries (Garber and Dahl 1984).

Wisconsin milk production in 1983 (23 billion pounds) was 17% of the U.S. total. Dairy farming dominates agriculture in the state, accounting for 59% of total cash receipts in 1983 (figure 12.1). The importance of dairying has changed little over the past twenty-five years. However, major changes in the importance of other commodities have taken place. In particular, cash

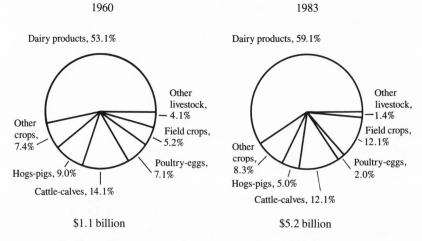

Fig. 12.1. Percentage of Wisconsin cash receipts from farm marketings by commodity. (Source: *Wisconsin Agricultural Statistics for 1961* and *Wisconsin Agricultural Statistics for 1984*, Wisconsin Department of Agriculture, Trade, and Consumer Protection.)

receipts from livestock products other than milk declined from 34.3% of the total in 1960 to 20.5% in 1983. Field crops increased their share of Wisconsin farm receipts from 5.2% to 12.1%, reflecting increasing state production of corn in excess of on-farm livestock feeding needs. In 1983, Wisconsin ranked seventh among states in corn production. Expanding production of soybeans has also increased cash receipts from field crop sales.

Though minor in comparison to dairying, vegetables and potatoes remain important cash crops in Wisconsin. In 1983, the state ranked fourth in potato production; first in production of processing beans, peas, and cabbage; and second in production of processing sweet corn. Other important horticultural specialties are tart cherries (third leading state), cranberries (tied with Massachusetts for first), and ginseng (leading state).

Table 12.1 indicates the geographical pattern of farming specialization within the state. Potato and vegetable production is concentrated in the irrigated areas of central Wisconsin. Much of the increase in field crop production has been in the west central and southern counties of the state. Dairy farming dominates in the other crop reporting districts.

Wisconsin's farming mix differs substantially from that of neighboring states and the United States (table 12.2). Due to the influence of dairying, Wisconsin is more livestock-intensive and less dependent on grain and oilseed sales as a source of farm income. This form of specialization has implications for the level and variability of farm income. Usually, greater specialization implies greater income variability. But, as emphasized later, the dairy price support program has tended to stabilize milk prices to the extent that Wisconsin's net farm income has been less volatile than that of most other states (table 12.3). In particular, Wisconsin did not ride the U.S. grain export boom-and-bust roller coaster of 1972–83. Note from table 12.3 that Wisconsin's share of U.S. net farm income increased between 1981 and 1983, while the level of income declined. This further indicates the relative imbalance among farm commodity prices because of different federal programs and market conditions.

Farm Structure

The 1982 farm census counted 83,000 farmers in Wisconsin based on the census definition of a farm as having sales of at least $1,000 in the census year. This is roughly half the number of farms in 1950, indicating a long-standing trend of declining farm numbers. Total land in farms in 1982 was 17.2 million acres, compared to 23.2 million acres in 1950. Harvested cropland dropped by about 3 million acres over the same time span, while irrigated acreage increased from 10,000 to 260,000 acres.

The distribution of farms by size in Wisconsin contrasts markedly with the

Table 12.1. Number and Size of Farms (1983), Percentage of Farm Cash Receipts by Commodity (1982) for Wisconsin Crop Reporting Districts

	Northwest	North Central	Northeast	West Central	Central	East Central	Southeast	South Central	Southeast
No. of farms	8,840	9,290	5,090	13,830	7,840	13,420	12,950	13,050	5,690
Ave. size of farm (acres)	213.9	195.7	199.1	226.3	217.8	164.5	230.7	190.9	202.2
Land in farms (1,000 acres)	1,890.9	1,818.2	1,013.6	3,130.3	1,707.6	2,207.6	2,987.5	2,491.3	953.0
Total cash receipts ($ million)	439.1	481.1	261.1	755.0	449.6	798.4	775.1	947.7	340.1
Percentage from									
Dairy products	65.1	71.0	66.6	59.6	46.9	67.7	53.7	47.1	39.6
Meat animals	11.6	14.0	15.4	15.2	14.9	16.3	27.2	21.5	15.0
Other livestock	9.6	2.4	0.1	3.8	1.1	2.0	1.3	2.8	7.0
Total livestock	86.3	87.4	82.1	78.6	62.9	86.0	82.2	71.4	61.6
Field crops	9.1	2.3	4.7	16.3	10.6	8.0	15.0	23.4	26.9
Vegetables	1.2	4.1	7.8	0.4	18.5	4.2	0.7	3.8	4.4
Other crops	3.4	6.1	4.4	4.6	7.9	1.8	2.1	1.4	7.1
Total crops	13.7	12.5	16.9	21.3	37.0	14.0	17.8	28.6	38.4

Source: 1984 Wisconsin Agricultural Statistics, Wisconsin Agricultural Reporting Service, Madison, June 1984.

Table 12.2. Percentage of Cash Receipts by Commodity, Wisconsin, United States, and Selected Midwestern States, 1983

Commodity	Wis.	Minn.	Iowa	Ill.	Mich.	U.S.
Livestock products	79.6	53.0	57.8	28.2	41.4	49.9
Meat animals	17.2	25.2	50.1	23.0	13.5	28.0
Dairy products	59.1	22.3	6.0	4.4	24.7	13.6
Poultry & eggs	2.0	4.7	1.5	0.6	2.8	7.0
Misc. livestock	1.3	0.8	0.2	0.1	0.5	1.3
Crops	20.4	47.0	42.2	71.8	58.6	50.1
Food grains	0.4	7.2	0.1	2.3	4.7	7.2
Feed grains	9.8	16.7	20.6	43.6	20.1	12.1
Tobacco	0.4	—	—	—	—	2.0
Oil crops	1.5	17.6	20.8	23.8	5.7	9.6
Vegetables	4.6	2.0	0.1	0.6	11.4	5.9
Fruits & nuts	1.3	0.1	—	0.2	6.3	4.4
All other crops	2.4	3.3	0.6	1.3	10.4	5.7

Source: *Economic Indicators at the Farm Sector: State Income and Balance Sheet Statistics,* ECIFS3-4, Economic Research Service, U.S. Dept. of Agriculture, January 1985.

Table 12.3. Net Farm Income, Wisconsin, United States, and Selected Midwestern States, 1964–83 (millions of dollars)

Year	Wis.	Minn.	Iowa	Ill.	Ind.	Mich.	U.S.	Wis. as % of U.S.
1964	410.1	341.4	758.2	536.1	268.4	249.6	10,492	3.9
1965	488.4	581.5	1,089.5	771.0	510.5	243.3	12,900	3.8
1966	608.2	664.9	1,164.7	865.4	456.4	309.0	13,960	4.4
1967	498.6	577.2	922.1	808.2	426.3	237.7	12,339	4.0
1968	564.5	594.2	873.9	594.6	377.0	245.8	12,322	4.6
1969	574.4	659.0	1,144.4	815.8	537.0	295.6	14,293	4.0
1970	576.6	815.5	1,080.8	629.8	363.7	277.8	14,381	4.0
1971	636.4	732.2	867.1	793.6	590.7	248.4	15,043	4.2
1972	681.5	909.4	1,332.0	897.5	493.5	371.7	19,507	3.5
1973	900.5	2,277.1	2,698.8	1,810.0	1,278.0	529.4	34,435	2.6
1974	729.7	1,581.4	1,589.2	1,616.9	724.0	589.7	27,309	2.7
1975	775.5	1,129.6	1,758.1	2,284.7	1,066.1	514.1	25,555	3.0
1976	664.8	603.9	926.0	1,502.4	1,033.3	399.0	20,129	3.3
1977	1,080.8	1,388.7	1,008.2	1,537.6	727.1	505.5	19,821	5.5
1978	989.9	1,410.9	2,065.3	1,437.1	827.3	466.0	27,651	3.6
1979	1,432.6	1,445.6	1,646.9	2,033.3	977.3	519.8	32,251	4.4
1980	1,430.0	1,191.2	836.4	520.5	590.6	437.5	21,239	6.7
1981	1,441.9	1,504.1	2,086.2	1,891.3	663.7	501.2	30,966	4.7
1982	1,188.0	991.6	863.0	934.8	476.8	429.5	22,339	5.3
1983	972.4	734.6	−217.4	−584.5	−129.7	347.6	16,100	6.0
Coefficient of variation (percent)								
	39.9	47.4	50.7	62.0	52.0	30.4	36.5	—
Correlation with U.S net farm income								
	.70	.91	.76	.74	.73	.91	—	—

Source: *Economic Indicators of the Farm Sector: State Income and Balance Sheet Statistics,* ECIFS3-4, Economic Research Service, U.S. Dept. of Agriculture, January 1985.

Table 12.4. Distribution of Farms and Commodity Sales by Farm Size, Wisconsin and United States, 1982

Farm Product Sales Class	Wisconsin				United States			
	No. of Farms		Sales		No. of Farms		Sales	
	No.	%	$ thousand	%	No.	%	$ thousand	%
Less than $2,500	10,768	13.1	11,302	0.2	536,327	23.9	558,106	0.4
$2,500–$4,999	6,472	7.9	23,593	0.5	278,208	12.4	999,220	0.8
$5,000–$9,999	7,884	9.6	57,061	1.2	281,802	12.6	2,008,512	1.5
$10,000–$19,999	8,940	10.9	129,310	2.7	259,007	11.5	3,694,306	2.8
$20,000–$39,999	11,304	13.7	333,164	6.9	248,825	11.1	7,142,112	5.4
$40,000–$99.999	22,957	27.9	1,518,602	31.3	332.751	14.8	21,641,795	16.4
$100,000–$249,999	11,808	14.4	1,706,472	35.1	215,912	9.6	32,930,351	25.1
$250,000–$499,999	1,581	1.9	520,207	10.7	58,668	2.6	19,851,024	15.0
More than $500,000	465	0.6	550,297	11.3	27,800	1.2	42,764,189	32.4
Abnormal farms	26	—	4,572	0.1	1,636	0.1	310,608	0.2
Totals	82,205	100.0	4,854,582	100.0	2,240,936	99.8	131,900,223	100.0

Source: U.S. Census of Agriculture 1982, various volumes.
Note: Percentages may not add up to 100.0 due to rounding.

U.S. distribution (table 12.4). Compared to all farms in the United States, more Wisconsin farms are of the size generally referred to as family farms; fewer are in the "hobby," or part-time and large farm categories. Forty-two percent of Wisconsin farms in 1982 had gross sales of $40,000 to $250,000. These farms accounted for two-thirds of total farm product sales. For the United States, the comparable numbers were 25% and 41.5%. Farms with gross sales in excess of $500,000 accounted for 11% of 1982 Wisconsin farm sales and 32% of U.S. sales. Small farms (1982 sales less than $10,000) represented 30.6% of Wisconsin's farms and 48.9% of U.S. farms.

The family farm concept in Wisconsin is clearly alive. The prototype farming operation is one or two families with at least one spouse engaged full time in the farming operation. Most of the farming labor is provided by family members. Farm income may be supplemented by off-farm earnings of one or more spouses.

Increasingly, however, other prototype farms are emerging. One is a part-time farm with both spouses engaged in off-farm occupations. In this case, farming is more an avocation than a vocation. It is questionable whether some of these small units can legitimately be called farms. Another emerging farm prototype is a large unit with the operator serving as a manager and hiring most of the necessary labor. Alternatively, this unit might be a corporation with several family members as stockholders. Neither of these prototypes is as prevalent in Wisconsin as in other states.

Financial Structure

Based on aggregate measures, the financial condition of Wisconsin agriculture is currently sound but deteriorating. Total equity on 1 January 1984

Table 12.5. Balance Sheet of the Wisconsin Farm Sector, 1 January 1984

Assets ($ million)		
Real estate	$15,320	
Livestock & poultry	2,585	
Machinery & motor vehicles	4,793	
Crops	1,657	
Financial assets	1,388	
Total assets		$25,743
Liabilities ($ million)		
Real estate debt	3,443	
Non-real estate debt	3,426	
Total liabilities		6,869
Equity ($ million)		$18,874

Source: *Economic Indicators of the Farm Sector: State Income and Balance Sheet Statistics,* ECIFS3-4, Economic Research Service, U.S. Dept. of Agriculture, January 1985.
Note: Excludes farm households.

was estimated to be about $19 billion, yielding a debt-asset ratio of 26.7% (table 12.5). Equity as of 1 January 1981 was $23.2 billion. Based on 1983 net farm income, return to equity was 5.1%. Debt ($6.9 billion) was split equally between long-term real estate loans and shorter-term obligations (equipment loans and borrowed operating capital).

Aggregate financial data mask considerable variations among farmers, however. A 1984 survey by the Wisconsin Agriculture Reporting Service indicated that 44% of Wisconsin farmers had no outstanding real estate loans and 42% had no non–real estate debt. Debt-asset ratios for farmers holding debt averaged 34.3%, up from 17.8% in 1979. Debt-asset ratios varied substantially according to the age of farmers, type of farming enterprise, and size of farm. The most highly leveraged farmers were young (under 35) dairy farmers with assets exceeding $1 million.

Many highly leveraged Wisconsin farmers are having difficulty obtaining new financing, owing to a recent combination of low earnings (from relatively low commodity prices and high interest payments) and declining asset values. Farmers who borrowed heavily to purchase land during the 1977–81 period of rapidly escalating land prices are particularly hard-pressed, as land devaluation has severely eroded equity positions. Fourteen percent of surveyed Wisconsin farmers were refused credit between January and May of 1984; 18% were delinquent on real estate loan payments; 25% were delinquent on non-real estate loan payments; and 29% were not current on installment payments to farm supply firms. Problems in obtaining credit increased in early 1985, and, in response, the Wisconsin legislature passed an emergency loan guarantee program for financially troubled farmers.

Wisconsin farmers use a variety of lenders (table 12.6). The Federal Cooperative Farm Credit System (Federal Land Banks, Intermediate Credit Banks,

Table 12.6. Wisconsin Outstanding Farm Debt by Lender, 1 January 1984 (millions of dollars)

Institution	Real Estate Debt	Non–Real Estate Debt
Federal Land Banks	1,648	—
Farmers Home Adm.	335	339
Life insurance cos.	146	—
All operating banks	519	1,148
Individuals and others	1,273	642
Production Credit Assoc.	—	1,137
Fed. Int. Credit Banks	—	82
Commodity Credit Corp.	—	236
Total	3,921	3,584

Source: *Economic Indicators of the Farm Sector: State Income and Balance Sheet Statistics*, ECIFS3-4, Economic Research Service, U.S. Dept. of Agriculture, January 1985.

Note: Includes farm household debt. Totals may not equal sum of items because of rounding.

and Production Credit Associations) is the largest lender, providing 42% of real estate loans and 34% of non–real estate loans. About a third of real estate debt is held by individuals, primarily as land contracts. Private banks hold 13% of long-term real estate debt and 32% of short-term debt.

Effects of Policy on Wisconsin Agriculture

To a large degree, agriculture in Wisconsin is dictated by climate, geography, and natural resources. These represent the constraints on production and marketing. But within these constraints, state and federal policies strongly influence the direction of agricultural development.

Four general areas of policy that have had a major effect on agriculture are discussed here. These vary substantially, both in their effect and in terms of how much influence the state has in their formulation.

Macroeconomic Policy

Except as measured by political influence in Congress, farmers and other Wisconsin residents have little control over broad national economic policies. Thus, it is frustrating to farmers that federal fiscal and monetary policy has, in large part, caused the acute financial problems facing farmers at this time.

The critical monetary policy decision affecting farmers was made in October 1979, when the Federal Reserve Board discarded previous goals of using changes in the money supply to regulate interest rates and initiated a new policy of tightly controlling money supply growth in order to reduce inflation and inflationary expectations. The Fed has achieved remarkable success in attaining this goal. The Consumer Price Index plunged from more than 13% in 1980 to less than 4% by 1983. However, the battle against inflation was won at the cost of high interest rates, particularly when expressed in real terms, that is, net of the rate of inflation. The prime rate rose to a record 19% in 1981 before falling to 11% in 1983. But the recent fall has not been accompanied by a fall in real interest rates, since the reduction in inflation more than offset the interest rate drop. Real interest rates of around 8% compare historically with rates of 2–3%.

The important fiscal policy change occurred with the passage of the Economic Recovery Tax Act of 1981, which led to a drop in federal tax receipts in fiscal 1982 with no accompanying reduction in government outlays. Resulting federal deficits have been in the $150 billion to $200 billion range. The magnitude of the federal deficit undoubtedly stimulated economic growth during the early 1980s, but at a cost of upward pressure on interest rates amplifying those stemming from monetary policy.

The effect of these macroeconomic policy changes on farmers has been on both the cost and revenue sides of their ledger. Interest expenses paid by U.S. farmers increased to over $20 billion in 1982, and in 1983 interest costs exceeded net farm income. Monetary and fiscal policy combined to yield a strengthening of the U.S. dollar against trade-weighted currencies of more than 45% between 1979 and 1984. The strong U.S. dollar reversed a ten-year upward trend in agricultural exports, during which time farmers brought into production an additional 50 million acres of cropland. Evaporating market outlets caused a burgeoning surplus and depressed commodity prices, in spite of government efforts to control excess capacity. Protected by high price supports, the dairy industry substantially increased production in response to low grain prices, causing unprecedented government purchases of manufactured dairy products.

Macroeconomic policy also affected farmland values. Low inflation rates sharply cut back speculative demand for land, and, coupled with falling commodity prices, caused a precipitous devaluation of land, much of which had been recently acquired by farmers. Both farmers and lenders found their balance sheets rapidly deteriorating.

At the same time that these changes in macroeconomic policy occurred, the agricultural sector was becoming increasingly sensitive to them. Interest rates affect farmers in their role as major borrowers of both real estate and operating capital. Technology has transformed agriculture from a labor-intensive to a capital-intensive industry. This heightens the impact of interest rate increases and limits farmers' ability to tighten their belts during bad times. Currently, farmers depend on overseas markets for about a third of their total production. Policies affecting the value of the U.S. dollar can generate wide swings in the cost of U.S. agricultural commodities to foreign buyers.

Agriculture's plight under current monetary and fiscal policy has not gone unnoticed by federal legislators, but timely remedial policy changes are unlikely. Macroeconomic policy affects every sector of the economy and every individual. Thus, tax increases, expenditure cuts, or reinflation that would benefit farmers would require sacrifices of too many other sectors and individuals (voters).

Tax Policy

Local, state, and federal governments levy taxes on farmers. Hence, the state has at least some control of tax effects on agriculture through its own tax structure and through local cost- and revenue-sharing practices.

There are two major issues relating to taxes and farming: (1) tax incentives for outside investment and farm expansion, and (2) the equity of property taxes as a source of revenue.

Tax laws treat farmers differently from other businessmen in permitting cash accounting, special treatment of capital assets, and special depreciation allowances. These provisions are generally supported by farmers, and, in many cases, were sought by them. But special tax treatment of farming has encouraged the use of farming for tax-sheltering purposes. Individuals can write off farm losses against nonfarm income and convert ordinary income into capital gains.

The incidence of tax-loss farming in the state is apparent from Department of Revenue statistics (see Wisconsin Legislative Fiscal Bureau 1985; Governor's Commission on Agriculture 1985). For the 1983 tax year, 7% of Wisconsin tax filers reporting farm losses in the range of $25,000 to $50,000 had Wisconsin adjusted gross income exceeding $75,000 and, as a group, averaged $180,000 in nonfarm income. Six percent of tax filers with farm losses over $50,000 had Wisconsin adjusted gross income of over $75,000 and averaged $383,000 in nonfarm income.

Tax sheltering allows nonfarm investors a competitive edge over bona fide farm operators, whose viability is dependent upon achieving profits. Tax sheltering tends to bid up the value of farm assets, since rates of return to nonfarm investors who invest in farming to shelter income are higher than for farm operators. Tax incentives also encourage increasing farm size. Specifically, investment tax credit and rapid depreciation induce adoption of equipment, structures, and technology that favor larger farming units.

The tax-equity issue in Wisconsin revolves around the question of what local services should be funded by property taxes. By the nature of their business, farmers are obligated to hold a large proportion of their assets as taxable property. Hence, they are saddled with a disproportionately large share of the total property tax levy. In 1981, 13% of statewide property taxes were collected on agricultural property, while farmers represented only about 3½% of all property taxpayers (Wisconsin Legislative Fiscal Bureau 1985). Wisconsin relies more heavily on property tax revenue for financing local services than competing agricultural states. Farm real estate taxes per acre in 1982 were $14.04 in Wisconsin, ranking the state seventh in the nation (U.S. Department of Agriculture 1984). Among major agricultural states, only Michigan and New York had land taxes exceeding Wisconsin's. In 1982, Minnesota levied property taxes of only $5.84 per acre, and Iowa, $8.63.[1]

Several forms of property tax relief are available to farmers, including homestead tax credit, the Farmland Preservation program, property tax credit for principal residences, and, in some cases, property tax exemption. However, most of these programs have restrictions or limitations that severely limit participation.

Wisconsin farmers are especially concerned about the use of property tax revenue to fund public schools. About 64% of total property tax collected in Wisconsin was used for elementary and secondary schools, and 7% for vocational, technical, and adult education.

Federal Price and Income Support Programs

Another set of policies vitally affecting Wisconsin agriculture but over which its citizens have little control are federal commodity programs. In 1982, 68.5% of Wisconsin farm cash receipts were from commodities for which a price support program was effective (Jesse 1984). The corresponding figure for the United States was less than 40%. The dairy price support program alone augmented dairy farmers' milk checks in 1984 by $1.10 per cwt., adding more than a quarter of a billion dollars to Wisconsin gross farm income.

The dairy price support program involves Commodity Credit Corporation (CCC) purchases of manufactured dairy products at prices that allow reasonably efficient processors to return the raw milk support price to dairy farmers. The program is, therefore, inactive whenever butter, nonfat dry milk, and cheese prices are above the CCC purchase prices. Overall, milk production in excess of demand is reflected by greater manufacturing, and, hence, accelerated CCC purchases.

Prior to 1981, price support levels were tied to parity.[2] Since that time, support levels have been specified legislatively without regard to parity. The announced raw milk support price applies to Grade B or manufacturing milk. Grade A milk is priced administratively through federal marketing orders which use Grade B milk prices as a base. Hence, all milk prices are affected by the price support program.

The cornerstone of price and income support programs for grain is the

CCC nonrecourse loan program. Pledging harvested grain as collateral, farmers may receive loans at the announced support price. If the market price rises above the support level, farmers can pay back their loan with interest and sell grain pledged as collateral. If the market price fails to rise above the support level, farmers grant title to the grain to the CCC and the loan is considered repaid. Recently, target prices and deficiency payments have been used in conjunction with the CCC nonrecourse loan program. Farmers are eligible to receive a deficiency payment equal to the difference between an announced target price and the market price in exhange for agreeing to "set aside" some of their normal grain acreage.

Federal price and income support programs have been subjected to sharp criticism recently for having side effects which, in combination, have far outweighed any benefits to farmers. Support payments have tended to benefit larger farms, accelerating trends toward concentration in the farm production sector. High support prices for grain have inhibited exports by making it more lucrative to store grain than to sell it. The programs have been costly, both in terms of taxpayer outlays for payments and consumer cost due to prices exceeding levels that would prevail without their use. The programs have generated distorted price signals to farmers, postponing necessary adjustments in resource allocation.

Public support for eliminating federal price and income support programs or making them more "market oriented" is strong. At issue, however, is how to achieve market orientation and how rapidly to move in that direction. In particular, the current financial plight of the farming sector suggests that a rapid termination of existing programs would cause considerable hardship. Wisconsin agriculture would be seriously disrupted by abrupt elimination of the dairy price support program.

Research, Extension. and Vocational Training

The state's agriculture has been strongly influenced by the research and extension activities of the Wisconsin Agricultural Experiment Station. Suitable varieties, species, and production and management practices have been developed to allow the state's farmers to remain competitive and to effectively exploit the state's resource base. In recognition of very high rates of return on research and extension expenditures, the state has consistently supported the Agricultural Experiment Station.

Agricultural research has not been without its critics. Some have criticized research emphasis on production efficiency, which, they argue, has tended to favor larger farms over traditional family operations. These critics have urged a reorientation of research toward increasing profitability rather than efficiency, and expanding research on the social impacts of agricultural technology.

Vocational training in agriculture is provided through three sources; high school Vo-Ag programs, Vocational, Technical, and Adult Education (VTAE), and UW–Madison's Farm and Industry Short Course (FISC). In 1983–84, 20,271 students at 271 Wisconsin high schools received Vo-Ag training. About 4,400 students are enrolled in VTAE agricultural programs. FISC enrollment is about 100 students per year.

The VTAE program serves as an informal "extension service"; many farmers seek management and technical advice from VTAE staff. There has been no formal attempt to integrate VTAE with UW–Extension or to delineate separate responsibilities.

Nearly half of VTAE funding is from property tax revenue. This has been criticized as inappropriate and inconsistent with funding of other postsecondary education in the state, which receives no local tax revenues.

Emerging Policy Issues

Agriculture in Wisconsin has changed to conform with changes in technology, food and fiber preference, and agricultural policy. These changes will continue and probably accelerate. Some forces driving future change are discussed below.

Changing Comparative Advantage

The Great Lakes states, including Wisconsin, have historically possessed a comparative advantage in dairy farming, especially production of milk for manufactured dairy products. The reasons for this comparative advantage are rooted in the region's location relative to major East Coast metropolitan areas and low milk production costs relative to other parts of the country. The traditional size of dairy unit, a herd small enough to be handled with family labor, was reasonably efficient given existing technology. Use of unskilled and usually unpaid family labor contributed to the production cost advantage. Finally, owner-managers of smaller, family-sized dairy units have been willing to accept less than market rates of return on investment and labor, apparently in exchange for nonpecuniary benefits associated with dairy farming.

Some recent changes have diminished the importance of these historical factors favoring dairying in the traditional areas. Population has shifted to the Sunbelt states—the Southwest and the Southeast. This has provided expanded fluid milk marketing opportunities for dairy farmers in these areas. Southwestern states have also benefited relative to the Upper Midwest by federal water projects which have subsidized the cost of irrigation. Through federal taxes, Wisconsin farmers and other residents are financing their southwestern competitors. Sunbelt dairy farmers, who purchase most of their grain and forages, have also disproportionally benefited from cheap grain prices vis-à-vis Upper Midwest dairy farmers, who produce their own feeds.

Recent technological changes have tended to favor large dairy farms. In particular, some new herd housing, feeding, and milking practices have involved substantial economies of scale. Innovations in herd health and nutrition have placed premiums on the ability to enhance management skills and to practice labor specialization. Traditional Wisconsin dairy farms, which combine crop production with milk production, have not been capable of fully taking advantage of some of these changes relative to highly specialized dairy farms in other parts of the country.

Emerging technologies may serve to widen the economic disparity between large and small dairy farms. Of special note is bovine growth hormone (bGH), which has experimentally increased milk production per cow by as much as 40%. Yield increases from the hormone depend, in part, on close monitoring of feeding. Hence, the technology may favor larger, specialized dairy farming units, that can economically use computerized feeding systems.

Given the current size distribution of dairy farms and differences in production and management practices, it is clear that Wisconsin and other Great Lakes states have a diminishing comparative advantage in dairy farming. The chances of Wisconsin losing its leading position in dairy farming are remote. An exodus of traditional family-sized units, however, seems likely, to be replaced by dairy farms that are large enough to efficiently utilize emerging technologies.

In a positive vein, Wisconsin may be gaining comparative advantage as a grain-producer. While the state has historically been on the fringe of the corn belt, changes in the availability and the cost of water could substantially change interregional relationships in corn and other feed grain production costs. Much of the recent expansion in U.S. corn acreage has been in areas over the shrinking Ogalala Aquifer. Population increases in parts of the Southwest are yielding growing pressures for market pricing of irrigation water in those areas. On the demand side, sales of U.S. feed grains in international markets will likely expand from current depressed levels, though perhaps not to the levels experienced in the late 1970s. In spite of an apparent world overcapacity, the potential for a rapidly expanding export market remains strong because of the large number of developing countries that have not yet converted from grain- to animal-based diets.

The Farm Structure Issue

The nature of Wisconsin's comparative advantage is crucial in ascertaining directions in farm structure. But major increases in labor productivity can be expected in both dairy and crop farming. Hence, there will be inexorable pressures on existing farming operations to either expand or exit.

The trend toward fewer and larger farms in the state yields several concerns: Is this trend being exacerbated by distorted economic incentives, such as federal commodity programs or tax-loss farming? What does the trend portend for food prices in the long run? What will happen to the quality of soil and water as farms become larger and ownership is possibly separated from management? How will local communities remain viable in the face of declining farm numbers?

While it is not possible to separate the structural effects of agricultural policies from those related to increasing productivity, the distinction is clearly important. Productivity-induced structural change is desirable, at least on grounds of economic efficiency. Policy-induced structural changes may be inefficient in the sense of permitting some farmers to operate with subsidized costs or revenues. More important, policy-related incentives are controllable and can be reversed.

There is ample evidence to suggest that increasing productivity has lessened the ability of smaller farming units to compete. That is, quite apart from tax policy and the distribution of commodity program benefits, there are differences in production costs between large and small farms. Also, while many technical efficiencies can be gained by modest-sized units, large farms have an additional cost advantage in purchasing and marketing. Hence, without special treatment, a continuing loss of farmers in the state is inevitable.

The economic implications of concentration in farming are not particularly alarming in the food production and distribution sector. Concentration is not likely to raise food prices. On the contrary, greater concentration in some commodity sectors, notably broilers and pork, can be correlated with lower real prices. Monopolization of the food production sector is simply not a realistic threat in the short run. Nor will continued trends in concentration likely cause gross neglect of land. While poor methods of soil and water conservation are more apparent when practiced on a larger scale, there is no evidence of a distinction among farm size classes with respect to resource husbandry.

It *is* likely that the continuing trend toward fewer and larger farms will create severe adjustment problems and high dislocation costs in some rural communities. The viability of many businesses in farm towns and villages is related to the number of farmers in the area, not the volume of production. Also, large farmers tend to make fewer local purchases of production inputs, preferring to negotiate volume discounts from direct distributors.

In municipalities heavily dependent on farming, a snowball effect is likely. A general loss of revenue combined with attrition of some businesses would be expected to increase the tax burden and/or reduce the quality of local services for remaining residents, thus accelerating the rate of exodus.

The viability of rural communities may depend to a large extent on whether displaced farmers can remain as nonfarmers. A standard pattern for retiring Wisconsin farmers is to retain life estate in their farmsteads or to move to a nearby town or village. This lends some stability to economic bases. Whether younger displaced farmers have this option depends on local employment opportunities.

The social implications of increasing farm concentration may be of considerably more concern than the economic implications. Unfortunately, such social costs as increasing population density in large metropolitan areas or a decline in rural qualities are impossible to quantify. But these are not trivial concerns. Agricultural fundamentalism is alive and well, as evidenced by the increasing involvement of rural-urban coalitions in espousing preservation of the family farm on grounds of the need to maintain rural values and "appropriate" population distributions.

Such organizations are frequently frustrated by the absence of state or federal farm structure objectives. In particular, federal agricultural legislation typically extols the virtues of "family farms" while the legislation itself is at best size-neutral; more likely, size-enhancing.

Options and Recommendations

Numerous questions result from an assessment of the evolution, current status, and likely future environment of Wisconsin agriculture. Only two of the questions are addressed here: (1) How can Wisconsin's regional comparative advantage be strengthened? (2) Should measures be taken to slow or reverse trends in concentration, that is, should the state intervene to assure the continued viability of Wisconsin family farms?

Strengthening Regional Comparative Advantage

The first basic question has two embedded assumptions. The first is that agriculture is important enough to the state of Wisconsin to justify special support programs. The second assumption is that without special support, Wisconsin's competitive edge in agriculture will decline. The first assumption is beyond debate, given the contribution of agriculture to the overall state economy. The second assumption seems equally valid. Recent changes in population distribution and relative milk production costs, combined with emerging technologies favoring large-sized operations and a large chronic surplus of milk, suggest that Wisconsin's long-term dominance in the U.S. dairy industry may be more tenuously held. In any case, a benign state position regarding Wisconsin agriculture will not strengthen its position relative to other states.

Some possible state actions that could improve the interregional position of Wisconsin agriculture follow:

1. Wisconsin should monitor conditions in other states to ensure that Wisconsin farmers are not being penalized by state actions. The most obvious example in this regard concerns property taxes. Wisconsin must align its property tax structure with that of competing states. Similarly, a competitive Wisconsin agricultural industry cannot afford to have environmental, farm income tax, agricultural zoning, or other regulations that impose higher costs on Wisconsin farmers than farmers face in other states.

2. Wisconsin should aggressively seek new farm product markets and support similar private efforts. New markets include exports, new products, and new food manufacturing firms. The state should encourage and assist producer-funded product development and promotion efforts. Much new market development work is going on through the Wisconsin Department of Agriculture, Trade, and Consumer Protection. These efforts need additional state support.

3. In conjunction with other midwestern states with common interests, Wisconsin should aggressively seek federal legislation that will permit the state to exploit natural advantages. This is not to suggest state lobbying efforts to obtain special handouts or lucrative commodity program benefits. It does suggest aggressive defensive action in opposition to legislation or federal regulations that negatively affect Wisconsin agriculture. As an example of such action, the state has recently testified against changes in federal milk marketing orders that would benefit other regions relative to Wisconsin. This is an appropriate and highly important role for the state.

4. The state should enhance the capability of the University of Wisconsin Extension Service and VTAE to conduct applied research and present educational programs on technology and management practices that will strengthen Wisconsin's competitive position. Particular emphasis should be on adapting practices proved to be cost effective in other regions or for different-sized operations. When new technologies are commercially available, Wisconsin farmers must be able to be the early adopters. Coordinated interdisciplinary research of the type that will be conducted within the University of Wisconsin Dairy Research Center is of special value in this regard.

Structure Modification

Without active intervention, trends toward fewer and larger farms in the state will undoubtedly continue and possibly accelerate. This will probably not result in large economic cost, at least as measured by increasing food cost or impaired long-run productive capacity. It will change the rural landscape, physically, economically, and socially. It will threaten the existence of rural communities that cannot provide employment opportunities for displaced farmers. In any case, it will probably reduce economic activity in rural communities as larger farmers bypass local suppliers in purchasing inputs and marketing their commodities. Perhaps most important, increasing concentration in farming will further diminish the size of the population holding traditional rural values that all but a few cynics respect.

The benefits associated with a dispersed farming sector are partly intangible and predominately subjective. In contrast, the benefits of large-scale agricultural enterprises are real and measurable as per unit returns above cost. Consequently, reversing or stabilizing trends in concentration requires that society be willing to incur the associated costs. Little is known about the cost of maintaining a dispersed agriculture by restricting economic incentives to farm growth. But they are not likely to be expensive in a relative sense, since the proportion of disposable income spent on food in the United States is smaller than for any other country.

If a dispersed agriculture is deemed politically desirable, the decision to implement structure modification policies must be made at the federal level. Wisconsin can do little unilaterally without risking deterioration in its competitive position.

Feasible means of promoting family-sized farming are noted below. These vary according to their potential effectiveness and their effect on economic efficiency in the farming sector.

1. Eliminate tax-related incentives to expand farm size. This is a reasonable policy goal on grounds of economic efficiency whether or not a farm structure goal is simultaneously being pursued. Farm asset values should reflect farm returns, not tax-sheltering strategies by high-income farmers and nonfarmers. Farm prices should reflect a competitive rate of return on equity, not a rate subsidized by tax losses.

2. Target federal farm program benefits toward family-sized farms. To the extent that commodity programs represent a political decision to redistribute income to farmers, it makes little sense to provide the bulk of these benefits to higher-income farmers. Targeting benefits has been attempted in the past through payment limitations. However, limitations have been set at such high levels as to be ineffective in differentially benefiting family-sized units. And, recent programs such as the 1983 payment-in-kind programs for grains and cotton and the 1984–85 dairy diversion program have not included limits on individual farm payments. More attention needs to be given to size-based eligibility requirements and income insurance for family farms.

3. Impose compulsory acreage or production quotas. Acreage or marketing allotments based on historical production levels can serve to freeze an existing structural configuration. Proportional cutbacks from established bases can, in turn, elevate prices to levels that would provide "reasonable"

levels of profits to family-sized farming units. The obvious problem with such an approach is that prices that yield reasonable levels of profits to the family-sized units could well yield exorbitant profits to larger farms. Incentives to increase productivity would be stifled if allotments were not transferable, and substantial windfall gains would accrue to original allotment-holders if they were.

Evidence from the Canadian dairy sector casts some doubt on the effectiveness of quotas in maintaining farm numbers. Ontario, which is the leading dairy province, has had fluid milk quotas since 1965 and manufacturing milk quotas since 1968. From 1966 to 1981, the rate of decline in the number of Ontario dairy farms was greater than in Wisconsin.

4. Prohibit farms larger than some specified size. Many states, including Wisconsin, restrict farm ownership by nonfarm corporations or aliens. Similar restrictions on farm size could be enacted. The effectiveness of such a policy in achieving a goal of family-sized farms is questionable, however, since subversion through fragmentation of ownership would probably be inevitable. Moreover, such stringent state control might be considered tantamount to socialism, and, in any case, could place Wisconsin at a competitive disadvantage relative to other states without comparable size restrictions.

NOTES

1. See Lampman and McBride, chapter 3 in this volume, for an expanded discussion of Wisconsin's dependence on the property tax.

2. Parity relates to the ratio of farm prices to farm costs relative to a base period (1910–14). The dairy price support program required milk prices to be supported at 75–90% of parity.

13

Natural Resource Policy

KATHLEEN SEGERSON AND DANIEL W. BROMLEY

Introduction

The use of Wisconsin's natural resources has been a topic of considerable interest over the last several years and will undoubtedly continue to be debated in the future. That debate will occur in many arenas, including the state legislature, the executive agencies, and the news media. In almost all cases, the policy problem is one of allocating a finite resource to meet several objectives that are often viewed as being incompatible. For example, policies designed to improve environmental quality are often accused of stifling economic growth by those who claim that the controls are too stringent, and that they thereby encourage existing firms to leave Wisconsin or discourage prospective firms from moving to the state.

This view of natural resource policy as an allocation problem highlights the fact that goals relating to natural resource use should not be defined along single-issue lines. The same people who enjoy the fruits of improved environmental quality—a scenic vista along the Mississippi River, a quiet canoe trip down the Bois Brule River, and the joy of catching a respectable (and edible) fish—also benefit from a healthy state economy. Thus, natural resource policy should be viewed as a challenge to satisfy objectives that are viewed as, but need not be, largely incompatible.

This is not to imply that formulating natural resource policy will not involve conflict. In fact, conflicts over resource use are the catalysts for policy formation. Thus, before turning to a more specific discussion of natural resource policy, we have chosen to devote the next section of this chapter to a brief discussion of the nature of the policy-making environment and the role of conflict in the policy process. Our hope is that this will aid in more fully understanding the sections that follow. The third section outlines some common characteristics of environmental problems. We then turn from these gen-

250

eral issues to a more specific discussion of natural resource policy in Wisconsin. The fourth section explores several important environmental policy problems, while the last section discusses areas in which the state's natural resources offer promise for stimulating economic growth. A final section presents some conclusions.

The Policy-Making Environment

The essence of the development of natural resource policy is bargaining to resolve competing goals and interests. One individual is harmed by the pesticide use of another; a downstream food-processing plant must pay to have water cleaned up after it has been defiled by an upstream factory; a rural resident must purchase bottled water because local groundwater is contaminated with aldicarb; an angler finds a favorite lake silting in because of the bad soil-management practices of upstream farmers; another angler is alarmed to find that fish populations are possibly harmed by acidic rainfall said to originate with coal-fired electric generating plants; and a forest owner sees the trees harmed by the same acid deposition. The problem is, quite clearly, one of costs being imposed on one interest group by another.

This way of viewing the problem is helpful in understanding the actions of the state, federal agencies, and the courts in natural resource policy. For it is citizen pressure, brought to bear on legislative bodies by those now bearing unwanted costs, that is the origin of new laws that must be enforced by administrative agencies such as the U.S. Environmental Protection Agency and the Wisconsin Department of Natural Resources. While the administrative agencies are the focus of considerable wrath regarding "government intervention," a more realistic view would reveal that the executive branch agencies are simply attempting to carry out legislative mandates. Indeed, it is not uncommon to find executive branch agencies being sued for an absence of zealotry in following environmental laws.

We emphasize the three-part nature of environmental policy—the offending party, the victim, and government—because the conventional perspective is that the Department of Natural Resources "interferes with the rights" of an individual for no apparent reason; in fact that reason is precisely the harm that certain individuals and groups are experiencing under the status quo use of natural resources.

The resolution of natural resource problems is made more difficult because the environmental legislation of the last decade has confronted and condemned as antisocial long-standing patterns of human behavior—and these include accepted business practices. The actions of industries, long the figurative, if not literal, patrons of communities, have suddenly been labeled villainous; small wonder that the owners and managers of these firms feel unfairly accused. And the workers, many of whom are the most avid in seeking restoration of the state's fishing waters, find themselves caught in the uncomfortable position of advocating environmental policy that may jeopardize their very means of existence.

The tensions are not confined to industrial activities. In agriculture, the use of chemicals to control pests and weeds is important to produce abundance, yet these same chemicals may pose a threat to others in the form of polluted drinking water. More interestingly, it may be the farmers themselves who are most at risk from such practices, since they obtain their drinking water closest to the places where the chemicals are being applied. Their actions as economic agents run counter to their interests as consumers.

Science plays an important role in the creation of natural resource problems, as well as in their resolution. The creative role follows from the myriad products now available that are often the root of recent problems—toxic chemicals, nonbiodegradable materials, and the antibiotics that allow large concentrations of livestock and hence large concentrations of animal wastes. The other side of science is that we can now have more definitive information on the probable causes of problems and so can be more precise in our search for solutions. In earlier times when illnesses and death were strictly the province of one's God, there was little interest in public policy directed at reducing the prevalence of these fates. When science permits us to establish causality between the incidence of cancer and certain industrial processes, then public policy is very much at center stage.

We have a policy environment, therefore, that is dominated by conflicts among individuals and groups, with federal and state agencies caught in the middle as brokers and agents in the political struggle over which interests will be given what degree of protection. This policy environment is both informed and influenced by the availability of scientific information that establishes, in many instances, the direct cause of the harm being experienced by certain groups. Finally, the policy environment is dominated by a struggle over the presumed "rights" of the various participants in the debate. That is, one group is certain that it has a "right" to clean air or water while another group insists that it has a "right" to continue its traditional business practices. It is left to the legislatures and the courts to decide whose interests will be given the legal protection of a "right" and whose interests will instead be interpreted to include a "duty" to protect someone else's newly codified "right." It is then up to the administrative agencies to create rules and procedures that will implement these decisions.

The inescapable conflicts of natural resource policy cannot help but influence the resolution of those problems. In contrast to some other areas of public policy, where the interests of various groups are not so obviously at odds, natural resource policy is dominated by this polarity and it influences profoundly the complexion of the policy process as well as the ultimate resolution. The challenge is to take these competing and often conflicting interests into account, not in an atmosphere of confrontation but rather in an atmosphere that tries to find as many common interests as possible and then develops compromises with as broad a base for acceptability as possible. The adversary posturing needs to give way to well-intentioned behavior that understands the legitimacy of the other side's position, and to a willingness to work together to achieve continued economic development consistent with a safe and healthy environment.

In addition, it is necessary for all parties with an interest in Wisconsin's environmental policy to understand that change is inevitable, and that what is done today—with today's knowledge and economic conditions—will most certainly require modification when tomorrow's conditions turn out to be different from those we are now accustomed to. Recognizing this necessity of choice, on a continual basis, will be helpful in facilitating the transitions that are surely required. It must be understood that businesses require some certainty over their immediate planning horizon, and that expensive adjustments to processes cannot always be easily or quickly implemented. At the same time, those responsible for creating environmental damage must recognize that the mere fact of their practices having always been part of their routine does not give them an inalienable right to continue to impose costs on others.

If policymakers in Wisconsin can design environmental policies that remove the incentives for adversary relations—and search for policies that encourage efficiency and equity—then natural resource integrity will continue to be one of Wisconsin's strongest appeals for continued economic growth.

Common Characteristics of Environmental Problems

Many environmental problems share three characteristics that are fundamental and must be recognized in the formation of effective policy. The first, as noted in the previous section, is the effect that the actions of one party can inadvertently have on other parties (i.e., the interdependence between the decisions made by one group and the well-being of another unsuspecting—and generally ungrateful—group). Second, in most cases, both the effects of a given activity and the cost of reducing it will vary from source to source depending on the nature of the physical environment that links the source party with the affected party. The third characteristic is the pervasive uncertainty that surrounds these questions of natural resource use.

Joint Costs

When the activities of one person or firm affect the well-being or output of other people or firms, economists say that an "externality" exists. Externalities exist in nearly all environmental problems, since some of the negative effects of certain actions are borne by people other than those who take and benefit from the actions. For example, in the case of nonpoint source pollution, farmers reap the benefits (in terms of reduced expenditures) of allowing "disposal" of animal waste through runoff or of raising crops with little regard for soil erosion; yet the costs of these activities are borne by a different group (e.g., recreationists who suffer losses in boating, swimming, or fishing pleasures due to increased eutrophication and sedimentation, or consumers whose water supplies have been polluted by runoff carrying animal waste or chemicals from fertilizers or pesticides). In the case of hazardous waste disposal, generators (or, more generally, consumers of the products whose production generates the wastes) have benefited from low-cost land disposal, while a large portion of the costs of that management technique have been borne by those living in the vicinity of the disposal sites, who pay in terms of both health effects and losses in property values.

The fundamental problem is that often those who benefit from an activity do not bear the full costs of the activity and weigh only their private costs against their private benefits in deciding whether or not an action is warranted. State and national policymakers, on the other hand, must think more broadly when evaluating the desirability of certain activities and weigh the total social costs, including those external to the perpetrator, against the total benefits.

This broader approach to (or definition of) the problem will generally yield different conclusions than would private decision making, and often the public sector must then step in to ensure that private decisions satisfy social objectives. Such attempts to "internalize" what would otherwise be considered by the private sector to be external costs are generally met with outcries of government "interference" in private decisions. The actions are viewed by those forced to internalize those costs as an unnecessary intrusion and curtailment of individual freedom. However, this loss of freedom by the perpetrator is matched by the new freedom of those previously forced to bear those external costs. It is an inescapable aspect of policy formation in the matter of externalities that one person's relief comes at the cost of another person's inability to continue some traditional practice. It thus pits citizens against one another in the legislative, administrative, and judicial processes.

Of course, the solution to this confrontation typically does not leave one group an absolute winner and the other an absolute loser; it is more a compromise between the two. This is as it should be, not only from the point of view of fairness or "equity" but very often in terms of economic efficiency as well. Solving an externality problem from an economic efficiency standpoint does not necessarily imply eliminating the activity generating the externality. For example, externalities from hazardous waste disposal do not suggest a ban on making products that generate hazardous waste; nor do they necessarily imply that the use of land disposal should be prohibited. In setting public policies regarding externalities, it must be recognized that there are costs associated not only with the presence of an externality but also with eliminating it. For example, the calculation of costs should include the loss of benefits from consumption of products that have generated hazardous wastes or the increased waste management costs if a more expensive alternative to land disposal must be used. Both kinds of costs, those of having the externality and those of not having it, must be balanced in determining the appropriate public policy response.

Site-Specific Costs and Benefits

To date, the typical approach to environmental policy in the United States has been to recognize that the activities of one group can impose costs on another group, and the response has often been to regulate those activities across the board (i.e., to impose mandatory controls or operating practices for those activities). For example, limits are set on allowable emissions for many pollutants, the use of "best available control technology (BACT)" is required, or standards are set for construction of facilities.

These across-the-board approaches often ignore cost differentials in pollution abatement. For example, the costs of reducing soil erosion can vary widely across farms because of different soil, weather, and topographic characteristics. Control on steep slopes will generally be more expensive than that on flat land, other things being equal. Likewise, the benefits of reduced erosion can vary widely. Runoff from farms located in close proximity to vulnerable waterways will generally impose greater external costs than that from more distant farms. Thus, reduced erosion may benefit some farms more than others. In the case of acid rain, emission sources that are upwind of lakes, streams, or land areas susceptible to the effects of acidification will have larger effects than those in a more benign location. As far as damages are concerned, a ton of sulfur dioxide emitted in one place may differ substantially from a ton emitted elsewhere.

Although it may be an obvious and well-recognized fact that damages resulting from a given activity and the costs of reducing it vary across locations, it is seldom incorporated into natural resource policies. When cost differentials are ignored, any given level of total abatement may not be achieved at least cost, since polluters with high incremental abatement costs will be forced to abate to the same level as those with low costs. If the associated administrative or transaction costs are low, a policy that results in more abatement by low-cost firms than by high-cost firms could reduce the total cost of a desired level of abatement. Likewise, discharge at different locations will have different ultimate effects because of variations in the physical link between points of discharge and damage points. If this fact is disregarded, a specific reduction in damages may not be achieved at the lowest possible cost to society, since polluters whose discharge causes a relatively low level of damage will be forced to abate to the same level as those causing much greater harm. Again, depending on administrative and transaction costs, a policy that recognizes differential benefits may be more cost effective.

Of course, cost effectiveness is not the only criterion to be used in deciding among policies. One of the original arguments for the use of across-the-board regulation was based on "fairness." It was argued that differential abatement requirements based on site-specific costs or benefits would put firms with high abatement requirements at a competitive disadvantage relative to firms with low requirements; thus it would be more "equitable" to have all firms reduce emissions by an equal amount (or percentage). However, this means that firms for which it is relatively inexpensive to reduce emissions are, in fact, affected less severely than are firms for which a reduction in emissions is quite expensive. Likewise, using uniform requirements where the benefits differ implies that states or regions where damages are low pay the price (in the form of excessive abatement) for keeping industries competitive in high-damage regions rather than having high-damage regions pay for competitiveness in the form of lower environmental quality. In other words, low-damage regions subsidize high-damage regions so that the latter can remain competitive. Thus, by holding a false conception of "fair treatment," the policy process can actually encourage solutions that are not only more expensive than necessary, but also quite unfair. This could be avoided by policies that recognize both differential costs and benefits.

There have been examples of regulatory programs that incorporate differential costs and impacts. In fact, the state of Wisconsin has taken the lead in several such attempts for control of point source water pollution, including the use of transferable discharge allocations and variable permits. These innovative approaches allow a specified reduction in pollutant loadings to be achieved at reduced costs. Of course, as noted above, the additional benefits that can result from site-specific regulation must be compared to any additional administrative or enforcement costs in determining appropriate policies.

Uncertainty

A third common characteristic of resource problems is pervasive uncertainty. This uncertainty takes several different forms. The first is physical uncertainty, which exists when the behavior of certain physical phenomena is not well understood. In the case of groundwater contamination from agricultural chemicals, we do not have enough information on groundwater movement to trace a particular contamination point back to a particular source. Likewise, knowing the exact source of contamination is often of little help in determining the ultimate destination of a contaminant. This aspect of uncertainty makes it difficult to design well-targeted and cost-effective policies for controlling groundwater contamination. The problems of nonpoint pollution and acid rain have similar elements of physical uncertainty.

A second form of uncertainty concerns the ultimate impacts of various levels of contamination on human health and ecosystem integrity. Again, using groundwater contamination as an example, we do not know the precise human and animal health effects that result from alternative levels of aldicarb in drinking water. Much debate has focused on the human response to different levels of particular contaminants, but to date the results are generally imprecise.

Technological uncertainty is a third important form of uncertainty. Many of the externalities that dominate debates on natural resource policy arise because of technical options that appear as part of a modern and industrialized economy. Chemicals, large machinery, and other man-made items generate many of the conflicts that natural resource policy must address. At the same time new technical knowledge and devices may hold the solution to current externalities. Since it is difficult to foresee the technological options that will exist in the future, we must forge policy in the absence of complete knowledge about future technical solutions as well as technical threats.

A final area of uncertainty concerns the behavioral dimension of citizens as they confront altered choices in their daily lives. What will farmers do if aldicarb is banned? What will electric utilities do if limits are placed on sulfur emissions? What will tourists do if Wisconsin's waters become more seriously polluted?

Environmental policy has generally addressed the uncertainty inherent in environmental problems through the use of compliance standards that are based on some notion of risk. However, if they are not contingent on changing environmental conditions, compliance standards generally lack the flexibility necessary to respond quickly to new information as it becomes available or new conditions as they arise. Furthermore, the use of compliance standards puts the entire burden of the associated risks on the victims or the public sector rather than on the polluters. In other words, polluters may not be held liable for damages as long as they are in compliance with the mandatory standards or regulations, and the potential effects of having regulations that turn out to be insufficient to protect the environment are borne by society at large. That is, the residual risk remains with the victims of pollution. Of course, if the regulations turn out to have been too stringent, the benefits are also reaped by society. Thus, in setting the regulations society gambles on the ultimate outcome, but given those regulations, polluters may be absolved of risk.

The alternative to the use of compliance standards is to mandate a level of resource quality and hold polluters responsible for any damages in excess of some specified targets. This places all of the risk associated with different levels of control on the polluting parties and provides the necessary incentives for pollution abatement. However, the difficulties of establishing who is legally responsible for an observed violation of the target resource quality level can limit the practical use of this approach.

Natural Resource Integrity

We turn now to more specific issues of natural resource policy in Wisconsin and begin with environmental issues relating to natural resource integrity. The state faces pressing environmental problems stemming from both the agricultural and the industrial sectors. These include soil erosion and siltation/sedimentation, fertilizer and pesticide runoffs, acid rain, and the many forms of waste disposal (i.e., solid waste, animal waste, industrial waste, and radioactive waste disposal). All of these activities pose substantial threats to the state's surface and groundwater resources. This section provides a brief description of some of these problems, the existing programs for addressing them, and some remaining policy issues.

We have chosen to focus on a limited number of issues regarding natural resource integrity that will confront Wisconsin citizens over the next five years. By selecting several issues for careful discussion here, we do not mean to imply that other resource problems are unimportant. However, space limitations prevent a thorough discussion of all concerns. We therefore focus on issues for which the political stakes are significant and where resolution will require a considerable measure of statesmanship on the part of our elected representatives. The issues covered and the programs designed to respond to them are presented in table 13.1.

Nonpoint Source Pollution

OVERVIEW OF THE PROBLEM. Among the most pressing problems threatening Wisconsin's environmental quality is nonpoint source pollution (NSP). The term "nonpoint source pollution" is generally used in reference to pollutants that enter waterways as the result of storm or snowmelt runoff that has picked up and transported those pollutants from dispersed sources. Some experts (e.g., Daniel and Forrest 1978) believe that nonpoint sources contribute about half the pollution of Wisconsin's water resources. Although substantial reductions in pollution from point sources have been achieved,

Table 13.1. Summary of Major Pollution Control Programs for NSP, Hazardous Waste, Acid
Rain, and Groundwater Contamination

Program	Major Provisions
Nonpoint Source Pollution (NSP)	
Federal	
Agricultural Conservation Program	Grants to farmers to control soil erosion
Rural Clean Water Program	Funding for demonstration projects to control rural NSP
National Urban Runoff Program	Funding for demonstration projects to control urban NSP
Sections 106 and 208 of Clean Water Act	Funding for development of state NSP control plans
Soil Conservation Service and Agricultural Extension Service	Technical assistance in implementing projects to control soil erosion
State of Wisconsin	
NSP Water Pollution Abatement Program	Cost-sharing funds for projects in priority areas
Animal Waste Management Program	Regulation of handling, storage, and disposal of animal waste
Wisconsin Farmers Fund	Cost-sharing funds for projects to control pollution from animal waste
Soil Erosion Control Program	Funding for implementation of soil-erosion-control projects
Hazardous Waste	
Federal	
Resource Conservation and Recovery Act	Regulation of transportation, treatment, and disposal of hazardous wastes
"Superfund" under CERCLA	Funding for response to unanticipated releases of hazardous wastes
Post-Closure Liability Trust Fund	Funding to cover federal government's postclosure liability
State of Wisconsin	
Hazardous Waste Management Act	Regulation of transportation, treatment, and disposal of hazardous wastes
Environmental Repair Fund	Funding for response to unanticipated releases of hazardous wastes
Waste Management Fund	Funding to cover state's postclosure liability
Acid Rain	
Federal	
Clean Air Act	Procedures for victims of acid rain to seek relief
State of Wisconsin	
Wisconsin Act 414	Limits on allowable sulfur oxide emissions
Groundwater Contamination	
Federal	
Various Statutes	Monitoring and identification of potential sources of groundwater contamination
Various Statutes	Regulation of use, transportation, and disposal of substances that are potential sources of contamination
State of Wisconsin	
Wisconsin Act 410	Groundwater quality standards and monitoring; procedures and funds for response to contamination

similar progress cannot be claimed for nonpoint sources (Wisconsin Department of Natural Resources 1984b).

The primary sources of nonpoint source pollution in Wisconsin are (1) animal wastes resulting from improper manure spreading, barnyard runoff, inadequate barnyard storage facilities, or direct deposition in waterways; (2) cropland erosion whereby soil particles, often with absorbed pollutants from pesticides or fertilizers, are dislodged and transported; (3) woodland grazing that decreases vegetative cover and thus invites soil erosion; (4) construction activities, which also can destroy ground cover and promote erosion; and (5) urban runoff that carries street litter and other deposited pollutants to waterways (Wisconsin Department of Natural Resources 1982).

In all of these cases, water traveling over (or percolating through) the land picks up pollutants and/or soil particles, either separately or in combination, and ultimately deposits them in the state's waterways. The detrimental effects of this process are many and varied. They include (1) increased murkiness of the water, which can impair normal photosynthesis processes; (2) increased sedimentation, which not only increases necessary dredging but also can interfere with habitat characteristics necessary for fish reproduction; (3) increased loadings of toxic metals, which can accumulate in the environment and affect fish reproductive cycles and ultimately enter the human food chain; (4) increased eutrophication of lakes and streams, which reduces their suitability for recreational activities; and (5) pollution of drinking water supplies, which can have obvious human health effects.

Although human activities are responsible for much of the NSP in Wisconsin, those activities can often be modified to minimize their detrimental effects. For example, in the case of agricultural activities that contribute to NSP, the use of certain management practices can be effective in reducing the transport of soil and pollutants to nearby waterways. Certain practices, termed "best management practices (BMPs)," are thought to be the most economical and practical means of controlling this transport. In the case of agriculture, they include the use of contour cropping, strip cropping, diversions, terraces, minimum till, no-till, barnyard runoff management, manure storage facilities, exclusion of livestock from woodlots, and streambank erosion control (Wisconsin Department of Natural Resources 1982). Control of urban sources can be enhanced by leaf collection and street sweeping, or the use of inflow and infiltration systems, retention basins, and porous pavement. Similar options are available to reduce construction-site runoff.

CURRENT POLICIES. The focus of public policies to control NSP has been to encourage the use of BMPs, with cost-sharing (federal, state, and/or county) available as an inducement to adopt these practices. At the federal level, the Agricultural Conservation Program (ACP), administered by the Agricultural Stabilization and Conservation Service, provides grants of up to

$3,500 to individual farmers for adoption of measures to control soil erosion and increase soil conservation. Although this program was not designed specifically to improve water quality, it can still be expected to be effective in controlling NSP when applied to land whose erosion causes transport of pollutants to waterways. Application to land not located in close proximity to waterways is likely to be less effective in reducing NSP.

Another program, the Rural Clean Water Program (RCWP), was specifically designed to improve water quality. It was intended to provide funds for adoption and maintenance of BMPs by critical polluters. Although this was originally expected to be an extensive program, funding for its implementation at the levels originally envisioned has not been forthcoming. Some short-term funding was made available for implementation of the program on an experimental basis, but no renewal of that funding is anticipated.

In addition to these two programs, the federal government assists in the control of agricultural NSP by providing loans through the Farmers Home Administration and technical assistance through the Soil Conservation Service and the Agricultural Extension Service to aid farmers in implementing projects for controlling soil erosion and NSP.

Federal programs also exist for addressing NSP from nonagricultural sources. These include the National Urban Runoff Program (NURP), which provided information on NSP from urban sources through a set of test projects, and funds available under the Surface Mining Control and Reclamation Act (SMCRA) for protection of water quality threatened by mining activities.

A mainstay of federal policy has been that, because problems of NSP are source- and site-specific, they are most appropriately addressed at the state and local level. Although federal funds authorized under sections 106 and 208 of the Clean Water Act were used by states to identify NSP and develop plans for its control, implementation of those plans has been left to the states, with limited federal funds available for cost-sharing.

In Wisconsin, implementation has been primarily through the Nonpoint Source Water Pollution Abatement Program, instituted in 1978. The program is similar to the federal programs in that its focus is the voluntary use of BMPs with cost-sharing to alleviate some of the associated expense. Cost-sharing funds are available only for projects in priority areas (i.e., areas designated to be critical NSP sources and where use of BMPs is likely to have an appreciable effect on local water quality). Initially, two types of priority area projects were identified, Priority Watershed Projects (approximately 100,000 acres in area) and Local Priority Projects (less than about 6,400 acres), although at present watershed projects are being emphasized. The DNR has thus far identified over twenty-five Priority Watershed Projects, with an estimated total cost of approximately $45 million for implementation of BMPs. Estimates indicate that the total cost to control the most significant sources of NSP in the state would be $600 million (1981 dollars) (Wisconsin Department of Natural Resources 1982).

The program provides for state cost-sharing of 50 to 70%, with a possible share of 80% for selected practices if county funds are provided for 10%. Thus, the landowner could be required to pay as little as 10% of the costs. There is no ceiling on the state expenditure per individual project except in the case of animal waste-storage facilities, where a limit of $6,000 is imposed.

In addition to this program for the abatement of nonpoint pollution, Wisconsin has recently instituted several other programs specifically designed to improve water quality. These include the Animal Waste Management Program and the Wisconsin Farmers Fund, both of which address pollution from animal wastes. The former provides a regulatory program for the handling, storage, and disposal of animal waste, while the latter provides cost-sharing funds for eligible farmers to reduce pollution from barnyard runoff or animal waste-storage facilities. Cost-sharing grants are limited to $10,000 per project or 70% of the cost. Total original appropriation for the fund for FY 1983–85 was $1 million. In addition, the Soil Erosion Control Program, created in 1982, indirectly addresses water pollution from soil erosion by providing assistance to counties for preparation of soil-erosion-control programs and state funding for implementation of eligible projects. The original appropriation for implementation was $600,000.

REMAINING POLICY ISSUES. Wisconsin currently has several programs in place whose purpose is to control nonpoint water pollution. The focus of these programs, particularly in the area of soil erosion, has been on voluntary implementation with cost-sharing. Although these are positive steps toward the control of NSP, whether or not they are sufficient to protect Wisconsin's waters is still unclear. For example, despite cost-sharing possibilities, landowner participation rates under the Nonpoint Source Water Pollution Abatement Program have been much lower than originally anticipated. Actual participation rates are only 11% to 38%, whereas original goals were 70% participation by the end of the second year (Wisconsin Department of Natural Resources 1984b). These low rates are disappointing, although perhaps not particularly surprising. Given the current financial stress facing many farmers, they may expect that the economic return to them from investment in BMPs would not be sufficient to justify participation. Although the low participation rates do not necessarily reflect the full effectiveness of the program, they do not bode well for the efficacy of this voluntary approach to control NSP.

Much of the difficulty in using a mandatory approach to control NSP stems from the three general issues discussed at the beginning of this chapter: joint costs, site-specific costs and damages, and uncertainty. Although NSP is a clear example of an externality or joint costs, both the costs and the benefits of control vary widely across sites. Thus, the efficient level of control that is mandated should also vary. Unfortunately, however, the relationship between on-site practices and off-site damages necessary to determine the efficient level of control cannot be predicted with certainty, and, even if it could be, the administrative costs of implementing site-specific mandatory controls might be extremely high. Thus, although a mandatory approach to NSP would probably be more effective than the current voluntary approaches, that increased effectiveness would come at a cost, namely, high administrative costs if site-specific controls are used, or lost efficiency under across-the-board controls.

Hazardous Waste Management

OVERVIEW OF THE PROBLEM. A second environmental problem arises from many of the modern industrialized processes that sustain our material standard of living and as a by-product generate substantial quantities of hazardous wastes. The U.S. Environmental Protection Agency estimated that in 1980 41.2 million metric tons of hazardous waste were generated in the United States. About 1.5% of this was generated in Wisconsin. In Wisconsin, these wastes include cleaning and metal-plating wastes, solvents, paint residues, and agricultural chemical wastes (Wisconsin Department of Natural Resources 1983).

Wastes can be classified as hazardous for any one of four reasons: ignitability, corrosivity, reactivity, or toxicity. Because of these characteristics, special care must be taken in disposing of these wastes to avoid human health, welfare, and environmental risks. Alternative hazardous waste management options include (1) waste reduction alternatives, such as source segregation, process modification, end-product substitution, and recovery and recycling; (2) treatment alternatives (i.e., treatment technologies, including incineration and biological treatment; and (3) disposal alternatives, such as landfills, surface impoundments, underground injection wells, and ocean disposal (U.S. Congress, Office of Technology Assessment 1983).

The first category, waste reduction alternatives, is aimed at reducing the volume of hazardous wastes that must ultimately be disposed of, while the second category includes techniques designed to reduce the hazard of the waste by transforming it into less hazardous substances (through, for example, incineration or application of biological processes). Of course, even if these first two alternative approaches are fully used, it is likely that there will still be a need for ultimate disposal of some waste. Surface impoundments are generally only temporary disposal approaches, while landfills, injection wells, and ocean disposal are intended to be permanent storage/disposal methods.

The Wisconsin Department of Natural Resources (1984a) estimates that, of the 125,000 tons of hazardous waste generated in Wisconsin in 1983, less than 3% was managed by in-state land disposal. This constitutes a large drop from 1981, when 33% of the 90,000 tons generated was disposed of by this means. Although out-of-state land disposal rose from 7.3% in 1981 to 18.4% in 1983, the total percentage of waste managed by land disposal still decreased. In contrast, the percentage managed by reuse, treatment, or recycling has increased from 50% to about 70% in two years.

Although these recent trends away from land disposal are welcomed, much of the problem of hazardous waste management stems from previous practices. Historically, land disposal methods were thought to be the least expensive waste management alternative and thus were commonly used. A survey by the Wisconsin Department of Natural Resources (1985) lists 2,717 abandoned landfills in Wisconsin alone. Recently, however, attention has focused on the fact that, when landfills are inadequately constructed, direct land disposal costs can represent only a small fraction of the total social cost of this alternative. If inadequate construction results in leaching from landfills, hazardous substances can enter groundwater supplies and pose serious threats to public health and welfare. Because landfill users have not historically been held liable for these social costs (perhaps in part because the effects were often not known until after the landfill had ceased operation), the full costs have not been considered in choosing among alternative disposal methods. The result of this divergence between the full costs of the landfill alternative and the private cost borne by landfill users or operators is a long list of more than 15,000 hazardous waste disposal sites requiring cleanup at a total cost of $10 billion to $40 billion (U.S. Congress, Office of Technology Assessment 1983). If these costs were reflected in the land disposal prices faced by waste generators, the perceived cost advantage of this approach might disappear. Of course, the waste reduction and treatment alternatives can involve environmental costs as well, and these costs must also be considered when choosing among society's alternatives for waste management.

CURRENT POLICIES.   Concern for the external environmental costs associated with land disposal has prompted legislative and regulatory action at both the federal and state levels. At the federal level, two major pieces of legislation have been passed that address hazardous waste management. The first is the Resource Conservation and Recovery Act of 1976 (RCRA), which required the EPA to establish a regulatory program with the following four components: (1) identification and listing of hazardous waste; (2) a national manifest system for tracking wastes; (3) standards for hazardous waste treatment, storage, and disposal facilities; and (4) a permit system for treatment, storage, and disposal facilities (U.S. Congress, Office of Technology Assessment 1983, 268). The second law is the Comprehensive Environmental Response,

Compensation, and Liability Act of 1980 (CERCLA), which establishes mechanisms to be used by the federal government to respond to releases of hazardous substances into the environment. The intent is to transfer liability for damages from the victims (or society at large) to the responsible parties. The legislation establishes two funds to be used for this purpose: (1) the Hazardous Substance Response Trust Fund (Superfund), which is used to finance actions taken in response to releases of hazardous substances; and (2) the Post-Closure Liability Trust Fund, which is used to pay for postclosure maintenance and damages from releases.

State response to the need for regulation of hazardous waste management followed shortly after the federal initiatives with passage of the Hazardous Waste Management Act. The law provided a mandate for stricter control over the transportation, treatment, and disposal of hazardous waste, much of which has been implemented through regulatory actions by the DNR. In particular, the DNR has numerous mandatory standards regarding facility siting and construction. In addition, the groundwater legislation passed in 1984 established an Environmental Repair Fund, to be used for cleanup of contamination from waste disposal facilities. This fund is analogous to the federal Superfund. The state's Waste Management Fund is now reserved for use in site-maintenance activities that are necessary after the owner's liability has expired. It is therefore now analogous to the federal Post-Closure Liability Trust Fund.

In addition to the above provisions that regulate facilities and generate revenue to be used in necessary cleanup operations, the state laws also include several provisions that encourage the reduction, recycling, or treatment of wastes. These include favorable depreciation and tax provisions for investment in pollution-control equipment. The DNR has found, however, that "existing incentives give preference to 'end-of-pipe' waste treatment rather than the reduction or recycling of hazardous wastes" (Wisconsin Department of Natural Resources 1983, 58).

REMAINING POLICY ISSUES. Most of the current hazardous waste policies focus on the cleanup of waste spills or of substances that are leaching from existing dumps. Estimates indicate that the cost of that cleanup can be extremely high. There are several issues that are likely to recur in this context. The first is the source of the funds used for cleanup. Although expenditures from the cleanup funds are supposed to be recovered from the responsible parties, in many cases the practical difficulties of identifying those parties and obtaining recovery make an alternative source of funds necessary. How those funds should be raised has been and is likely to continue to be an important issue.

A second related issue is whether a policy of recovery of fund expenditures from the responsible parties is appropriate. If recovery were not sought, the funds would provide a form of public insurance to private firms, with the firms' contribution to the fund being an "insurance premium." If firms are unable to purchase private environmental liability insurance, such publicly provided insurance might be appropriate, especially in the case of cleanup due to past disposal, where few incentive problems exist. It would shelter firms from some risk and thus provide them with greater certainty. However, to allow for as much cleanup as would occur under a recovery approach, a firm's fund contribution would have to be higher under the insurance approach.

The third related issue is the question of how clean is "clean" (i.e., to what extent sites should be cleaned up). Because of the uncertainty surrounding the long-run effects of exposure to hazardous waste, the appropriate trade-off between the costs and benefits of additional cleanup is difficult to determine. Yet, in each case a decision regarding the extent of cleanup must be made, and, because funds are scarce, additional cleanup at one site implies less cleanup at another.

The above issues all relate to cleanup of existing hazardous waste problems. It is likely, however, that cleanup costs will far exceed the cost of waste reduction or recycling. It thus seems appropriate for the state to take more concrete steps to encourage these alternatives to waste disposal. Although progress has certainly been made in this area, more must be done to avoid incurring even larger costs in the future.

Acid Rain

OVERVIEW OF THE PROBLEM. A third environmental issue that has received considerable attention is acid rain. Acid rain is a term used to refer to rain (or, more loosely, any deposition, whether wet or dry) with a pH level of less than 5.6. Acid precipitation results when emissions of sulfur and nitrogen oxides are transformed in the atmosphere into sulphuric and nitric acids that dissolve in cloud droplets and raindrops and are deposited back on the ground through precipitation.

Examination of the primary sources of sulfur and nitrogen oxide emissions provides an indication of the activities that might be responsible for acid rain. DNR estimates of emissions of sulfur oxides in Wisconsin in 1980 indicate that, of the total of 726,325 tons emitted, 95% were from point sources, 3% were from groups of smaller sources (e.g., residential furnaces), 1% were from motor vehicles on highways, and less than 1% were from natural sources. Moreover, about 90% of the emissions from point sources were from the combustion of coal by, for example, electric utilities and paper mills (Wisconsin Legislative Council 1982).

In the case of nitrogen oxides, DNR estimates indicate that in 1980 emissions from point sources totaled 200,000 tons while emissions from vehicles on highways were 173,000 tons. Estimates of natural (and therefore total) emissions were not available (Wisconsin Legislative Council 1982). As in the case of sulfur oxides, coal combustion was a large source of emissions.

Although these estimates provide an indication of possible causes of acid rain, the fact that airborne pollutants can be carried long distances (hundreds or perhaps even thousands of miles) implies that emission sources within the state may not account for all possible sources. Likewise, emissions generated within the state may be carried to other states.

The concern over acid rain stems from its potential damages, which can be classified into four categories: (1) aquatic effects; (2) terrestrial effects; (3) human health effects; and (4) effects on man-made materials. Aquatic effects result from decreases in pH levels of lakes and streams due to acid precipitation, which are thought to affect fish populations either by inhibiting their reproductive processes or by increasing the levels of potentially toxic metals in the water. Terrestrial effects can result from the direct effect of acidic precipitation on plant foliage and growth and its indirect effect on soils. Increased acidity of drinking water supplies and atmospheric concentration of sulfur compounds can affect human health, and the increased acidity of the rain itself is thought to accelerate the corrosion of certain man-made materials, which would imply not only increased maintenance or replacement costs but also possibly irreversible damage to historical or cultural monuments.

In general, lakes in northern Wisconsin tend to be more susceptible to the effects of acidification than those in the southern part of the state because the underlying bedrock in the north provides less buffering capacity to offset those effects than that in the south (Wisconsin Legislative Council 1982). Early evidence suggests, however, that although the buffering capacity of some lakes in the north appears to have decreased, on average the alkalinity (which provides the buffering capacity) of the sampled lakes has actually increased. But difficulties in interpreting the cause of the increases (Wisconsin Legislative Council 1982) suggest caution in drawing conclusions regarding the seriousness of acid rain in Wisconsin. At this point, it appears reasonable to operate on the premise that, although there is no evidence of extensive damage to date, the potential for damage implies that continued concern over acid rain is warranted.

CURRENT POLICIES. The response to acid rain has come at both the federal and state level. In 1980, the United States and Canada signed a Memorandum of Intention, stating the intentions of both governments to address and resolve their dispute over acid rain in a timely manner. The Acid Precipitation Act of 1980 created the Acid Precipitation Task Force, which was charged with coordinating a ten-year, $50 million research program on acid rain. In addition, based on the results of this research, it called for control of acid rain through use of existing laws. The major law that was in place and could be invoked in cases of acid rain was the Clean Air Act. In addition to several provisions for controlling local point source pollution (such as ambient air quality standards and new source performance standards), the Clean Air Act also provides recourse for victims (either other states or other countries) of the long-range transport of air pollutants. However, petitions by the states of New York, Pennsylvania, and Maine to get the EPA to take action under these provisions against some Midwest states have recently been denied by the EPA, suggesting that future attempts to use existing authority under the Clean Air Act to combat acid rain are not likely to be very effective. Legislation that would provide more effective control has been introduced into the U.S. Congress many times, but thus far without success.

At the state level, three recent acts passed by the legislature in 1983 are specifically directed toward acid rain. Both Act 413 and Act 421 focus primarily on research. The first appropriated $400,000 for a DNR study of the cost of reducing sulfur dioxide emissions, while the second authorized the DNR to conduct a lake acidification experiment on Little Rock Lake. Act 414 is more directly related to control of acid rain. It establishes a combined limit of 500,000 tons per year on total sulfur dioxide emissions allowable from "major" utilities and requires submission of operation plans specifying how this limit will be met. In addition, it establishes a goal (675,000 tons/year) for total sulfur dioxide emissions from all stationary sources but includes no specific requirements (other than those relating to major utilities) for meeting that goal.

REMAINING POLICY ISSUES. At the federal level, no policy designed to deal specifically with acid rain control exists, although the federal government has provided funding for acid rain research. The purported reason for the lack of an explicit control strategy is uncertainty regarding the precise causes and effects of acid rain. Because there are still unanswered questions about the transport of acid rain precursors and how their deposition affects both ecosystems and human health and welfare, the Reagan administration has chosen to advocate further study rather than the implementation of control policies. In so doing, it appears to be avoiding making a decision under conditions of uncertainty. However, it is important to recognize that the decision to do nothing now is still a decision, and one made under uncertainty, since the long-run effects of not controlling current emissions are also unknown. Whether uncertainty is a legitimate reason for inaction or not depends partly on the cost of making a wrong decision (i.e., the cost of imposing controls that turn out to be unnecessary versus the cost of not controlling emissions when we should have).

Because acid rain is a long-range pollutant, the appropriate level for control strategies is the national, or in some cases the international, level. In the absence of this, however, Wisconsin should strive for at least a regional approach. Since its acid rain is not caused entirely by in-state emissions, unilateral actions to control emissions will be less effective in reducing in-state damages than a regional control strategy would be. Thus, if possible, the state should try to work with neighboring Midwest states to devise acid rain control policies that will provide mutual benefits.

Groundwater Pollution

OVERVIEW OF THE PROBLEM. The above three problems have generally been viewed as source-specific in the sense that efforts to control them have focused on the pollution source. In the case of groundwater pollution, however, because of uncertainty about pollution sources, long lag times before a pollution problem is detected, and the slow rate of natural cleansing, attention has necessarily been directed not only at preventing but also at cleaning up the pollution. Thus, although groundwater pollution is a possible consequence of the specific problems of hazardous waste disposal and NSP discussed above, we treat it separately here since it has often been viewed so in policy arenas.

In Wisconsin, groundwater is in abundant supply, but it is also in great demand for domestic, industrial, and agricultural use. Groundwater provides over 25% of manufacturers' water needs, nearly all of the water used in irrigation, and drinking water supplies for about 94% of Wisconsin's cities and villages.

Potential sources of groundwater pollution include the use of agricultural pesticides and fertilizers, leaking underground storage tanks for chemicals or gasoline, leaching from landfills, and faulty septic systems. Recently, the DNR found that the "quality of Wisconsin's groundwater is generally excellent," although "localized groundwater quality problems have developed" (Wisconsin Department of Natural Resources 1984b, 50). The most publicized problem has been the discovery of the agricultural pesticide aldicarb in wells in central Wisconsin. In addition, volatile organic chemicals (VOC) have been detected in a few isolated wells, although only 14 of the 897 wells tested had confirmed presence of VOC (Wisconsin Department of Natural Resources 1984b). Finally, occurrences of high nitrate concentration and gasoline contamination have been detected as well.

CURRENT POLICIES. Despite the localized nature of pollution from these sources, the importance of groundwater as a drinking water supply, the difficulty of cleaning up contaminated groundwater, and the slow rate at which it cleanses itself give reason for concern over what appear to be localized problems. At the federal level, response to these concerns has been mainly in the area of detecting groundwater contamination. The Clean Water Act (CWA), the Safe Drinking Water Act (SDWA), the Resource Conservation and Recovery Act (RCRA) and the Comprehensive Environmental Response, Compensation, and Liability Act (CERCLA) include provisions for monitoring groundwater and identifying potential sources of groundwater contamination. A study by the Office of Technology Assessment, which examined (among other things) federal efforts to correct groundwater contamination, concluded that few federal statutes provide for corrective action, that cleanup standards are generally not specified in regulations, and that federal agency experience with such actions is limited (U.S. Congress, Office of Technology Assessment 1984, 197).

An exception is in the case of contamination from hazardous waste, where both RCRA and CERCLA include provisions for corrective action. Finally, in terms of preventing groundwater contamination, several federal statutes regulate the use, transport, and disposal of substances that, if handled improperly, could pose a threat to groundwater quality. These include radioactive materials, hazardous wastes, pesticides, and toxic substances. However, the OTA study concludes that the various federal programs are not consistent in terms of either the scope of the groundwater resources that are covered or the extent of degradation that is permitted (U.S. Congress, Office of Technology Assessment 1984).

At the state level, the Wisconsin legislature responded to concern over groundwater contamination by passing comprehensive groundwater protection legislation (1983 Wisconsin Act 410). The legislation has four major components: (1) establishment of groundwater quality standards; (2) requirements for groundwater monitoring; (3) provisions for compensation for contaminated wells; and (4) the establishment of funds for cleanup of contamination and to finance state agencies' activities relating to groundwater. The standards are based on a two-tiered approach; the lower limits, termed "preventive action limits (PALs)" signal the possibility of an impending contamination problem, while the higher "enforcement standards" indicate contamination at the level that threatens public health or welfare. Appropriate actions in terms of curtailing the responsible activities are required when these second standards are exceeded. Detection of standard violations is facilitated by the monitoring system established by the act. When contamination is discovered in private wells, the act provides funds for compensation for up to 80% of the eligible costs of well replacement. An annual appropriation of $500,000 in general-purpose revenues has been provided for this purpose. In addition, as noted previously, the legislation created the Environmental Repair Fund to provide money for cleanup of environmental damage. This fund is financed by fees paid by nonapproved sites and a nonapproved-site tonnage-fee surcharge. Finally, it also creates a Groundwater Fund, financed by fees on activities that could potentially affect groundwater (such as fees on pesticide manufacturers, waste disposal tipping fees, and fees for the review of plans to store petroleum products). This money is to be used to cover state agencies' expenses in implementing the legislation.

REMAINING POLICY ISSUES. To date the federal approach to groundwater contamination has focused on detection rather than correction. Again, the explanation lies at least in part in the site-specific nature of groundwater problems and the uncertainty surrounding the sources and effects of contamination. For example, the contamination of groundwater by aldicarb is a problem in Wisconsin and Long Island, but not in some other parts of the country. Likewise, the effects of that contamination will depend upon how the groundwater is used, a factor that can also vary considerably across sites. In addition, the effect of different human activities on groundwater quality and the resulting effect on human health are difficult to predict with accuracy. These factors combine to make control at the federal level problematic.

In the absence of a federal control policy, the states must act individually to protect groundwater quality. In light of water shortages in other parts of the country, the continued availability of clean groundwater in Wisconsin contributes not only to sustaining activities that currently depend on its use, but also to the possible attraction of future economic growth. Thus, Wisconsin's groundwater resource is a valuable economic as well as environmental asset and we should take steps to protect it. The recent implementation of the two-tiered set of quality standards is a promising start. However, it is still a reactive approach aimed at correcting a problem rather than a proactive approach to prevent one, and how effective it will be in controlling contamination remains to be seen.

Natural Resource Potential

The state's natural resources serve not only as a source of aesthetic pleasure that should be protected to ensure adequate levels of ecological integrity and human health and welfare; if used wisely, they can also be the source of continual income and employment generation. In essence, natural resources are productive assets, similar to labor or capital assets, that are inputs into the production of either tangible goods (such as forest products) or intangible services (such as recreation) now and in the future. As with any asset, they must be managed wisely both in the short run to ensure full realization of their potential to contribute to the state's economy and in the long run to provide a suitable environment for human existence and development.

In this section we briefly discuss three areas in which the state's natural resource base generates income and employment within the state: forestry, mining, and tourism/recreation. We recognize that other resources, such as the state's fishery resources, contribute to the economy as well. However, space limitations have forced us to focus our attention on a small subset of the economically important resources. Land and soil resources relating to agricultural production are not discussed here. For information on Wisconsin's agricultural resources, the reader is referred to chapter 12 in this volume.

Forestry

OVERVIEW OF THE RESOURCE. The 14.8 million acres of commercial forestland in Wisconsin provide a number of benefits, including watershed protection, wildlife habitat, amenities, and, of course, a source of raw materials for the production of wood products. Proper management of the forest asset must balance these various uses, recognizing the importance of each. However, since removals for growing stock and sawtimber currently average only 50–60% of net growth, it appears that increased utilization of forestland for production of wood products need not diminish the other benefits being derived from the forests. Therefore, we focus here on the use of forestlands as a source of raw material.

Wisconsin's forest products industry (SIC categories 24–26) has a substantial impact on the state's economy. It employs approximately 75,000 people, with another 200,000 employed in secondary wood-using industries. One estimate (Stier and Vick 1984) is that every 1 million cubic feet of timber harvested in the state ultimately generates 444 in-state jobs. Forest products industries are the largest source of employment in 24 of Wisconsin's 71 counties. This employment generates substantial income. For example, in 1982 Wisconsin's forest industries paid nearly $1.4 billion in payroll from shipments valued at over $8 billion.

Despite this impact on the state's economy, the full potential of Wisconsin's forests is not currently being realized. Forests that grew to replace the original pinery are beginning to mature and could sustain harvests nearly twice the current levels; yet over half of the state's total wood-fiber demand is supplied by wood imported from other states and Canada. Two factors have contributed to this situation. First, 80% of the forests are hardwoods, while there is excess demand for softwoods. Second, nearly 60% of Wisconsin's forestlands are owned by farmers and other private nonindustrial owners, with two-thirds of the land in holdings of 100 acres or less. These lands are often not managed for timber production, and about 40% of all private owners do not harvest their timber resource at all. Thus, harvest rates are well below their potential levels.

CURRENT POLICIES. Programs to assist private nonindustrial forestland owners in managing and harvesting their timber resources do exist. For example, at the federal level the Agricultural Conservation Program (ACP) and the Forestry Incentives Program (FIP) both provide financial assistance to small woodlot owners for forest management, while the Rural Forestry Assistance Program (RFA) finances the provision of technical assistance.

In addition, Wisconsin has state-level tax laws designed to encourage appropriate timber management. The original law was the Forest Crop Law (FCL), enacted in 1927. This provided property tax relief for qualifying private forestland owners by greatly reducing the per acre tax and deferring taxation of the value of the timber until the time of harvest. In exchange, landowners were required to institute forest management practices for twenty-five or fifty years and allow public access for hunting, fishing, and other recreation. The Woodland Tax Law (WTL), enacted in 1954, extended a similar form of property tax relief to small (10 to 40 acres) woodlot owners. Although the annual per acre tax under the WTL was twice the rate under the FCL, it did not tax the timber at the time of harvest, shortened the commitment of the landowner to fifteen years, and did not require that public access be allowed. Very recently, these two laws have been replaced by a single law, the Managed Forestlands Act. As before, the law provides property tax relief to forestland owners who actively engage in forest management. However, landowners now have the option of closing up to 80 acres of their land to public access and paying a $1 per acre surcharge for acres closed.

REMAINING POLICY ISSUES. Despite these economic incentives to practice improved forest management, harvest rates on private nonindustrial lands are still well below their potential. Only 6% of the land in this category has been registered and committed under the FCL and WTL, while approximately two-thirds of the industry-owned land is committed. Since nonindustrial land is sold on average every ten years, it is not surprising that landowners are reluctant to commit their land to management practices for long periods of time. In addition, the public access requirements of the Forest Crop Law may have provided a significant disincentive for landowners to participate in the program, especially if they hold their forestland for reasons other than the value of the timber. The recent changes embodied in the Managed Forestlands Act that give landowners a choice between allowing public access and paying a higher per acre tax (but one that is still below the tax paid on land that is not enrolled) may reduce this disincentive. However, the disincentive effects of the long-term commitments would still remain. A precise estimate of the effectiveness of such a change requires detailed information on reasons for nonparticipation.

Although changes in the tax laws might enhance utilization of the resource, they must be coupled with a commitment to this goal by both the Department of Natural Resources as the resource management agency and the Department of Development as the economic development agency. Since most of Wisconsin's forests are hardwoods, markets for this hardwood resource must be expanded. Both the existing transportation channels and the large resource base suggest that Wisconsin could expand its export markets. To increase the value-added within the state, this expansion should focus on hardwood lumber or other wood products rather than logs. The state could provide incentives to encourage consideration of this expansion. Expanded markets coupled with increased harvest from private nonindustrial lands could significantly increase the economic returns from Wisconsin's forests.

Mineral Resources

OVERVIEW OF THE RESOURCE. In addition to a large forestry resource, Wisconsin also has some potential for substantial mineral production. Although the long history of metallic mining in the southwestern part of the state ended in 1979, recent discoveries of mineral deposits by Kennecott Copper Company and Exxon, USA, in other parts of the state have renewed interest in metallic mining in Wisconsin. In addition, 1983 saw the beginning of leasing lands for oil and gas exploration in the northwestern counties. Although the probability that commercial quantities will be discovered is quite low, there is still the potential for a significant impact on the state's economy.

Since mining operations tend to be capital-intensive rather than labor- intensive, the economic impacts will come mainly in the form of increased state taxes and royalty payments to landowners. This is not to imply that the employment effects would be insignificant to the local economies, since mining of the Exxon deposit would generate about 700 jobs (in an area in which there are presently about 15,000 jobs) and the Kennecott mine would generate about 80 new jobs. However, especially in the case of oil and gas production, the employment effects would be less than the tax and royalty impacts.

CURRENT POLICIES. Royalty rates on mining proceeds are specified in individual contracts with landowners. For metallic mining in Wisconsin, they generally range from 3% to 7% of net smelter return. The contracts for oil and gas leasing in Wisconsin generally include a $1 per acre/year rental fee for the land leased and, in the event of a discovery and production, a royalty payment of one-eighth of the value of the oil and gas produced.

In addition to royalties, state revenue is also generated by mining operations through state taxes. In Wisconsin, the mining proceeds tax, instituted in 1977 and subsequently modified, is a progressive tax on net income from mining of metallic minerals. Since the tax is based on a production-related measure of net income, it should have a less negative effect on production decisions than the more common severance tax, which is based on gross value of the resource, generally at the wellhead. A gross value tax can render some production unprofitable that would not be so in the absence of the tax. A net value tax, such as the mining proceeds tax, avoids this disincentive effect, since the amount of the tax decreases as profitability declines.

REMAINING POLICY ISSUES. There are several ways in which the state could respond to the potential for increased mining or drilling operations. With regard to tax policy, if oil and gas are discovered in Wisconsin, the state should consider treating these resources in a manner similar to metallic minerals by applying a net value tax rather than simply a gross value severance tax to minimize production disincentives. Such a tax is potentially more difficult to administer because of the need to determine production costs, but the benefits in terms of improved incentives are likely to outweigh that cost.

With regard to royalties, evidence from other parts of the country suggests that the standard procedures for setting royalty rates in Wisconsin would not capture a substantial portion of the economic rents or profits that would be generated by the mining operations. For example, the federal leasing procedures in the Outer Continental Shelf, where competitors bid for leases by offering up-front lump-sum payments for the rights to exploration and production of an area, indicate that a system of competitive leasing will capture more of the profits for the landowner than negotiations with an individual company. Likewise, the system of competitive leasing used for state and county lands in Minnesota appears effective in capturing additional rent. Under this system, competitors bid for the leases by offering percentage royalty payments in the event of a discovery and production that exceed the minimum required royalties. Even though the number of bids for tracts in Minnesota has been small, the evidence suggests that the mere threat of competition results in higher offered royalty rates. To be effective and minimize transaction costs, it is likely that the use of a competitive system would have to be fairly widespread and standardized. However, experimenting with either of these competitive leasing systems might allow landowners in Wisconsin to capture more of the profits from mining operations.

Recreation/Tourism

A third industry that is linked to natural resources and provides substantial income and employment for the state is the hospitality-recreation-tourism industry. This industry generates gross sales of over $3 billion annually in Wisconsin and employs about 150,000 people. Although it is impossible to estimate precisely the extent to which these sales are linked directly or indirectly to the use of natural resources, it is likely that a substantial portion are derived from activities associated with fishing, hunting, boating, hiking, camping, scenic excursions, and the like. All of these activities depend upon the existence of high-quality air, water, forest, or fish and wildlife resources.

Thus, the future of this industry is closely tied to the questions of environmental quality discussed above.

Conclusions

As Wisconsin's economy continues to undergo structural adjustments in the years ahead, it is doubly important that the state search for new ways to benefit from existing economic opportunities. A fuller use of our timber resources would seem to represent an important dimension of that strategy. The added prospects of enhanced recreational opportunities and mineral exploration should not be overlooked. However, the development of these opportunities will place a special burden on policies to maintain resource integrity.

Wisconsin has been a front-runner in the implementation of environmental policies, particularly in the areas of nonpoint source pollution and groundwater contamination. In both of these areas the costs and benefits of control vary widely across sites and physical uncertainty is prevalent. As a result, the federal government has encouraged state-level control and Wisconsin has responded accordingly. Although the effectiveness of the voluntary approach to the control of NSP and the two-tiered standard approach to groundwater pollution has yet to be proven, their implementation reflects a recognition of the seriousness of these problems and a commitment by the state to address them.

The battle is not over yet, however. If these approaches prove ineffective, difficult choices will remain. For example, if aldicarb levels in groundwater exceed the upper limits, will the state be willing to pay the economic cost of a reduction in or ban of aldicarb use? If the voluntary approach to NSP control is insufficient to protect the state's waterways, will the state be willing to pay the economic cost of mandatory controls? In the area of hazardous waste, is the state willing to pay the short-run costs necessary to encourage waste recycling and reduction to avoid the long-run costs of waste disposal cleanup? These and other similar choices must inevitably be made, because of the need to balance the costs associated with preserving environmental quality against those associated with not preserving it.

NOTE

We are grateful to Professors Duncan Harkin and Jeff Stier and to many members of the staff at the Wisconsin Department of Natural Resources for discussions relating to and comments on earlier drafts of this manuscript.

REFERENCES

INDEX

References

Adams, James F. 1980. *Understanding Adolescence*. 4th ed. Boston: Allyn and Bacon.

Advisory Council on Intergovernmental Relations. Various years. *Significant Features of Fiscal Federalism, Annual Report*. Washington, D.C.: U.S. GPO.

Advisory Council on Intergovernmental Relations. 1981. "The Condition of Contemporary Federalism: Conflicting Theories and Collapsing Constraints." Report A–78, August. Washington, D.C.: U.S. GPO.

Advisory Council on Intergovernmental Relations. 1982. "Tax Capacity of the Fifty States: Methodology and Estimates." Report M–134, March. Washington, D.C.: U.S. GPO.

Alan Guttmacher Institute. 1981. *Teenage Pregnancy: The Problem That Hasn't Gone Away*. New York: Guttmacher.

American College Testing Research Services. 1979–80, 1985. *ACT High School Profile Report*. Iowa City, Iowa: ACT Testing Program.

American Hospital Association. 1981–86. *Hospital Statistics*. Chicago: AHA.

Anderson, Gerard, and Judith Lave. 1984. "State Rate-Setting Programs: Do They Reward Efficiency in Hospitals?" *Medical Care* 22: 94–98.

Armington, Catherine, and Marjorie Odle. 1982. "Small Business—How Many Jobs?" *Brookings Review* 1 (Winter): 14–17.

Ashby, John. 1984. "The Impact of Hospital Regulatory Programs on Per Capita Costs, Utilization and Capital Investment." *Inquiry* 21: 45–59.

Atkinson, Graham, and Jack Cook. 1981. "Regulation Incentives Rather Than Command and Control." In *A New Approach to the Economics of Health Care*, M. Olson, ed. Washington, D.C.: American Enterprise Institute.

Bane, Mary Jo, and David Ellwood. 1983. "The Dynamics of Dependence: The Routes to Self-Sufficiency." Cambridge, Mass.: Urban Systems Research and Engineering, Inc. Mimeo.

Bassi, Laurie, and Orley Ashenfelter. 1986. "The Effect of Direct Job Creation and Training Programs on Low-Skilled Workers." In *Fighting Poverty: What Works and What Doesn't*, Sheldon H. Danziger and Daniel H. Weinberg, eds. Cambridge, Mass.: Harvard University Press.

Birch, David. 1979. *The Job Generation Process*. Cambridge, Mass.: MIT Program on Neighborhood and Regional Change.

Birch, David, and Susan MacCracken. 1984. *The Role Played by High Technology Firms in Job Creation*. Cambridge, Mass.: MIT Program on Neighborhood and Regional Change.

Blum, Walter J., and Harry Kalven, Jr. 1952. *The Uneasy Case for Progressive Taxation*. Chicago: University of Chicago Press.

Browne, Lynn. 1983. "Can High Technology Save the Great Lakes States?" *New England Economic Review* (November/December): 19–33.

Bumpass, Larry L. 1984. "Children and Marital Disruption: A Replication and an Update." *Demography* 21 (February): 71–82.

Butler, David, and Austin Ranney, eds. 1978. *Referendums: A Comparative Study of Practice and Theory.* Washington, D.C.: American Enterprise Institute.

Capital Times. 1973. "Bidwell Plans Hearings on Lucey Budget's 'Dark Spots'," 9 April.

Capital Times. 1975. "Finance Panel Angers Senators," 2 May; "Lucey Huddles with Senate Dems to Save Fading Budget," 5 June.

Chambers, David L. 1979. *Making Fathers Pay: The Enforcement of Child Support.* Chicago: University of Chicago Press.

Christenson, Bruce. 1984. "American Indians in Wisconsin—1980." Paper presented at the Conference on American Indians in the North Central Area, 9–10 July, Stevens Point, Wis.

Coelen, Craig, and Daniel Sullivan. 1981. "An Analysis of the Effects of Prospective Reimbursement Programs on Hospital Expenditures." *Health Care Financing Review* 3 (Winter): 1–40.

Cohen, Carol E. 1986. "1984 State Tax Wealth: Preview of the RTS Estimates." *Intergovernmental Prospective* (Summer): 24–28.

College Board Admissions Testing Program. 1980, 1985. *Wisconsin College-Bound Seniors, 1980, and 1985.* Evanston, Ill.: The College Board.

Daniel, Tom, and Mary Forrest. 1978. "Nonpoint Pollution: What Does It Mean for Wisconsin's Waters?" University of Wisconsin–Extension, Bulletin no. 62962, November.

Danziger, Sandra K. 1984. "The Impact of the Reagan Budget Cuts on Working Welfare Mothers in Wisconsin." Institute for Research on Poverty, Discussion Paper no. 761–84, University of Wisconsin–Madison.

Danziger, Sandra K. 1986. "Breaking the Chains: From Teenage Girls to Welfare Mothers, Or, Can Social Policy Increase Options?" Institute for Research on Poverty, Discussion Paper no. 825–86, University of Wisconsin–Madison.

Danziger, Sandra K., and Ann Nichols-Casebolt. Forthcoming. "Teen Parents and Child Support: Eligibility, Participation, and Payment." *Journal of Social Service Research.*

Danziger, Sheldon, and Peter Gottschalk. 1985a. "How Have Families with Children Been Faring?" Institute for Research on Poverty, Discussion Paper no. 801–85, University of Wisconsin–Madison.

Danziger, Sheldon, and Peter Gottschalk. 1985b. "The Poverty of *Losing Ground.*" *Challenge* (May/June): 32–38.

Danziger, Sheldon, Robert Haveman, and Robert Plotnick. 1981. "How Income Transfer Programs Affect Work, Savings and the Income Distribution." *Journal of Economic Literature* 19: 975–1028.

Danziger, Sheldon, Robert Haveman, and Robert Plotnick. 1986. "Antipoverty Policy: Effects on the Poor and the Nonpoor." In *Fighting Poverty: What Works and What Doesn't,* Sheldon H. Danziger and Daniel H. Weinberg, eds. Cambridge, Mass.: Harvard University Press.

Dimancescu, Dan, and James Botkin. 1986. *The New Alliance: America's R&D Consortia.* Cambridge, Mass.: Ballinger.

Donoghue, James R. 1979. "Local Government in Wisconsin." In *Wisconsin Blue Book, 1979-80*. Madison: Wisconsin Legislative Reference Bureau (compiler).

Dowling, Williams. 1974. "Prospective Reimbursement of Hospitals." *Inquiry* 11: 163-80.

Drilias, Deborah. 1985. "Wisconsin's Brain Drain: An Exodus of the Very Best." *Wisconsin Business Journal* (May): 40-47.

Duncan, Greg J., and James N. Morgan. 1983. *Five Thousand American Families— Patterns of Economic Progress*. Vol. 10. Ann Arbor: Survey Research Center, Institute for Social Research, University of Michigan.

Eby, Charles, and Donald Cohodes. 1985. "What Do We Know about Rate-Setting?" *Journal of Health Policy, Politics and Law* 10: 299-327.

Ferguson, Ronald, and Helen Ladd. 1986. "Economic Performance and Economic Development Policy in Massachusetts." Discussion Paper D86-2, State, Local, and Intergovernmental Center, John F. Kennedy School of Government, Harvard University, Cambridge, Mass.

Fetter, Robert, et al. 1980. "Case Mix Definitions by Diagnosis-Related Groups." *Medical Care* 18: 1-53.

Friedman, Bernard, and Mark Pauly. 1983. "A New Approach to Hospital Cost Functions and Some Issues in Revenue Regulation." *Health Care Financing Review* 4 (March): 105-14.

Garber, Caroline, and Wilmer Dahl. 1985. "Agriculture's Contribution to the Wisconsin Economy." In *Wisconsin's Agricultural Economy: An Urban-Rural Perspective*. Madison: Wisconsin Department of Agriculture, Trade, and Consumer Protection.

Garfinkel, Irwin, and Sara S. McLanahan. 1986. *Single Mothers and Their Children: A New American Dilemma*. Washington, D.C.: Urban Institute Press.

Garfinkel, Irwin, and Marygold Melli. 1982. *Child Support: Weaknesses of the Old and Features of a Proposed New System*. Vol. 3. Institute for Research on Poverty Special Report no. 32-C, University of Wisconsin-Madison.

Gosling, James. 1980. "The Wisconsin Budgetary Process: A Study of Participant Influence and Choice." Ph.D. dissertation, University of Wisconsin-Madison.

Gosling, James. 1985. "The Wisconsin State Budgetary Process: An Interpretive Description." Robert M. La Follette Institute, Policy Paper no. 3, University of Wisconsin-Madison.

Governor's Commission on Agriculture. *Final Report, June 1985*. Madison: Office of the Governor.

Green Bay Press-Gazette. 1971. "Keppler Predicts No Merger Vote until September," 6 August.

Greenberger, Ellen. 1986. "Adolescents at Work: Policy and Research Implications." Paper presented to the Society for Research on Adolescence, Madison, Wis.

Groves, Harold. 1970. *The Tax Philosophers*. Madison: University of Wisconsin Press.

Hellinger, Fred. 1976. "The Effect of Certificate of Need Legislation on Hospital Investment." *Inquiry* 23: 187-93.

Hofferth, Sandra L. 1985. "The Relationship of Teen Childbearing to Single Parent Families and Poverty." Paper presented at Association for Public Policy Analysis and Management, Seventh Annual Research Conference, October, Washington, D.C.

Institute for Research on Poverty. 1986. "U.S. Census Extract." IRP, University of Wisconsin–Madison. Mimeo.

Ippolito, Dennis. 1981. *Congressional Spending.* Ithaca, N.Y.: Cornell University Press.

Jesse, E. V. 1984. "The President's Economists Grade U.S. Agricultural Policy." *Economic Issues.* Department of Agricultural Economics, University of Wisconsin–Madison, July.

Joskow, Paul. 1981. *Controlling Hospital Costs: The Role of Government Regulation.* Cambridge, Mass.: MIT Press.

Kale, Balkrishna D. , and Paul R. Voss. 1986. "Toward an Understanding of Population Growth in Wisconsin in the 1980s." *Proceedings of the Conference on the Small City and Regional Community.* Vol. 7. Stevens Point: Center for the Small City, University of Wisconsin–Stevens Point.

Krause, Harry O. 1981. *Child Support in America: The Legal Perspective.* Charlottesville, Va.: Michie, Co. Law Publishing.

Lampman, Robert J., and Timothy D. McBride. 1984. "Changes in the Pattern of State and Local Government Revenues and Expenditures in Wisconsin, 1960–81." Robert M. La Follette Institute, Policy Paper no. 2, University of Wisconsin–Madison.

Landry, David J. 1987. *The Effect of Migration on the Educational Composition of Wisconsin's Population.* Population Series 80–6, Applied Population Laboratory, University of Wisconsin–Madison, January.

Lang, Robert. 1985. "Tax Reduction and Reform Provisions of Enrolled Assembly Bill 85." Legislative Fiscal Bureau, memorandum to the Wisconsin State Legislature, Madison, Wis., 9 July.

Ley, Michael. 1985. "Wisconsin's Experience with Tax Reform and Simplification: A Progressive Report." Speech before the National Tax Association, June.

Lipscomb, Joseph, Ira Raskin, and Joseph Eichenholz. 1978. "The Use of Marginal Cost Estimates in Hospital Cost-Containment Policy." In *Hospital Cost Containment,* H. Zubkoff et al., eds. New York: Prodist.

Lurie, N. O. 1980. *Wisconsin Indians.* Madison: The State Historical Society of Wisconsin.

McIntosh, Melanie. 1986. "Planning Paper: The Wisconsin Approach to Problems Associated with Adolescent Pregnancy and Parenthood." Madison: Division of Policy and Budget, Wisconsin Department of Health and Social Services.

McLanahan, Sara. 1985. "Family Structure and the Reproduction of Poverty." *American Journal of Sociology* 90 (January): 873–901.

Marini, Margaret Mooney. 1985. "Work Experience, Occupational Aspirations, and Later Employment." Paper prepared for the National Academy of Sciences, Washington, D.C.

McLaughlin, Catherine. 1987. "HMO Growth and Hospital Expenses and USC: A Simultaneous-Equation Approach." *Health Services Research* 22: 183–205.

Melli, Marygold. 1984. "Child Support: A Survey of the Statutes." Institute for Research on Poverty, Special Report no. 33, University of Wisconsin–Madison.

Milwaukee Journal. 1971. "Lucey Riding Herd on Budget, Merger," 18 April; "Assembly Rejects Bid to Cut Merger from Budget Bill," 10 June.

Milwaukee Journal. 1973. "GOP 'Sunshine' Budget Intends to Scorch Lucey," 23 March; "State's Joint Finance Committee Needs Some Major Changes," 4 October.

Milwaukee Journal. 1977. "State Budgetary Process Is Indefensible; This Is a Goofy Way to Do Business," 23 June.

Milwaukee Journal. 1981. "Legislators Strip Policy Items from State Budget Bill," 19 March.

Milwaukee Sentinel. 1973. "Senate Budget Action Cooked Up in Restaurant," 20 July.

Milwaukee Sentinel. 1975. "Assembly to Bar Budget Changes," 7 May.

Mitchell, Samuel, Michael Morrisey, and Frank Sloan. 1987. "Is Rate Setting the Best Path to Controlling Costs?" *Health Affairs* 6 (Summer): 170–72.

Morrisey, Michael, Frank Sloan, and Samuel Mitchell. 1983. "State Rate Setting: An Analysis of Some Unresolved Issues." *Health Affairs* 2 (Summer): 36–47.

National Association of State Development Agencies. 1983. *Directory of Incentives for Business Investment and Development in the United States*. Washington, D.C.: Urban Institute Press.

National Center for Health Statistics. 1986. *Monthly Vital Statistics Report,* Vol. 35, no. 4, Supplement, 18 July.

National Council of State Legislatures. 1983. "A Comparison of Wisconsin's Budget Procedures to Other States: Selected Issues." Denver, Colo.: NCSL.

Nichols, Donald. 1987. Testimony before the Ways and Means Committee, Wisconsin State Assembly, 12 May.

O'Connell, Martin, and Carolyn C. Rogers. 1984. "Out-of-Wedlock Births, Premarital Pregnancies and Their Effect on Family Formation and Dissolution." *Family Planning Perspectives* 16 (July/August): 157–62.

Oellerich, Donald. 1982. "The Absent Parents' Ability to Pay: A New Measure of State IV-D Child Support Enforcement Programs for AFDC Households." In *Child Support: Weaknesses of the Old and Features of a Proposed New System,* Irwin Garfinkel and Marygold Melli, eds. Vol. 3. A report prepared for the Division of Economic Assistance, Wisconsin Department of Health and Social Services, Madison, Wis. (Also available as Institute for Research on Poverty Special Report no. 32C, University of Wisconsin–Madison.)

Oestricher, John C. 1986. "Panel Contains Costs." Letter to the Editor. *Business Journal,* 4 August.

Passel, J. S., and P. A. Berman. 1985. "Quality of 1980 Census Data for American Indians." Paper presented at the Annual Meeting of the American Statistical Association, Las Vegas, Nev., August.

Population Estimates and Vital Rates. 1983, 1984. Wisconsin Division of Health. Madison: Wisconsin Department of Health and Social Services.

Preston, Samuel H. 1984. "Children and the Elderly: Divergent Paths for America's Dependents." *Demography* 21 (November): 435–58.

Rhodes, Terry A. 1985. "State Budget Process." Madison: Wisconsin Legislative Fiscal Bureau.

Riche, Richard, Daniel Hecker, and John Burgan. 1983. "High Technology Today and

Tomorrow: A Small Slice of the Pie." *Monthly Labor Review* 106 (November): 50–58.

Salkever, David, and Thomas Bice. 1976. "The Impact of Certificate of Need Controls on Hospital Investment." *Milbank Memorial Fund Quarterly* 54: 185–214.

Salkever, David, Donald Steinwachs, and Agnes Rupp. 1986. "Hospital Cost and Efficiency under Per Service and Per Case Payment in Maryland: A Tale of the Carrot and the Stick." *Inquiry* 23: 56–66.

Sawhill, Isabel. 1976. "Discrimination and Poverty among Women Who Head Families." *Signs* 2: 201–11.

Schramm, Carl J. , Steven Renn, and Brian Biles. 1986. "Controlling Hospital Cost Inflation: New Perspectives on State Rate Setting." *Health Affairs* 5 (Fall): 22–33.

Sharkansky, Ira. 1968. "Agency Requests, Gubernatorial Support, and Budget Success in State Legislatures." *American Political Science Review* 62: 1220–31.

Simborg, Donald. 1981. "DRG Creep: A New Hospital-Acquired Disease." *New England Journal of Medicine* 304: 1602–4.

Simons, Henry. 1938. *Personal Income Taxation: The Definition of Income as a Problem of Fiscal Policy.* Chicago: University of Chicago Press.

Sloan, Frank. 1983. "Rate Regulation as a Strategy for Hospital Cost Control: Evidence from the Last Decade." *Milbank Memorial Fund Quarterly* 61: 195–221.

Sloan, Frank, and Bruce Steinwald. 1980. "Effects of Regulation on Hospital Costs and Input Use." *Journal of Law and Economics* 23: 81–109.

Sorkin, Alan. 1971. *American Indians and Federal Aid.* Washington, D.C.: Brookings Institution.

Stanley, Sam, and R. K. Thomas. 1978. "Current Demographic and Social Trends among North American Indians." *Annals of the American Academy of Political and Social Science* 436: 111–20.

Statistical Abstract of the United States. Various years. Washington, D.C.: U.S. GPO.

Stier, Jeffrey C. , and Gerard L. Vick. 1984. "An Economic Perspective on the Wisconsin Hardwood Veneer and Plywood Industry." Department of Forestry, Forest Resources Analysis Paper R3270, University of Wisconsin–Madison, June.

Sweet, J. A. 1984. "Components of Change in the Number of Households, 1970–1980." *Demography* 21: 129–41.

Thornton, Russell. Forthcoming. *As Snow before a Summer Sun: The Demographic Destruction and Survival of North American Indians.* Norman: University of Oklahoma Press.

U.S. Bureau of the Census. Various years. *Government Finances.* Washington, D.C.: U.S. GPO.

U.S. Bureau of the Census. Various years. *1960 Census of Population.* Washington, D.C.: U.S. GPO.

U.S. Bureau of the Census. Various years. *1970 Census of Population.* Washington, D.C.: U.S. GPO.

U.S. Bureau of the Census. Various years. *1980 Census of Population.* Washington, D.C.: U.S. GPO.

U.S. Bureau of the Census. 1977. "Gross Migration by County: 1965 to 1970." *Current Population Reports,* Series P-25, no. 701. Washington, D.C.: U.S. GPO.

U.S. Bureau of the Census. 1979. *State and Metropolitan Area Data Book.* Washington, D.C.: U.S. GPO.

U.S. Bureau of the Census. 1984. "Projections of the Population of the United States, by Age, Sex, and Race: 1983 to 2080." *Current Population Reports,* Series P-25, no. 952. Washington, D.C.: U.S. GPO.

U.S. Bureau of the Census. 1985. "Child Support and Alimony, 1983." *Current Population Reports,* Series P-23, no. 141. Washington, D.C.: U.S. GPO.

U.S. Bureau of the Census. 1986. *State and Metropolitan Area Data Book.* Washington, D.C.: U.S. GPO.

U.S. Commission on Civil Rights. 1981. "Child Care and Equal Opportunity for Women." Washington, D.C.: U.S. GPO.

U.S. Congress, Office of Technology Assessment. 1983. *Technologies and Management Strategies for Hazardous Waste Control.* Washington, D.C.: U.S. GPO.

U.S. Congress, Office of Technology Assessment. 1984. *Protecting the Nation's Groundwater from Contamination.* Report OTA-O-233. Washington, D.C.: U.S. GPO.

U.S. Congress, Office of Technology Assessment. 1985. *Medicare's Prospective Payment System.* Washington, D.C.: U.S. GPO.

U.S. Congress, Office of Technology Assessment. 1986. *Indian Health Care.* Report OHA-H-290. Washington, D.C.: U.S. GPO.

U.S. Department of Agriculture. 1985. *1984 Handbook of Agricultural Charts.* Report AH-637. Washington, D.C.: U.S. GPO.

U.S. Department of Labor, Bureau of Labor Statistics. 1986. *Employment and Earnings.* Washington, D.C.: U.S. GPO.

U.S. House of Representatives, Committee on Ways and Means. 1985. *Background Material and Data on Programs within the Jurisdiction of the Committee on Ways and Means.* Washington, D.C.: U.S. GPO.

U.S. Office of Management and Budget. Various years. *Special Analysis G: The Budget of the United States.* Washington, D.C.: U.S. GPO.

Van der Gaag, Jacques. 1982. "On Measuring the Cost of Children." *Children and Youth Services Review* 4: 77–109. (Also available as Institute for Research on Poverty, Reprint no. 447, University of Wisconsin–Madison.)

Ventura, Stephanie J. 1984. *Trends in Teenage Childbearing, United States 1970–81.* Washington, D.C.: National Center for Health Statistics.

Voss, Paul R. 1985. *Migration of Low Income Families and Individuals.* Madison: Applied Population Laboratory, Department of Rural Sociology, University of Wisconsin–Madison.

Voss, Paul R., Stephen J. Tordella, and Robert Manchin. 1984. *Wisconsin Business Climate Study: April 1984.* Part 3. Madison: Wisconsin Department of Development.

Wander, Thomas W., F. Ted Herbert, and Gary Copeland. 1984. *Congressional Budgeting: Politics, Process, and Power.* Baltimore: Johns Hopkins University Press.

Wax, M. L. 1971. *Indian Americans: Unity and Diversity.* Englewood Cliffs, N.J.: Prentice-Hall.

Wennberg, John, Kim McPherson, and Philip Caper. 1984. "Will Payment Based on Diagnosis-Related Groups Control Hospital Costs?" *New England Journal of Medicine* 311: 295–300.

Wildavsky, Aaron. 1979. *The Politics of the Budgetary Process.* Boston: Little, Brown.

Wisconsin Agriculture Reporting Service. 1984. *Agricultural Finance Survey, Wiscon-*

sin, May 1984. Madison: Crop Reporting Board, Statistical Reporting Service, and Wisconsin Department of Agriculture, Trade, and Consumer Protection.

Wisconsin Blue Book, 1979–80. Madison: Wisconsin Legislative Reference Bureau (compiler).

Wisconsin Bureau of Health Statistics. N.d. Loose table 16, for 1970 and 1980. Madison: Division of Health, Wisconsin Department of Health and Social Services.

Wisconsin Department of Administration. 1983. *Wisconsin Population Projections: 1980–2010.* Madison: Demographic Services Center.

Wisconsin Department of Administration. 1987. *Wisconsin's Strategic Development Commission: An Update.* Madison: DOA, 10 September.

Wisconsin Department of Development. 1984. *The Job Generation Process in Wisconsin: 1969–1981.* Madison: DOD.

Wisconsin Department of Development. 1986. *Economic Development Lending Activities of the Wisconsin Housing and Economic Development Authority: 1986 Annual Report.* Madison: DOD.

Wisconsin Department of Development. 1987a. *An Economic Analysis of Wisconsin Regions.* Madison: DOD.

Wisconsin Department of Development. 1987b. *Analysis of State Investment Board Investments to Enhance the Wisconsin Economy.* Madison: DOD.

Wisconsin Department of Development. 1987c. *Final Report—Governor's Advisory Committee on Business Incentives.* Madison: DOD.

Wisconsin Department of Development. 1987d. *Models of State Entrepreneurial Development Programs.* Madison: DOD.

Wisconsin Department of Development. 1987e. *Wisconsin Long-Range Economic Forecast: 1985–1995.* Madison: DOD.

Wisconsin Department of Health and Social Services. Various years. *Public Health Statistics.* Madison: Wisconsin Division of Health, Bureau of Health Statistics.

Wisconsin Department of Health and Social Services. 1984. *Wisconsin Maternal and Child Health Statistics, 1982.* Madison: DHSS.

Wisconsin Department of Natural Resources (Bureau of Water Quality Management). 1982. *The Wisconsin Nonpoint Source Water Pollution Abatement Program: A Report to the Governor and Legislature.* March. Madison: DNR.

Wisconsin Department of Natural Resources (Bureau of Solid Waste Management). 1983. *Alternatives to Hazardous Waste Land Disposal.* July. Madison: DNR.

Wisconsin Department of Natural Resources. 1984a. "Providing Hazardous Waste Management in Wisconsin: An Assessment of State Needs and Management Options." Prepared by Mary Ann Heidemann. September.

Wisconsin Department of Natural Resources. 1984b. *Wisconsin Water Quality: Report to Congress, 1984.* Report WDNR-SWQS-84-7. Madison: DNR.

Wisconsin Department of Natural Resources. 1985. "Locating and Repairing Abandoned Waste Sites: A Report to the Legislature on Wisconsin's Environmental Response and Restoration Program." January.

Wisconsin Department of Revenue, Division of Research and Analysis. 1979. *Wisconsin Tax Burden Study.* Madison: DOR.

Wisconsin Expenditure Commission. 1986a. *The Migration Impact of Wisconsin's AFDC Benefit Levels.* Madison: Wisconsin Department of Administration, Documents Section.

Wisconsin Expenditure Commission. 1986b. "State Expenditure and Revenue Trends: 1958–59 to 1983–84." June.

Wisconsin Hospital Rate-Setting Commission. 1985. *Rules of the Hospital Rate-Setting Commission.* Wisconsin Administrative Code, October.

Wisconsin Legislative Council. 1982. *Acid Rain: A Background Report.* Staff Brief 82-7, July. Madison: Legislative Council.

Wisconsin Legislative Fiscal Bureau. 1985. "The Role of Farming in the Wisconsin Tax Structure." In *Wisconsin's Agricultural Economy: An Urban-Rural Perspective.* Madison: Wisconsin Department of Agriculture, Trade, and Consumer Protection.

Wisconsin Legislature. 1974. *Report of the Special Joint Committee on the Budgetary Process.* Madison: Legislature.

Wisconsin Legislature. 1979. *Bulletin of Proceedings of the Wisconsin Legislature.* Madison: Legislature.

Wisconsin Local Property Tax Relief Commission. 1987. *Final Recommendations Approved by the Local Property Tax Relief Commission.* Madison: LPTRC, 18 September.

Wisconsin's Agricultural Economy: An Urban-Rural Perspective. 1985. Proceedings and Background Papers, 19–20 January, Wingspread, Racine, Wis. Madison: Wisconsin Department of Agriculture, Trade, and Consumer Protection.

Wisconsin Secretary of State. 1975. *Laws of Wisconsin.* Madison: Office of the Secretary of State.

Wisconsin State Journal. 1979. "'Benevolent Dictator' Rules Demos' Caucus," 24 June.

Wisconsin State Journal. 1983. "Senate Democrats Back Health Care Costs Limits," 3 June; "The 1983–84 Version," 26 June.

Wisconsin State Journal. 1987. "Senator Urges Limit on Aid to Business," 17 February; "Recession World Trade Help Development Strategy Evolve," 9 May.

Wisconsin Statistical Analysis Center. 1970, 1980, 1984. *Wisconsin Crime and Arrests.* Madison: Wisconsin Divison of Corrections.

Wisconsin Strategic Development Commission. 1985a. *Final Report.* Madison: SDC.

Wisconsin Strategic Development Commission, Task Force on Agriculture. 1985b. *Production Agriculture in Wisconsin.* Madison: SDC.

Wisconsin Vital Statistics. 1984. Madison: Wisconsin Department of Health and Social Services.

Wisconsin Youth, Work and the Economy—What Now? 1981. Madison: Wisconsin Department of Industry, Labor, and Human Relations.

Witte, John F. 1985. *The Politics and Development of the Federal Income Tax.* Madison: University of Wisconsin Press.

Witte, John F. 1986. "A Long View of Tax Reform." *National Tax Journal* 39 (September): 255–61.

Wolfgang, Marvin E., Robert M. Figlio, and Thurston Sellin. 1972. *Delinquency in a Birth Cohort.* Chicago: University of Chicago Press.

Worthington, Nancy, and Paula Piro. 1982. "The Effects of Hospital Rate-Setting Programs on Volumes of Hospital Services: A Preliminary Analysis." *Health Care Financing Review* 4 (December): 47–66.

Youth Policy and Law Center. 1983. *The Violent Offender.* Madison: YPLC.

Index